D-65'S LIGHTROOM WORKBOOK

WORKFLOW, NOT WORKSLOW IN LIGHTROOM 4

D-65
1143 Vintner Blvd
Palm Beach Gardens, FL 33410

Library of Congress Control Number: 2012934647

ISBN 13: 978-0-9852489-0-1

ISBN 10: 0985248904

www.D-65.com

*This book is dedicated
to all of our students,
who always teach us,
while providing the inspiration
to keep on teaching*

Seth and Jamie

CONTENTS

| ACKNOWLEDGEMENTS

There are so many folks who helped make this project a reality. First we must thank all of our readers and workshop participants who looked forward to another edition.

The photographic inspirations come from mentors and friends Jay Maisel, Susan Meiselas and Eric Meola.

None of this would have been possible without the support of a core group of friends and colleagues of the Pixel Mafia and especially the close support and friendship of some of the most intelligent digital minds in the world, Seth's fellow partners in Pixel Genius; Jeff Schewe, Martin Evening, Andrew Rodney, Mac Holbert and the late Mike Skurski and Bruce Fraser.

There is of course the entire Adobe family as well. Never have we worked with a company where one truly feels like family. There are so many brilliant minds and wonderful people including Shantanu Nurayen, Mark Hamburg, Maria Yap, Melissa Itamura, Julie Kmoch, Becky Sowada, Melissa Gaul, Palib Jyotee Hazarika, Jingyuan Bai, Simon Chen, Kjetil Drarvik, Brian Kruse, Ying Liu, Peter Merrrill, Andrew Rahn, Kevin Tieskoetter, Jianping Wang, Max Wendt, Ben Zibble, Yu Zhao, Qiang Zhu, Kelly Castro, Tony Francesconi, Dan Gerber, Paul Kleczka, Shoji Kumagai, Baichao Li, Xin Lu, Craig Marble, Chuntang Pan, Tomoko Shinji, Mark Soderberg, Becky Sowada, Dan Tull, Jeff Van de Walker, Benjamin Warde, Xiokang Wu, Xin Wu, Phil Clevenger, Phil Lu, Melissa Itamura, Julieanne Kost, David Franzen, Michelle Qi, Heather Dolan, John Kwon, Adriana Ohlmeyer

Extra thanks to: Tom Hogarty, Sharad Mangalick, David Auyeung, Whitney McCleary, Pam Sogge

Extra extra thanks to: Eric Chan, Thomas Knoll, Zalman Stern

Additional Special thanks to Kathy Waite

A very special extra thanks to Rob van Tuin, our web designer and Angela Paniza, our book designer, Greg Gorman for the wine and friendship, George Jardine for continued support and friendship and Nancy Leigh and Jim Sorensen, RR Donnelley our printer.

We could never have done this without the loving support of each other, and from our family.

Seth and Jamie

| FOREWORD

Having been an analog photographer since 1968, I was not only
a late bloomer, but also a major disbeliever in digital. Of course, I
loved the digital point and shoot cameras but the "pro" cameras at
3 megapixels just couldn't compete with the images I was realizing
with my Hasselblad's or even my 35mm Canons. My Los Angeles
based lab encouraged me early on to take *Photoshop* classes.
I asked "What for? Wasn't *Photoshop* a good excuse for poor
photography?" I then realized all of my analog imagery for motion
pictures campaigns was being scanned and finished up in *Photoshop*.
I figured it finally must be time to learn *Photoshop*.

Barely understanding all of the digital technology, *Photoshop* seemed
an endless maze of controls and options – confusing to someone
who was used to traditional darkroom techniques. Being more of an
old school photographer with a puritanical sense of aesthetics as far
as what should be done to the image, I was at a loss with all of the
choices *Photoshop* had to offer.

Before I launch into my dissertation on *Lightroom,* I must first
backtrack a bit to tell you how I first met Seth Resnick. Both of us
being Canon Explorers of Light and avid wine lovers, we welcomed
the Explorers of Light events where Seth and I often had a field
day with the grape juice. Our ongoing love affair with wine was the
foundation for a terrific relationship, which now includes, as well,
Jamie and Luci. Knowing that Seth was also a photographer and
not just another digital geek, made for a much more interesting
connection between us. I clearly remember the very first time I heard
Seth's three hour presentation on workflow. I believe it was in Dallas
at a digital imaging conference. Going in, I thought to myself, either I
am going to be bored out of my mind or this is going to be way over
my head. Well I am sure you know where this is going – it was neither!
It was interesting, informative and totally made sense. So many
questions in the back of my mind were being answered. It was as
though someone had turned on the lights. I think because Seth also
came from an analog photographer's background, his mindset was
more straightforward. His approach from capture to keywording to
final output and storage all made sense. In terms of workflow and the
proper application of what to do with one's images once they were
downloaded, literally all came together.

Finally, along comes this new program from Adobe called *Lightroom*. I was an early alpha tester. Being known as a photographer who shoots a lot of images when working, Mark Hamburg , senior architect of *Lightroom*, was curious as to which programs I was using to get the job done.

In the early days, I was working with IView Media Pro and Photo Mechanic, along side *Photoshop* to get the job done from my workflow point of view. Having to go between three different applications was, after all, confusing as well as frustrating. The idea of *Lightroom* was to present one stand alone application designed by photographers for photographers. A program that in addition to managing your pictures, offered one the basic tools of a traditional darkroom but pared down to improve the speed and efficiency of the application. Processing my images never became more intuitive. As *Lightroom* has grown and improved its capabilities and potential, I found a need to better understand how to work with the tools and the various modules that *Lightroom* was now offering.

What better way to understand all of the new bells and whistles, so to speak, than to have Seth and Jamie's bible in hand! After all, it was Seth who first taught me so clearly the importance of a strong and effective workflow. Seth has taught with me in Mendocino at my digital photographic workshop for the past six years and I can tell you that, as soon as the day is done, with a very good glass of wine in hand from my cellar, Seth is feverishly downloading, keywording and backing up his imagery. His workflow is impeccable.

Not only has *Lightroom* built a great Library and Develop module but also the printing capabilities through *Lightroom* are fantastic and save the photographer so much time with all the available presets. In addition to all of my printing needs, I produce all of my slideshows as high definition QuickTime movies with accompanying soundtracks from iTunes. It is amazing the amount of work I can accomplish in a single app!

Lightroom 4 is very exciting and offers even more for those of you that shoot pictures of things other than people such as a map module for geotagging and even a book module that allows you to output and publish your own books through Blurb.

Finally, I have gotten my old school clients to relinquish their desires for contact sheets although *Lightroom* produces them quickly and efficiently. Now I simply create a web gallery and send my clients a link where they can review and edit the imagery in a more timely and eco-friendly atmosphere.

With *Lightroom 4*, Seth and Jamie share with us many new upgraded features that many of us have been complaining to the engineers about. The architects of *Lightroom* have actually been listening which is a good thing for us - the end users! With the new Develop module we can soft proof - something that was sorely missed in LR3. No more wasting of paper – sorry Epson! Soft proof is a killer addition and finally some of the dysfunctional retouching tools in LR3 now really work like Clarity. Fill Light is gone but replaced with new sliders to control exposure, contrast, highlights and shadows. My black and white's never looked so good! I can also import and adjust my Hassleblad files with ease. For me, these are probably the most important tools and leave it to Seth and Jamie to show you the right way to get the most out of them. They do so in a simple, clean-cut easy way to understand.

One of the things I appreciate most about Seth is his extraordinary eye. So many times, we shot similar setups together with our models in Mendocino and I can tell you each of our styles of photography are unique unto ourselves. Seeing the same subject and same location from two completely different points of view keeps everything fresh and alive. The manner in which Seth and Jamie have written this book is much the same way. It is fresh and alive and keeps you turning the page to see how a proper digital darkroom and workflow should unfold.

Greg Gorman
Bologna 2012

| INTRODUCTION

What is D-65?

D-65's services include digital workflow workshops, webinars, one-on-one training and tech support, and consulting for photographers, studios, agencies, and corporate art departments. We've been doing this for over a decade, and have taught thousands of photographers.

D-65 set the standard for digital workflow. Seth Resnick is the Co-founder of D-65. Chosen as one of the 30 most influential photographers of the decade by Photo District News Magazine, Seth Resnick is one of North America's most prolific corporate, editorial and stock photographers. Seth is greatly in demand for his beautiful graphic images in both natural and created light. Resnick has been published in the world's most prestigious magazines. His credits include over 2500 publications worldwide and his clients constitute a virtual list of Corporate America. Resnick is at the forefront of digital innovation working with Adobe, NEC, Canon, OnOne, LowePro Xrite, Epson and others to help them formulate more useful products for photographers. Resnick is one of 78 photographers worldwide named as a Canon Explorer of Light. He is a member of the prestigious X-rite Colorati program, LowePro Professional, OnOne Masters, as well as an Alpha/Beta and feature consultant for *Adobe Photoshop* and *Lightroom*.

This book is based on the D-65 workshops, which are a dynamic resource for photographers of any level. Our 4-day intensive, hands-on workflow workshop equips pro photographers art directors, photo editors, image heavy bloggers, and the advanced amateur with the tools to manage their workflow efficiently, effectively, and effortlessly.

We teach you detailed workflow utilizing the 7 modules of *Lightroom* 4, to vastly improve your digital asset management, processing and image delivery skills. You'll learn the fundamentals of *Lightroom* and become an expert in keeping every image you shoot organized, edited and archived through keywording, metadata and collections. You'll optimally develop and enhance your images with presets and synchromization. And have the ability to move between *Lightroom* and *Photoshop* with ease while delivering quality images to friends, family or clients.

By the end of our book, workshop, or consultation you will have the skills to create your own successful workflow in *Lightroom 4*.

If you read our first, or second book, The *Photoshop Lightroom Workbook, Workflow not Workslow* in *Lightroom 2,* or D-65's *Lightroom* Workbook Workflow, Not Workslow in *Lightroom 3,* you will already know why we love *Lightroom.*

If you haven't read our earlier books, or been to one of our workshops or webinars, *Lightroom* is a one-stop solution for digital workflow. It utilizes the power behind *Adobe Camera Raw*, combining image processing and a digital asset management system under one roof. The aim of *Lightroom* is to be simple and to streamline workflow.

If you're reading this, we're happy to offer a Special Discount Code for our workshops, $200.00 off our published price. Enjoy! Discount Code: **LR4Book**

TIP: **The Lightroom 4 catalog upgrade process does not erase or remove your previous Lightroom catalogs. The upgrade process will modify previews of an upgraded catalog. Returning to a previous version of Lightroom will require that the previews be re-rendered. This can be a lengthy process for those with hundreds of thousands of images.**

UPGRADING FROM *LIGHTROOM 3* TO *4*

If you were working in *Lightroom 3* you will need to upgrade your *Lightroom 3* Catalog or create a new catalog. If you have a single catalog in the default location, *Lightroom 4.0* will automatically open that file and upgrade it. If you have multiple catalogs, or a catalog that is not in the default location you will need to upgrade each one manually.

(see Figures 1A, 1B and 1C).

The time this process will take is dependent on the size of your existing catalogs. This operation CANNOT be cancelled. Do not force quit this operation or *Lightroom* will become corrupted. Any catalog that is updated in 4 will no longer be able to open in 3. During the upgrade process, *Lightroom* can be set to always load a catalog on startup and automatically check the integrity of the new catalog.

FIG 1A

FIG 1B

FIG 1C

When you upgrade an existing catalog, you will notice that the original catalog remains and a new catalog and previews are created. This can cause some confusion because the new catalog will be designated with the number 2 after it. (Figure 1D) Because of this we physically delete the original catalog and rename the new catalog and Previews to Lightroom_4_Catalog. lrcat and Lightroom_4_Catalog_Previews.lrdata. (Figure 1E)

FIG 1D

FIG 1E

Lightroom_Catalog_-2 Previews.lrdata

Lightroom_Catalog_.lrcat

Lightroom_Catalog_-2.lrcat

Lightroom_4_Catalog.lrcat

Lightroom_4_Catalog Previews.lrdata

All keyboard shortcuts and screen shots in this tutorial are Macintosh. If you are using the Windows version see chart below.

Windows:	Mac:
Alt	Option/Alt
Control	Command
Right Click	Control Click
Enter	Return

Minimum Requirements to run *Lightroom 4*

MAC

- Multicore Intel® processor with 64-bit support

- Mac OS X v10.6.8 (Snow Leopard) or v10.7 (Lion)

- 2GB of RAM

- 1GB of available hard-disk space

- 1024x768 display

- DVD-ROM drive

- Internet connection required for Internet-based services*

WIN

- Intel® Pentium® 4 or AMD Athlon® 64 processor

- Microsoft® Windows Vista® with Service Pack 2 or Windows 7 with Service Pack 1

- 2GB of RAM

- 1GB of available hard-disk space

- 1024x768 display

- DVD-ROM drive

- Internet connection required for Internet-based services*

DIGITAL CONCEPTS

| MEMORY CARDS

Flash memory cards are an overlooked but a very important part of digital workflow. After all, the flash memory card is the modern day equivalent of your film. In the same way that you didn't use just any film, even though they were all color or black and white, all memory cards are not created equal. Some of the important criteria are speed, data verification, technical support, warranty, and size. SanDisk, Toshiba and Samsung are among the largest flash memory chip suppliers. Toshiba is actually a partner with SanDisk.

There is also a second component within a memory card known as the controller. SanDisk and Lexar produce the majority of the controllers. Technically, it is the combination of the controller and the flash memory that ultimately determines the efficiency and the performance of the card.

MEMORY CARD SPEED

The speed itself is dependent on more than just the card. The architecture of the camera is also a factor. A card that is super fast in one camera could be slow in another camera. This all depends on how the controller interchanges data with the specific camera.

CHOOSING THE RIGHT SIZE MEMORY CARD

Flash memory cards have been increasing in size, and are now available up to 128 GB. D-65 advocates using more than one card on every shoot and no larger than 32 GB cards. Why? The memory card is likely to be the first place you can encounter a problem. Any glitch or failure with the memory card can wreck a shoot. For this reason, D-65 chooses to match the memory card to the RAW file size produced by the camera. Quite simply, the larger the file the larger the card but we will not yet go larger than 32 GB.

Don't fall into the trap of believing that more storage on a card is better. You would never shoot a film-based job on only one really long roll of film just in case the lab ran into problems. For this reason, D-65 recommends using multiple cards per job. You can size the card specifically for a camera. While a 128 gig card may seem like a great convenience, you are putting all of your "digital eggs" in one basket. The key is not to have too many images on one card in case of failure.

HOW LONG WILL MY MEMORY CARD LAST?

All cards have a lifespan, as is the case with all digital products. While the manufacturers are reluctant to post specific numbers, all cards will eventually die, as the cells in the card start to expire.

Do not assume that a card will last for 300,000 erase and write cycles. It is a good idea to introduce new cards on regular intervals and at least every three years.

ALWAYS FORMAT THE MEMORY CARD IN YOUR CAMERA... EVERY TIME

You must format your memory card in the camera. Do not just remove or delete the images using the computer or camera software. This may lead to data loss. Why?

All cards run with their own operating system and have their own native file structure. These media typically need to be formatted to a FAT16 file structure while many computers use a FAT32 file structure. If you manipulate the images on a card using a FAT32 computer, this information will be written to the card. So, you will have a FAT16 device with FAT32 information. Not a desired result, and such an easy problem to avoid.

To avoid data loss:

- Always format compact flash cards in your camera.

- Reformat the card every time you remove it from the camera.

- Do not take the card out of your camera, check the images on a computer and then put the card back in the camera and continue shooting.

- Never fill a memory card. If there is not enough space to write the last file, the entire card may get corrupted. Leave a few shots (3 or 4) at the end of each card. This greatly reduces the risk of card failure.

- Never open the card slot on the camera to remove or check a card while the camera is still writing data to the card. For those shooting in burst mode it may take 10 seconds or more for the data to completely write to the card.

| EDITING IN CAMERA

While it is generally safe to delete files as you shoot in the camera, there is an exception to this rule that can lead to data loss.

Do not delete files at the end of the card to create extra space for more shooting.

The data is very vulnerable when the cards are close to filled. It is almost a guarantee that you will encounter data loss if you delete files at the end of the card. It is acceptable to do a rough edit while you are shooting, using the LCD on the camera back. Do not be overzealous with your editing; remember the limitations of the LCD display. However, it is a good idea to delete obvious "out takes" in camera to reduce editing time later.

| SHOOTING AT THE OPTIMUM ISO

Every digital camera has an optimum ISO setting. The best capture quality will be obtained using that ISO. In fact, the only camera setting that will significantly impact the quality of the RAW capture is the ISO. The nomenclature on the menus of cameras tends to confuse photographers. We all ask the questions, "Should I shoot on Adobe RGB, turn on noise reduction? Sharpening?" The reality is that none of these apply when shooting in RAW mode. The only settings that apply when shooting RAW are shutter speed, f-stop and ISO.

When shooting film, photographers typically pick a higher ISO when they need speed or when the light is reduced. In the world of digital capture, D-65 suggests shooting at the optimum ISO whenever possible because there is a direct correlation between digital noise and higher ISO.

The higher the ISO, the more potential there is to generate noise.

Noise is a level of electronic error usually resulting from amplification of the signal from the sensor. While there are various ways to mask noise, the best solution is to try to prevent it before it occurs. Up until recently, D-65 was adamant to try to shoot at the optimum ISO for the camera. Although camera manufacturers claimed excellent results at higher ISOs, we found that most cameras produced less than optimal quality at ISO 400 or above.

Recently, because of better insulators in micro components and all around better technology, both Nikon and Canon have changed our way of thinking with the high end cameras. We have seen spectacular results at ISOs above 3200. As time goes on, ISO may become less and less of an issue.

In general, a camera with a maximum ISO sensitivity of 800 will gather light twice as fast at that sensitivity as it would at 400. If you can make a shot at 1/100th of a second at 400 ISO with a particular setup in the camera, the camera will take the same shot at 1/200th of a second with the same setup at 800 ISO. There is, however, a penalty of increased noise at higher ISO sensitivities.

You should always set the ISO no higher than is necessary to produce the best quality image.

| WHITE BALANCE

The white balance indicates the color of the light in which an image was captured. Our eyes automatically adjust to changes in white balance by making the brightest area of the scene white. As you may recall, shooting film under fluorescent lighting looked green, while to the human eye, it never appeared green. While no camera is capable of the white balancing accomplished in the human brain, digital cameras do an admirable job.

Digital cameras have sensors with red, green and blue filters. There are twice as many green filters as red and blue filters in digital cameras because our eyes are most sensitive to green wavelengths. Digital is trying to mimic the way your eyes see.

Unlike film, a digital camera gives you full control over white balance. Obtaining a specific white balance value can be accomplished in many ways. Some cameras allow you to set custom white balance values. While it is true that you can always adjust the white balance of a RAW file after the fact, having to do this will slow down your workflow. Achieving the correct white balance in camera will speed up your workflow.

Many cameras have an AWB mode. In our minds, this stands for Average White Band, and not Auto White Balance. The photographer, not a computer chip, should take control and determine the desired color temperature. For example, many of us like to shoot at sunrise and sunset. The light at these times, known as golden light or National Geographic light, is exceedingly warm. Setting your camera to AWB at this time will correct this light to look more like light at high noon.

On the next page we have an example of the same image shot with two different white balance settings. The scene is a vendor selling squid in an outdoor market. It is a cloudy day, and there are fluorescent tubes and a red incandescent light bulb hanging over the squid, along with a green and white awning. It is the type of image that in the days of film would be nearly impossible to correct. In Figure 1.1, the camera is set to daylight. In Figure 1.2, we have done an in-camera custom white balance to achieve the correct white balance that we wanted.

FIG 1.1
As Shot

FIG 1.2
Custom White Balance
Done in Camera

X-Rite ColorChecker

If custom white balance isn't an option for you, another way
to obtain an accurate white balance is to place an X-Rite
ColorChecker (www.xrite.com) in the scene.

To do this, place the X-Rite ColorChecker in the frame and
capture the image. When you process the file in *Lightroom,* use
the White Balance tool in the Develop Module and click on the
second patch from the left in the bottom row. The white balance
will be corrected instantly.

Click on this patch for white balance in a frame

FIG 1.3

To use the custom white balance in the camera, focus on an area of the image that has white with detail (such as the underbelly of the squid in the upper left-hand corner of the image in Figure 1.2). While white with detail will not give the exact same reading as an X-Rite ColorChecker, it will be very close in most situations.

Color balance is very subjective. We all see color differently. It is technically determined in our brain. No two people see the exact same shade of red in a red ball. If you were shooting clothing for a clothing manufacturer, then we would always recommend using an X-Rite Passport ColorChecker. The manufacturer will want the yellow sweater to look exactly or as close to the real thing as possible. Going to a beach at sunset and shooting a portrait for an editorial piece is another story. You would likely want the warm light on your subject, which is not "technically" white balanced at all.

In the days of film, we used an 81A filter on the lens or a sun CTO filter on the strobes to warm up the scene and make it look like afternoon sunlight. Many editors hired us specifically for this look, while other editors didn't like the look of our warm portraits at all, thinking the skin tones were too orange. Neither look is right or wrong; it is just personal preference.

UNDERSTANDING HISTOGRAMS

One similarity between film and digital is that whether you are shooting with a digital camera or on film, getting correct exposure is essential for getting great results. Your creativity and composition may be great, but unless it is exposed correctly, you have nothing at all. With film it is pretty easy to simply look at transparency and judge whether it was exposed correctly or not.

Some photographers and photo editors assume that exposure is not a problem with digital, because you see your results immediately. Although this is a great advantage, it doesn't actually solve all the problems. Once you start looking at and understanding the technical merits of a digital file, the world that you thought you knew changes very quickly.

Figure 1.4 below contains only pure black and pure white. The histogram for this image, Figure 1.5 looks like a pair of goalposts.

FIG 1.4
As Shot

FIG 1.5
Histogram showing pure black and pure white

Most digital cameras today use a sensor that simply counts photons. They produce a charge that's directly proportional to the amount of light that strikes them. The cameras for the most part use a series of array filters. The red-filtered elements produce a grayscale value proportional to the amount of red light reaching the sensor; the green-filtered elements produce a grayscale value proportional to the amount of green light reaching the sensor; and the blue-filtered elements produce a grayscale value proportional to the amount of blue light reaching the sensor.

A RAW digital file is truly a linear file. Ironically, data is captured in a linear progression very much the same way as traditional f-stops work with film. F 2.8 allows twice the light as F 4.0 and 4.0 is twice 5.6 and so on. So without getting too geeky here, one half of the data of a 12-bit capture (4096 levels) or 2048 levels is in the brightest stop (highlights), 1024 in the next stop, 512 in the next stop and so on until one gets to the shadows which contain only 64 levels. The darkest stop of the digital file has the least amount of data and thus shows the greatest amount of digital problems, mainly noise, which looks like static on a television screen.

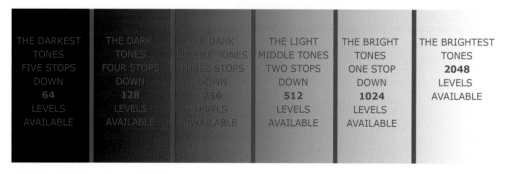

| THE DARKEST TONES FIVE STOPS DOWN 64 LEVELS AVAILABLE | THE DARK TONES FOUR STOPS DOWN 128 LEVELS AVAILABLE | THE DARK MIDDLE TONES THREE STOPS DOWN 256 LEVELS AVAILABLE | THE LIGHT MIDDLE TONES TWO STOPS DOWN 512 LEVELS AVAILABLE | THE BRIGHT TONES ONE STOP DOWN 1024 LEVELS AVAILABLE | THE BRIGHTEST TONES 2048 LEVELS AVAILABLE |

FIG 1.6
One half of the data of a 12-bit capture (4096 levels) or 2048 levels is in the brightest stop (highlights), 1024 in the next stop, 512 in the next stop and so on until the shadows that contain only 64 levels.

Since the most information in a digital capture is in the first brightest stop, the very act of underexposure reduces the quality of a digital file.

From a pure technical position, you should expose digital capture so that the most data is present. As a general rule, this means that a properly exposed digital file is slightly overexposed.

Let's think about film for a moment. When shooting transparencies, we typically underexposed to increase saturation and color. The problem here is that if we simply underexpose in camera, we will lose valuable data in our RAW files. Essentially, digital exposure is exactly the opposite of transparency film. In digital capture we want to make a judgment call on the overexposure side rather than the underexposure side. It is during processing that we can achieve our rich, saturated color, rather than during exposure where we would sacrifice the quality of the file.

D-65 is not saying to always slightly overexpose in digital. With film, the "correct exposure" is the correct exposure. However, many times that "correct exposure" is a slight underexposure in order to achieve the desired saturation and color. We don't however always underexpose film. Similarly, we don't always overexpose digital files.

⏐ WARNING: USING THE HISTOGRAM DISPLAYED ON THE BACK OF YOUR CAMERA

Not to further confuse the issue, but there is also a lesson here for the photographer. Many cameras have a histogram display on the back of the LCD on the cameras that warn when a highlight is about to be blown out and many photographers adhere strictly to the histogram. However, the LCD preview and the histogram on the back of the camera do not represent any real information regarding how your RAW capture will look. The camera does an "on the fly" conversion to sRGB.

The histogram is a luminance histogram of the sRGB preview, not a true representation of your file. As a general rule for some of the most widely used professional cameras, the overexposure warning is off by at least one stop. This prevents you from blowing out the highlight, but it typically also eliminates the brightest stop with the most information. The camera manufacturers set the threshold for this display too low, which will lead you to underexpose your image.

If you look at Figure 1.6, and realize that the histogram in the back of the camera is blinking at level 1024, instead of 2048 (one stop early), and if you are like most photographers, you are worried by the blinking histogram. So you back off one more stop. You are now at level 512. You have successfully eliminated two-thirds of the information in this image. The blinking light is useful in that it really means you have at least one stop to the right before you are blowing out any highlights. One amazing quality about *Lightroom* is the ability to recover almost two stops of blown-out highlight detail captured by the sensor, but not visible in the camera LCD.

Beware of the camera's histogram and LCD!

| EXPOSING FOR DIGITAL

Determining exposure for digital capture is quite different than exposing for film. Digital camera sensors have a wider dynamic range and are much more sensitive to light than many films. You can use less created or strobe light with digital than you would with film. Lighting digital capture the same way you would light film will generally result in an image that looks overly lit.

Another common exposure problem is that people will base their exposure on a gray card and as a result shoot at that ambient light value. A light meter reading taken off a subject of known reflectance like an 18% gray surface is only giving you a base exposure.

With digital, it is vital to actually expose for the color as well as the ambient light. Colors change and vibrate depending on the exposure. Our best suggestion is to shoot at the same ISO value so that your brain gets used to the colors produced under similar light conditions. Ideally, shoot on manual so that you learn the light instead of letting the camera make the decision for you.

D-65 determines what color in a scene we want to accentuate. Our exposure is based on that particular color. For example, an image with bright, vibrant yellow and very dark blue will have a different exposure value depending on whether you are accentuating the yellow or the blue, regardless of the ambient light which is constant throughout the frame.

The key to getting a digital file that is technically good is essentially to shoot in a RAW mode and overexpose slightly and then bring it down during the processing phase. In the end you can still end up with a red that looks like the Jay Maisel Red and in fact with a good RAW processor, you can actually achieve a better quality image with more detail and even more vibrant colors and saturation, but getting there is essentially the opposite of what we did when exposing film.

One thing that a photo editor must keep in mind is that if a photographer delivers a RAW file and it is exposed correctly for the greatest amount of data, the file will most likely be overexposed. A photo editor may naturally think that the photographer should learn how to expose if his own knowledge is based on working with film but the slightly overexposed digital file is actually the best one.

| 16 vs. 8: IS THERE A BIT OF DIFFERENCE?

Understanding the difference between 8-bit and 16-bit is a critical part of digital. *Lightroom* and *Photoshop* are all about 16-bit corrections and yet commercial printing is all about 8-bit. Why do you need to care about bits, especially if you end up printing in 8-bit and know that 16-bit images are twice as big as 8-bit ones?

Let's start with some basics: in digital imaging the number zero is the complete absence of color while the number 255 is represents the maximum level of a color. 8-bit RGB images use 0 to 255 to represent each channel of red, green and blue. Therefore, (255,0,0) is equal to red and (0,255,0) is equal to pure green, while (0,0,0) equals black and (255,255,255) equals white. Zero through 255 gives 256 total distinct values that each of these three channels can have. If you multiply 256 times 256 times 256, you get 16.7 million different combinations for an 8-bit image.

Now with 16-bit, we get 65,536 values for each channel instead of only 256. So 65,536 x 65,536 x 65,536 gives us 281 trillion total possible colors. It's confusing if we make it so technical, huh?

So let's put all this in simple English and use fruits to describe 8-bit to 16-bit. Fruit and *Lightroom* go hand and hand and will actually make total sense.

Before we explain it is important to understand that altering pixel data is a destructive process. Quite simply, everything we do in *Photoshop* hurts pixels. In fact the best way of using *Photoshop* is the method that produces the least amount of destruction.

To make this easy we are going to use the concept of fruit. In this case 256 (8-bit) will be represented by apples and 65,536 (16-bit) will be represented by strawberries. Imagine that instead of pixels we had fruit deriving the images in Figures 1.7 and Figure 1.8). Apples represent 8-bit and strawberries represent 16 bit. Conceptually we are making rows of fruit instead of pixels, so we have 256 apples making up the image in the 8-bit model and 65,536 strawberries making up the 16-bit model.

Knowing that *Photoshop* is destructive, if we went ahead and did a levels adjustment on the 8-bit model we would have a hole, or in pixel terms a gap in data, in the image the size of one apple. If we did the same adjustment on the 16-bit model, we would have a hole, or gap in data, the size of one strawberry. We could do many more adjustments on the 16-bit model, with each adjustment causing another strawberry-sized hole before we had a hole the size of one apple.

FIG 1.7

16 bit = 65,536 strawberries

FIG 1.8

So as we edit in 16-bit mode, we will still lose data, but much less than we would in 8-bit. (It takes a lot of strawberries to make a hole the size of one apple.)

Can you see the difference between 16-bit and 8-bit? Yes and no. First, let's look at the histogram of the image with no changes, Figure 1.9.

FIG 1.9

In the histograms in Figure 1.10 and Figure 1.11 choosing auto contrast, auto levels and a curves adjustment on both a 16-bit (FIG 1.10) and 8-bit (FIG 1.11) file will show a drastically different histogram. The histogram with the 8-bit file clearly shows gaps of data (apples vs. strawberries).

FIG 1.10
Histogram of image with adjustments done in 16-bit.

However, if someone were to show you a printed image, it may be very tough to decide whether it was 16-bit or 8-bit. There is one good example that is many times a tell-tale sign. In places like Miami where we have a nice blue sky, the sky in a print should go from a nice light blue to a much darker blue at higher altitude. In a print, you may notice that the sky goes from light blue and then there is a line or what looks like banding going to a darker blue. Typically what you are seeing is an image where the adjustments were done in 8-bit instead of 16-bit. The stripes or banding are missing gradations of tone, so instead of a nice even light to dark blue it appears as light blue and then a much darker blue.

So the bottom line is to work in 16-bit whenever possible.

FIG 1.11
Histogram of image with adjustments done in 8-bit.

I FILTERS

While many photographers use all kinds of filters with film-based cameras, it is generally not a good idea to use them with digital. Why?

The glass in a lens is not flat and the lens is composed of many different elements and element groups. This glass has a meniscus curve. A meniscus curve is similar to the shape of a kneecap. Light will pass through the glass lens with a meniscus curve, hit the sensor and then bounce straight out through the lens.

Putting a filter, like a skylight filter which is generally a screw mount, can wreak havoc. The glass on the filter is most likely not a meniscus curve and light will pass through the filter, hit the sensor, and then reflect back on the sensor instead of passing through the filter. Skylight and UV filters are also altering the wavelength of light that hits your sensor.

The conversion of photons to pixels by the sensor is based on calculations from pure, natural light. In simple English, changing the light with a UV filter will effect contrast in the final image because the sensor has no way of knowing there is a UV filter on top of the lens. A polarizing filter is the only filter that is acceptable for digital, because achieving the effects of a polarizer in *Lightroom* or *Photoshop* is nearly impossible.

So how do you protect your lens? Use the lens cap! Jay Maisel uses Velcro strips to keep the lens cap attached to each lens. Otherwise you may find them in your washing machine after they fall out of your back pocket.

┃ YOUR PHYSICAL WORK ENVIRONMENT

A frequently overlooked but important part of digital workflow is the room that houses your computer. Your physical working environment must be considered part of your color management system. Following are some suggestions for maximizing the impact of your workspace.

- **Control ambient light when correcting color.** While many people work only in totally dark rooms while correcting colors, it is difficult to work in total darkness for long time periods. In reality, total darkness isn't practical and too much ambient light competes with the light emitted from the monitor. So you will need to find a balance that works for you in your environment.

- **Use a monitor hood.** Shield the monitor from ambient light by using a hood on its top and sides. These two areas should be shielded to a distance of 12". The inside of the monitor hood should be a matte black color. These hoods can be purchased from stores catering to the graphics design trade or made using directions found on the Internet.

- **Configure a neutral computer desktop.** Your computer desktop should be as neutral a color as possible. A solid gray is optimum. Your desktop should not be configured to display an image of your child or favorite travel destination.

- **Neutral walls reduce color cast.** The visible walls around your monitor should be a neutral color; gray is ideal.

- **Keep CPUs and monitors away from sources of direct heat or cold.**

| MULTIPLE WORKING BACKUPS

The most popular means of storing data is on hard drives. It is not a matter of if they will die, or fail. It is only a matter of when they will die. All data must be backed up regularly. For workflow, D-65 suggests a minimum of a secondary hard drive to use as a backup, and to perform backups of your current work on a regular basis.

| SUMMARY

- Not all memory cards are created equal, and bigger isn't necessarily better. Choose the correct memory card for your camera and for your needs. Don't forget to format your memory card every time you take it out of the camera.

- Only edit in camera when your memory card is not close to being full.

- The best image quality will be obtained when shooting at the optimum ISO for your camera. Noise is inherent at higher ISOs.

- The only filter acceptable for digital is a polarizer.

- Achieving the correct white balance may be subjective.

- X-Rite ColorCheckers can give a photographer the technically correct white balance.

- Your work environment is a critical component to your overall workflow and image quality.

- The histogram of an image shows the range of tone within an image. There is no such thing as a good or bad histogram. It simply reflects the tonal range of the image.

- Digital is linear capture, meaning we are capturing degrees of brightness. Twice the light or brightness equals twice the data or information.

- With digital capture, it is better to make a judgment call to overexpose, rather than underexpose.

- The histogram on the back of the camera is an sRGB histogram representing luminance only, and is typically off by one stop.

- It is essential to have a backup for digital imaging.

FILE FORMATS AND SHOOTING RAW

I SHOOTING IN RAW MODE

RAW is the digital capture format that provides photographers with the ultimate flexibility and allows them to produce the optimum file for delivery to clients and reproduction. The RAW format provides the most data, which is the basis for generating the best final image. This format contains all of the actual data captured by the camera's CCD or CMOS sensor. Finally and most importantly, capturing RAW format files gives you a true original: a digital negative. You can always return to your original and process it differently.

In the world of film-based shooting, once the film was processed, there were very limited options to fix a poorly processed or improperly exposed roll of film. However, with digital capture in RAW format, the photographer can manipulate the actual pixel data after the fact to achieve the desired results. This could be as simple as adjusting white balance or increasing contrast in the image, or as complex as manipulating individual color channels to improve hue and saturation. You do not have the ability to make these types of changes to JPEG or other file types without negatively impacting image quality.

Some photographers choose to capture JPEG format files because it is faster. Yes, shooting JPEG files is faster, but has some inherent problems. The JPEG format uses a lossy compression technique that results in pixel data being thrown away even during image captures. This loss of original pixel data lessens the quality of the image. The JPEG algorithm throws away approximately 3800 values of brightness from the image and uses destructive compression to shrink an image into a smaller size at the expense of quality. In fact, a JPEG has one third of its luminance data discarded. Unfortunately, the most commonly implemented capture format for digital cameras is JPEG. Although appropriate in limited circumstances, the difference in quality is very noticeable at higher ISOs where increased noise and hue problems are clearly visible. Most importantly, every time you capture in JPEG format, you have lost your ability to have a real original, and have restricted your color space.

The differences between capturing all the data, as in shooting RAW, or capturing just some of the data, as in shooting JPEG, are pretty dramatic. **Figure 2.1** reveals an image that was shot in RAW and processed as a TIFF. Notice the intense and rich color. This is what we would want the image to look like if we were showing it to a client or a teacher.

Next, take a look at **Figure 2.2** and notice the difference in color and tone. This image was shot in the highest JPEG mode in camera. The colors are severely muted. If you were to shoot both JPEG and RAW and you were going to send your teacher or client the JPEG files as an example of what you shot, you would see that they look very different from the version you shot as RAW. For this reason D-65 stresses that you shoot RAW and then if need be, convert to profile in *Photoshop* or *Lightroom* so that the color of the final image even in a JPEG will look the same as in the master file.

FIG 2.1
An image that was shot in RAW and processed as a TIFF. Notice the intense and rich color.

FIG 2.2
This image was shot in the highest JPEG mode in camera. The colors are severely muted.

The differences between an image with all the data and a compressed file like a JPEG go far beyond just the color. Look at **Figure 2.3 (A)** and **Figure 2.4 (A)** and notice the jagged edges revealed in the JPEG file compared to the full size TIFF file. Also notice the histogram for each file. You can clearly see data loss in **Figure 2.4 (C)** which is the histogram from the JPEG file.

FIG 2.3 (A)

FIG 2.3 (B)

FIG 2.4 (A)

FIG 2.4 (B)
Section of the JPEG file enlarged showing the effects of JPEG compression.

FIG 2.4 (C)

| THE IMPORTANCE OF DNG

Shooting digitally allows a photographer to combine editing with shooting—providing the power to see in real time and improve the image. Personally, we haven't shot any film in more than seven years, and doubt we will ever shoot film again. For what we do, digital is simply better.

But our intellectual property—and the intellectual property of all photographers—is at risk. Why? Almost every digital camera today creates a file, which is in a proprietary RAW format. A RAW file contains all of the data and information the chip in the camera is capable of capturing. Unlike JPEG, which is a lossy compression format that discards data and is only available as an 8-bit file, RAW preserves all of the color data and metadata. Using a RAW format, you can always go back and reprocess to different specifications without losing any quality.

In the old film-based world, when the film was processed, right or wrong, there was no going back. With the RAW format, however, the photographer is able to act as the "lab technician" and tweak the pixel data to achieve both tonal control and white balance.

You simply can't do this with JPEG or other compressed formats without a loss of image quality. Simply put, RAW is the format that is needed to produce the optimum file for delivery to clients and reproduction.

| THE MANY FACES OF RAW

Here, however, is the problem: there are many different and proprietary RAW formats. Each digital camera manufacturer has created one or more proprietary formats for RAW files; some manufacturers even change those proprietary formats between their individual camera models. We have NEF, TIF, CRW, and CR2—just to name a few RAW file extensions. And each camera company has created converters to change these RAW file formats into usable files such as JPEGs, PSDs, and TIFFs.

An additional factor is the evolution of operating systems. As these operating systems change—Mac 9.2 to OSX to Tiger, Panther, Leopard ,Snow Leopard and Lion for instance—software that's compatible with those systems at the very minimum needs updating.

Suppose you have a 4-year-old camera that you used to photograph the greatest project of your life. Of course, you shot RAW because the RAW format is superior to all others. And you did everything right; you even backed up those files to all the media types several times. You now turn on your new computer and find that your camera manufacturer's converter has not been updated to the new operating system and won't run. Your greatest job can no longer be accessed. As operating systems change and as the world of digital capture grows, the potential for disaster increases.

Other problems can also arise. For instance:

* The photographic world is experiencing mergers and acquisitions as are many other sectors of our economy. Suppose your camera manufacturer merges with another company—as with Hasselblad and Imacon—or simply changes and almost disappears like Polaroid or Kodak. Suppose they simply go out of business due to tough economic times or are ravaged by an earthquake and tsunami .You may indeed own the copyright to your data files, but it could become a classic case of having no software to open them.

• Currently, to open RAW files, you can use the camera manufacturer's converter or a third-party software such as Adobe's *Lightroom, Capture One* by Phase One or *Adobe's Camera Raw.* From the perspective of digital photographers, the third-party manufacturers are typically the crème de la crème. Every time a new camera comes out, an engineer from the third-party manufacturer is required to reverse engineer the camera to try to adapt it to their software and then create an update for all their users. The lag time waiting for an update, however, can easily be six months. With all the new cameras coming out at such a rapid pace, it's possible that you could have the latest camera, but that your software of choice may not be updated.

| UNIVERSAL DNG?

With this in mind, Thomas Knoll—the guy who wrote the *Photoshop* program—and a group of other engineers from Adobe have produced a format designed to be universal—Digital Negative, or DNG.

Officially released in September 2004, DNG preserves all of the needed proprietary metadata and color information from the camera manufacturers, and also provides a universal means of archiving the data for all future generations. It does not replace the proprietary file, but rather creates a new file renamed as a DNG, so that you wind up with your original RAW file as well as a copy of the RAW as a DNG. The long term goal is that the camera manufacturers will utilize DNG as their RAW format, and do away with all the proprietary formats—so that all RAW files coming out of digital cameras are DNG.

The ability for us to create art is based on licensing and re-licensing our creations for future generations. If future generations can't even open our creations, digital photography itself is at a risk of demise. In the D-65 workflow, we always archive a DNG.

| FILE FORMATS

While there are many file formats including JPEG2000 and PDF, *Lightroom* supports the following file formats. What follows below is a basic description of each format.

- **RAW:** Raw formats contain unprocessed data from a digital camera's sensor. Most camera manufacturers save image data in a proprietary RAW format.

- **DNG:** Digital Negative (DNG) is a publicly available archival format for RAW files. By addressing the lack of an open standard for the RAW files created by individual camera models, DNG helps ensure that photographers will be able to access their files in the future. You can convert proprietary RAW files to DNG from within *Lightroom* and *Photoshop* and with the standalone free application DNG Converter.

- **TIFF:** Tagged Image File Format (TIFF, TIF) is used to exchange files between applications and computer platforms. TIFF is supported by virtually all paint, image-editing, and page-layout applications. However, most other applications, including older versions of *Photoshop* (pre-*Photoshop CS*), do not support documents with file sizes greater than 2 GB. Most image editing applications will also recognize all the metadata contained in a TIFF file, making it the industry standard. The TIFF format provides greater compression and industry compatibility than *Photoshop* format (PSD) but has several save options and takes longer to save than a PSD. In *Lightroom*, you can export TIFF image files with a bit depth of 8 bits or 16 bits per channel.

- **PSD:** *Photoshop* format (PSD) is the standard *Photoshop* file format. To import and work with a multi-layered PSD file in *Lightroom*, the file must have been saved in *Photoshop* with the Maximize PSD and PSD File Compatibility preference turned on. You'll find the option in the *Photoshop* file handling preferences. *Lightroom* saves PSD files with a bit depth of 8 bits or 16 bits per channel. Adobe applications all recognize PSD. Most other image editing applications will also recognize PSD, but in some cases those applications may not be able to read all of the metadata within the file.

- **JPEG:** Joint Photographic Experts Group format (JPEG, JPG) is commonly used to display photographs and other continuous-tone images in web photo galleries, slideshows, presentations, online services and on camera LCDs. JPEG is an 8-bit RGB image that compresses file size by selectively discarding data. When shooting the JPEG format in camera, there is a loss of about 20% of the data on capture. And every time a JPEG is saved, there is additional loss. Making changes to the JPEG file and saving it over and over again will eventually lead to a file that can no longer be opened in *Lightroom* or *Photoshop*, because each time you save a JPEG, random pixels are thrown away.

- **MOV:** Common multimedia format often used for saving movies and other video files; uses a proprietary compression algorithm developed by Apple Computer; compatible with both Macintosh and Windows platforms. MOV files can be organized and managed in *Lightroom* but they can't be edited.

- **XMP:** Extensible Metadata Platform (XMP) is a type of metadata.

Metadata is a set of standardized information about a photograph, such as the author's name, resolution, color space, copyright, and keywords applied to it. Most digital cameras contain information about a file, such as height, width, file format, and the time and date the image was taken. You can use metadata to streamline your workflow and organize your files.

Lightroom supports the IIM standard of metadata originally developed by the International Press Telecommunications Council (IPTC). Wire services used this standard to identify transmitted text and images. IPTC includes entries for descriptions, categories, credits, and origins and its definitions are the basis for XMP.

XMP facilitates the exchange of metadata between Adobe applications and across publishing workflows. For example, you can save metadata from one file as a template, and then import the metadata into other files.

File information is stored using the Extensible Metadata Platform (XMP) standard. In the case of *camera RAW* files that have a proprietary file format, XMP isn't written into the original files. To avoid file corruption, XMP metadata is stored in a separate file called a sidecar file. For all other file formats supported by *Lightroom* (JPEG, TIFF, PSD, and DNG), XMP metadata is written directly into the files.

SUMMARY

There are seven file formats that we discuss in *Lightroom*: RAW, DNG, TIFF, PSD, JPEG, XMP and MOV.

RAW and DNG are the only formats that contain all of the information the sensor is capable of capturing.

There is currently no standard RAW format. This creates standardization and archiving issues.

DNG is an open source solution to proprietary RAW formats. Digital needs to be as stable as film. Only a standard file format can assure this for the future.

COLOR SPACES FOR DIGITAL WORKFLOW

| THE FOUR COLOR SPACES FOR DIGITAL

There are four major color spaces that we will discuss: sRGB, Adobe 98, ColorMatch and ProPhoto. First, think about color spaces as boxes of Crayola crayons. sRGB is the smallest box of crayons. It has 256 tones. The ColorMatch space can be thought of as a much bigger box than sRGB but not as big as Adobe 98. The large box that many people choose can be thought of as Adobe 98. It is like the big box of crayons with many shades of the same color. Finally, there is the ProPhoto color space, which is so big that there are more colors than you can fit into the box.

| UNDERSTANDING RAW DIGITAL CAPTURE

RAW files contain no color profile upon capture. Once you bring RAW files into an image processing software like *Lightroom,* a color space needs to be designated. ProPhoto is the default color space for the Develop Module in *Lightroom.* ProPhoto is D-65's choice for processing RAW files. We also set up our Color Settings in *Photoshop* with ProPhoto as our working RGB. Why?

Digital cameras today have come a long way in a very short time. Today's sensors are capable of capturing a very wide tonal range. Unfortunately, the majority of photographers simply don't take advantage of the capabilities of their camera's sensor and inadvertently throw out very important color information without even realizing it.

Note that:

- Your camera captures a wider range of colors than you can see. The profile associated with the camera determines the colors available to be processed.

- Your camera captures a wider range of colors than your monitor can display. The profile associated with the monitor determines what colors presented to it are actually displayed.

- Your camera captures a wider range of colors than your printer can print. The profile associated with the printer determines which of the colors presented to it will be printed.

Let's start with how most cameras actually capture color or rather don't capture color. The camera sensor actually doesn't capture color at all. The sensor captures in grayscale only. It captures the intensity of the light in grayscale.

There are colored filters on the sensor so that a given pixel only sees light through a single colored filter of either red, green, or blue. Assuming you are shooting RAW, the job of the converter such as *Lightroom, Adobe Camera Raw* or *Capture One,* is to interpolate that data and render it as color.

If the pixel being interpolated was a "red" pixel, that value is assigned to red. If the pixel being interpolated is a "green" pixel, that value is assigned green, and if the pixel being interpolated was a "blue" pixel, the value assigned is blue. With these three values, a color equivalent number can be calculated.

Every camera requires a profile or formula that can be used to translate the "zeros and ones" that become color equivalent numbers. Monitors and printers must recognize those numbers. This translation is essentially the goal of your working color space.

Okay, so in basic English, the color world we perceive with our eyes is captured by our cameras as light intensity in grayscale, translated into color by a special translator like *Lightroom,* and then passed on to our monitors, printers and all other devices.

| WORKING SPACE FOR DIGITAL

The majority of photographers use Adobe 98 as their working space. While delivery in Adobe 98 may be the so-called "standard" for delivery, it is not necessarily the ideal working space for digital photographers shooting RAW. Why?

ProPhoto can hold all the color the camera can capture, plus more. As cameras improve, they will capture even more colors. Every other color space including Adobe 98 will clip color from today's cameras. So the obvious question is, "What is clipping?"

In digital imaging, when a color falls outside the gamut or range, then we say that the color has been "clipped." If we did nothing about the color, then it would be left out of the final image. If we left these lost colors unattended, then our final image would come out looking flat, due to the missing hues.

One of the biggest complaints of digital photographers is the loss of reds. Well, when colors clip, red is the first to go. ProPhoto preserves the widest range of reds.

A monitor can display colors that cannot be printed. Paper, as well, can render colors the monitor cannot display. Why limit printed colors just because your monitor can't display them?

Epson and Canon printers can print colors that are outside the Adobe 98 space. Using a ProPhoto space will obtain a greater range of tones and colors. The bottom line is that **Adobe 98, or any color space except ProPhoto, does not preserve all the colors you get from the camera.** Once the file is converted, the extra shades are gone forever.

We must also look towards the future. Most of today's monitors can't typically display all of the color in Adobe 98. Some of today's more expensive monitors and the monitors of tomorrow do and will display the full range of Adobe 98, if not more. For anyone using Adobe 98, you must ask yourself the question, "Why would you want to eliminate extra color and tone just because your monitor of today can't show it?"

COLOR SPACE FOR THE WEB

The standard color space for the web for most monitors is sRGB. The reason for this is because when the standards were defined, sRGB was the largest space for any monitor. As monitors get better, there may be less of a need for sRGB.

COLORMATCH COLOR SPACE

Another color space worth paying attention to is ColorMatch. ColorMatch was defined by the old Radius PressView monitors, which were an industry standard quite some time ago.

ColorMatch is very close to the gamut of CMYK (Cyan/Magenta/Yellow/Black). Many photographers have difficulty converting to CMYK and complain about correct color when the client does the CMYK conversions from Adobe 98 for press. Since ColorMatch is very close to CMYK, it makes a lot of sense to deliver in ColorMatch if CMYK is out of the question.

Note: There is a problem delivering in Adobe 98 for most client/photographer relationships. Here's why:

In the old days, when we delivered film, the art director or pre-press house scanned the film and made a proof. Today, most art directors will receive a digital file in Adobe 98 from a photographer. This is where the problem starts.

Delivering in Adobe 98 is sort of like saying, "See all this color? Well, you can't have it." CMYK is a much smaller color space than Adobe 98. Delivery in Adobe 98 just about guarantees that the proof will not look like the image on the art director's monitor.

The blame then falls on the photographer shooting digital. If delivery occurred in ColorMatch, which is smaller than Adobe 98 and very similar to CMYK, the proof will look very much like what is on the art director's monitor. The digital photographer will definitely be hired again.

I USING COLOR SPACES AND PROFILES IN WORKFLOW

With this in mind, it makes sense for digital photographers shooting RAW to make their *Photoshop* Working Space ProPhoto, to process their RAW files as 16-bit ProPhoto, and to store their archive files as ProPhoto.

ProPhoto is perfect for the digital photographer, but it is not ready for prime time TV for the rest of the world. Because the majority of the world is in Adobe 98, you certainly don't want to deliver files to clients in ProPhoto. For client delivery, you may want to convert down to a color space the client can handle.

Most clients are used to Adobe 98. D-65's recommendation is to use the ProPhoto color space during RAW conversion, and then convert and deliver in Adobe 98 or ColorMatch. This will allow the photographer to gain greater tonal range and color and preserve it, achieving a better file. Converting the file to Adobe 98 or ColorMatch will preserve the greater tonal range and color while allowing the client to use the color space to which they are accustomed.

I WHY PROPHOTO?

- ProPhoto can hold all the color the camera can capture.

- As cameras improve, they will capture even more colors.

- When colors clip, red is the first to go. ProPhoto preserves the widest range of reds.

- A monitor can display colors that cannot be printed. Paper can render colors the monitor cannot display. Why limit printed colors just because your monitor can't display them?

- Epson and Canon printers can print colors that are outside the Adobe 98 space. Using a ProPhoto space will obtain a greater range of tones.

- The bottom line: Adobe 98 or any color space except ProPhoto does not preserve all the colors you get from the camera. Once the file is converted, the extra shades are gone forever.

I COLOR SPACES FOR CLIENT DELIVERY

Ideally, we would deliver images in CMYK using the International Color Consortium (ICC) profile supplied by the client or printer. Having the actual CMYK profile when we do our color conversions will produce the best results. However, much of the world disregards color profiles and/or doesn't understand color management. D-65 has a solution for these people, too.

If we are going to deliver RGB images, D-65 will deliver files in ColorMatch. ColorMatch most closely resembles what will be produced by CMYK output. Delivering files in Adobe 98 may look better on the screen, but may contain more colors than can be printed. So what you see is not going to be what your client will get in print.

For images being used on the web or in multimedia presentations, D-65 will deliver files in the sRGB color space. This limited space is the de facto standard for the web.

I DEMONSTRATION OF PROPHOTO

This is an image with a ProPhoto color space and a graph of the image in the color analysis program, Chromix ColorThink. See **Figures 3.1 (A), 3.1 (B), 3.2, 3.3.**

FIG 3.1 (A)
Image in the ProPhoto color space.

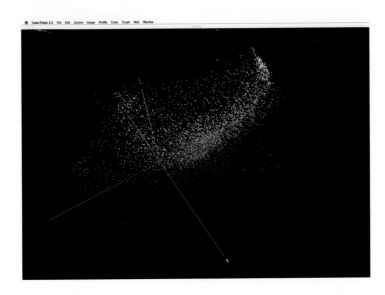

FIG 3.1 (B)
The image shown in
FIG 3.1 (A) showing
a map of the image
color in the application
Chromix ColorThink

This graph displays our image plotted in Adobe 98. Notice how much of the image is out of gamut, or outside the map of Adobe 98. See the yellows out of gamut right here.

FIG 3.2

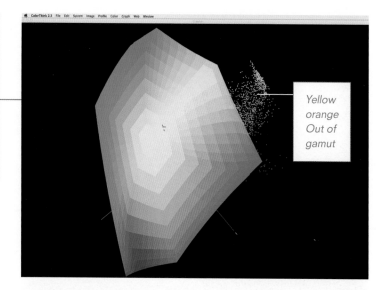

Yellow orange Out of gamut

The graph displays the image mapped in ProPhoto and you will notice that ALL of the color is contained within the ProPhoto space.

FIG 3.3

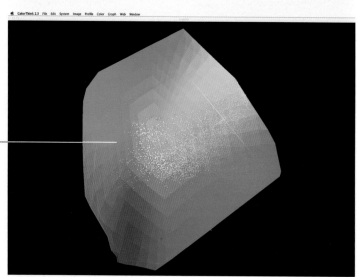

| WHEN TO ASSIGN OR CONVERT PROFILES

One big problem with color management that always surfaces is how to handle files with different tagged color profiles or without any color profile at all.

- When opening a file, always assign a profile to an untagged (missing a profile) file. If a file comes in without a profile, use your working RGB.

- Convert from a source color profile to a destination color profile when you want to retain the color in a file, but need it in a different color space. For example, you would convert a ProPhoto file to sRGB when it is being used on the web. It will still look like the ProPhoto file, but will be tagged sRGB.

- A big misconception is that you can "go up" or increase the color space of a file. While *Photoshop* will allow you to convert from sRGB (a smaller space) to ProPhoto (a larger one), the effect will be one not of additional colors, but only more tones of the same colors.

Lightroom has really simplified many of the tough choices associated with color processing. For one, *Lightroom's* Develop Module uses a very wide color space, essentially ProPhoto RGB but using a gamma of 1.0 instead of 1.8. A gamma of 1.0 matches the native gamma of RAW camera files and ProPhoto is able to contain all of the colors that your camera is able to capture. Since ProPhoto is really a 16-bit space, *Lightroom* uses a native bit-depth of 16 bits per channel.

It makes sense to process your RAW files in ProPhoto and to store your archive file as ProPhoto. For client delivery, you will want to convert to the client-provided CMYK profile or, for a webpress, U.S. Web Coated (SWOP) v2 is a good default if you can't get the ICC profile from the printer. Use ColorMatch RGB for print or sRGB for the web. D-65 does not deliver images in the ProPhoto color space because most clients would not know how to handle it.

Images in *Lightroom* can be in any color space and will be color-managed provided the image has an embedded profile. If the image(s) you are working on do not have an imbedded profile, *Lightroom* will automatically assign sRGB without a warning dialog box.

SUMMARY

- There are four important color spaces for digital photographers. They are from smallest to largest: sRGB, ColorMatch, Adobe 98 and ProPhoto.

- It makes sense to work in ProPhoto for digital imaging, but deliver in ColorMatch or convert to CMYK for print.

- If your images are going onto the web, sRGB is the correct color space.

- *Lightroom's* native color space is 16-bit ProPhoto.

- Assign a profile when an image is not tagged with one.

- Convert to profile when going from a larger color space to a smaller color space.

- While Adobe 98 may be the so-called standard, it isn't necessarily the best color space for digital photographers capturing in RAW.

CHAPTER 4
LIGHTROOM'S DESIGN

The basic architecture of *Lightroom* brings a rather unique
concept to software development. While *Lightroom* itself is one
application, its construction is modular in nature. *Lightroom* is
currently built with seven modules: Library, Develop, Map, Book,
Slideshow, Print and Web. *Lightroom's* modules are like five
separate applications working in a nested-together fashion. Each
module comes with its own set of tools, templates and panels.
(Figure 4.1).

FIG 4.1
Lightroom's Library Module

I MODULES

The modules are located on the top right corner of the *Lightroom* window. Clicking on the name of the module allows you to move between each module (**Figure 4.2**).

FIG 4.2
Lightroom's
Seven Modules

I PANELS

On the left and right side of each screen are panels. Each panel contains functions specific to that module. Generally, the panel on the left side contains content and templates (**Figure 4.3**) while the panels on the right contain the tools for each module (**Figure 4.4**).

FIG 4.3
Slideshow Module
Left Side Panel

FIG 4.4
Slideshow Module
Right Side Panel

I TOOLBAR

The toolbar is located underneath the grid or loupe view of your image(s). It contains controls specific to each module and can be customized by the drop-down menu located at the right side of the toolbar. Your screen size will depend on how many tools can be seen on your toolbar. To view more tools, you can collapse the side panels with the Tab Key. The Library Module Toolbar is shown in **Figure 4.5**. If you think your version of *Lightroom* doesn't have a Toolbar, try hitting the T key. The T key is the keyboard shortcut for showing and hiding the Toolbar.

FIG 4.5
Library Toolbar showing drop-down menu of available tools

| FILMSTRIP

The filmstrip at the bottom of the screen is a view of the current selection in the Library. The Filmstrip displays the photos you are working on as you move between modules. It displays selections from the currently selected Library folder, collection, keyword set, or contents of the Quick Collection.

One great little tip is that you can move forward or backward through your previously viewed images by using the Left or Right Arrows.

FIG 4.6
The *Lightroom* Filmstrip with Go Back Arrow highlighted

| *LIGHTROOM* KEYBOARD SHORTCUTS

There are some terrific basic keyboard shortcuts that will definitely speed up your workflow in *Lightroom*. We have outlined some in **FIG 4.7**.

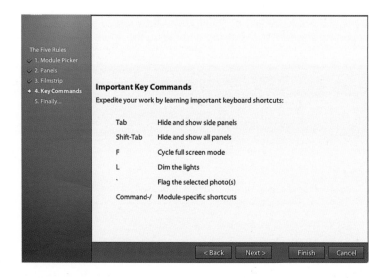

FIG 4.7
Some Important
Keyboard Shortcuts

- Tab will hide and show side panels (**Figure 4.8** and **Figure 4.9**)

FIG 4.8
Library Module Grid View with Show Panels

FIG 4.9
Library Module Grid View with Hide Panels

- The G key is Grid View (**Figure 4.10**) and the E key is Loupe View (**Figure 4.11**)

FIG 4.10
Library Module Grid View G Key

FIG 4.11
Library Module Loupe View E Key

- Shift-Tab cycles to full screen (**Figure 4.12** and **Figure 4.13**)

FIG 4.12
Normal View in Library Loupe

FIG 4.13
Shift Tab brings Loupe View Full Screen

- Pressing the F key will switch to full screen mode and pressing it again will switch to absolute full screen mode, hiding the system bar and hiding the Dock (**Figures 4.14 – 4.16**).

Sometimes people get fooled, because in absolute full screen mode they can't get to their desktop and they think that *Lightroom* has taken over their system and f....' them. **This is a good way to remember what the F key does.**

FIG 4.14
Pressing the F key will change this view to full screen mode

FIG 4.15
Pressing the F key changed this view to full screen mode (System bar and Dock are showing)

FIG 4.16
Pressing the F key again switches this view to absolute full screen mode (System bar and Dock are hiding)

- *Lightroom* can "turn out the lights," meaning that it can dim the technical sections of the screen so that you can view the image more clearly. Pressing the L key once will dim the lights darkening the interface. Pressing the L key again will turn the screen black and pressing it again will take you back to the default (see **Figures 4.17** thru **4.19**). Under *Lightroom* Preferences you can set the shade of gray and the opacity used in dimming.

FIG 4.17
Lights On

FIG 4.18
Lights Dim

FIG 4.19
Lights Out

| ADDITIONAL LIBRARY KEYBOARD SHORTCUTS IN *LIGHTROOM*

- Using Control–Plus (+) and Control–Minus (-) will reduce and increase the size of the thumbnails in the grid

- The spacebar toggles between Fit and user set zoom views in loupe mode

- The spacebar in the grid view will change the view to loupe

- The D Key takes you from the Library Module Grid View into the Develop Module

- Command–Option–Up Arrow will take you to the previous module

- Command–F will activate search

- Command–K will activate the keyword entry field

- Command–Right Slash (/) takes you to the keyboard shortcuts for each module – this is GREAT!

I CREATING CUSTOM WORKSPACES
   IN *LIGHTROOM*

You can create custom workspaces allowing you to display only the panels you want, when you want to see them, to maximize your image size or screen real estate (**Figure 4.20**).

FIG 4.20
Control-Clicking on a panel allows you to custom configure the panel to show or hide

You can manually extend panels, making the sliders larger or smaller. To do this, mouse down on the edge of the panel, and a crosshatch will appear. Drag the cross hatch to the right or left to expand your image size (**Figure 4.21**). This is particularly useful in the Develop module because it allows you to extend the length of the sliders, which provides more accuracy and finesse. Note the extended panels on the right in **Figure 4.22**.

Mouse down and drag to extend a panel.

FIG 4.21

FIG 4.22

I CREATING A FULL SCREEN WORKSPACE

D-65 likes to use the F key and the Tab key to create a full screen workspace. We sometimes find it annoying, however, that the panels on the right and left roll over when you don't want them to roll over. An option that we find useful to correct this annoyance is to press down the Control key (or right-click with a mouse) and at the same time, click on the Panel Group Icon (designated by the little gray triangle pointing to the left and right of the panels). Choose Manual or Auto Hide. (**Figures 4.23**). Both allow you to show the panels instead of having them roll over. You can also synchronize the behavior with the opposite panel.

FIG 4.23
Control-Clicking on the Panel Group Icon to set panels to open and close using Manual

- **Auto Hide and Show:** Displays the panel as you move your mouse to the edge of the application window. Hides the panel as you move the mouse away from the panel–this is the default.

- **Auto Hide:** Hides the panel as you move the mouse away from the panel, but to open the panel, you must use the Tab key or click on the little grey triangle.

- **Manual:** You must open the panel manually by using the Tab key or clicking on the little grey triangle.

- **Sync with Opposite Panel:** This synchronizes both panels so that you do not have to configure each panel separately.

| *LIGHTROOM* PRESETS

Lightroom comes with preconfigured presets, and the user can also create their own presets. Presets are settings that can be created and saved to accomplish various tasks in each module of *Lightroom*. Creating and using presets is an excellent way of speeding up your workflow.

Where Presets are Stored in *Lightroom*

If you have created any presets in *Lightroom* and would like to move them to another computer, they are stored in: User Library>Application Support>Adobe>Lightroom.

Preset Locations for *Lightroom* in Windows

Presets are stored on Windows machines in: Documents and Settings>[username]>Application Data>Adobe>Lightroom.

On Windows Vista and Windows 7 the path is: Users>[username]/AppData>Roaming>Adobe>Lightroom.

For easy access, you can get to this folder by going to the Edit>Preferences>Presets and choosing Show *Lightroom* Presets folder.

FIG 4.24
Easy access to
Lightroom's presets

Moving Presets from One Computer to Another

It is easy to create a preset on one computer and use it on another computer. Copy the preset that you would like to move to another computer and place it within the corresponding folder on your second machine. Make sure never to delete any of the folders that hold the presets. You can also select a preset, right-click and export that preset. That preset can then be imported onto another computer.

Help Available from Every Module

Help and Keyboard shortcuts for each and every module are available under the Help menu while you are in that module.

FIG 4.25
Help and Shortcuts for
each module

SUMMARY

* *Lightroom* is comprised of seven modules, each
designed for a specific task. The functionality of
each module is controlled by a toolbar, panels and
templates. There are many useful keyboard shortcuts
and presets to boost workflow.

CHAPTER 5
SETTING UP *LIGHTROOM'S* PREFERENCES AND CATALOG SETTINGS

All software comes with pre-configured default preferences. Many of us just assume that the defaults are appropriate and start using the software. The defaults may be fine for some, but disastrous for others. In order to truly streamline your workflow, it makes sense to configure your preferences and options so that they best suit your needs and to do so before you start using the software. With this in mind, this chapter will cover all of *Lightroom's* preferences, catalog settings and a few other configurable options so that your *Lightroom* will really fly and your workflow will be more efficient.

| *LIGHTROOM'S* PREFERENCES

Now, let's setup *Lightroom's* preferences. Go to the *Lightroom* main menu bar to Lightroom>Preferences. We will go through each of the preferences panes.

FIG 5.1
To set up Lightroom's preferences, go to the *Lightroom* main menu bar to Lightroom>Preferences.

	Lightroom	File	Edit	Library	Photo	Metadata	View	Window	Help

About Adobe Photoshop Lightroom 4.0 Beta...

Preferences...   ⌘,
Catalog Settings...   ⌥⌘,
Identity Plate Setup...
Edit Watermarks...

Services   ▶

Hide Lightroom   ⌘H
Hide Others   ⌥⌘H
Show All

Quit Lightroom   ⌘Q

| GENERAL PREFERENCES

By default, *Lightroom* will load your most recent catalog. D-65 suggests keeping all your photos in one catalog. However, you may want to create more than one catalog if you cannot hold all of your images in one location, or if you'd like to organize your system differently. You can choose to load another *Lightroom* catalog at any time from this general preferences menu. You can also choose another catalog by holding down the option key when starting *Lightroom*.

FIG 5.2
D-65's suggested setup for *Lightroom's* General Preferences

I PRESETS PREFERENCES

Default Develop Settings. D-65 chooses not to apply auto tone or auto mix. While we may use auto at times, we prefer to start out with our images "as shot," and manually decide how to process them. The reason we do choose "Make defaults specific to camera serial number and ISO setting" is that we might choose to apply a develop preset on import, which is camera- and ISO-specific. If this camera model or ISO should change, with these checked, the develop preset would not be applied.

Location. If you have more than one catalog, you might want to choose to "Store presets with catalog." We like to have our presets available all the time, no matter what catalog we choose or if we create a new catalog. Therefore, D-65 does not check "Store presets with catalog."

Lightroom **Defaults.** Restoring any of the presets listed will restore them to the way *Lightroom* is configured out of the box.

This is useful if you have deleted or made changes to some of the default presets in *Lightroom*. A great way to move custom presets from one computer to another is by clicking the "Show *Lightroom* Presets Folder."

FIG 5.3
D-65's suggested setup for *Lightroom's* Presets Preferences

I EXTERNAL EDITING PREFERENCES

Edit in *Adobe Photoshop CS6*: One of the totally cool features of *Lightroom* is the ability to open a file from *Lightroom* directly into *Photoshop*. This can be done using *Lightroom's* Photo Menu>Edit in *Adobe Photoshop CS6,* or keyboard shortcut, Command-E. You can then save that same file directly back into *Lightroom* next to or stacked with the original. You even have the ability to pick a second application for editing. For example, maybe you have a plug-in that only works in *Photoshop CS5*. You can pick *Photoshop CS5* as your second application. You will then have the choice to open a file in *Lightroom* directly into CS6 or CS5 from *Lightroom's* Photo Menu.

Why would you use the external editing feature? Suppose you shot a skyline of seven frames and they are all in *Lightroom*. You want to use CS6's stitching capability to create a panoramic. You would select all the images in *Lightroom*, choose Command-E to open them in CS6, and create your panoramic in CS6. When you close the file, it automatically creates a new panoramic file in *Lightroom*. Without this feature, you would have had to export each file individually from *Lightroom* and then open each file in *Photoshop*, and import the new panoramic file back into *Lightroom*. The external editing feature is a huge timesaver because you are basically able to bypass the import dialog altogether.

The File Format preference is for the files you are going to create in *Photoshop* or your designated external editing application. D-65 chooses a 16-bit ProPhoto RGB PSD or TIFF, because these are the types of files we create for working in *Photoshop*.

TIFF maybe more compatible with keeping up with changes in metadata in all applications. This is recommended for best preserving metadata in *Lightroom*. The first thing any application is going to update is to a TIFF standard.

Additional External Editor: OK, so why would you want a second editor? One reason a second editor may be desirable is if you want to use *Photoshop* plug-ins. Historically, all plug-ins needed to be rewritten for CS3 and many developers still have not updated some of the plug-ins even though we are up to CS6. If you wanted to use a plug-in that hasn't yet been updated, you may want to choose CS3, CS4, or CS5 as a second editor. If you work on images in several applications, you even have the ability to create a preset for additional editors, specifying the file type, color space, and bit depth per each application preset.

Edit Externally File Naming: We do not apply an export naming convention because we rename during our *Lightroom* workflow, and we like to keep those same names for our exported files.

Edit Externally File Naming: New in *Lightroom 4* Stacks are now enabled in collections. They work the same as folder stacks.

NEW

FIG 5.4
D-65's suggested setup for *Lightroom's* External Editing Preferences

I FILE HANDLING PREFERENCES

Import DNG Creation: If you choose to import as a DNG, instead of copying or moving the camera proprietary RAW file, we suggest the preferences listed in **Figure 5.5**. We choose to import the proprietary RAW file and export a DNG. This way, our proprietary RAW file will match the DNG file. We do this because although we love DNG and believe that it will be here to stay, it is still not universally adopted. Our concern is that if we imported as DNG and DNG was not adopted, that we might have to go back and re-tweak all of our proprietary RAW files. We don't ever want to even think about that scenario. Our hope is that one day DNG will be adopted universally and we would simply be able to import our DNG files and toss our proprietary RAW files.

Some folks like to embed the original proprietary file in the DNG. We do not do this because it takes much longer to embed the file and it would take equally long to extract the file if needed. If DNG isn't adopted, we would have to extract original proprietary RAW files from every file. Ouch.

Reading Metadata: If you are using other applications or have used applications in the past that separate keywords with a period or slash character, then you should check "Treat "." as a keyword separator," and "Treat "/" as a keyword separator." *Lightroom* uses commas (",") to separate keywords. This preference makes it very easy to import and utilize keywords applied to images even if the keywords are not separated by commas and were generated in another application.

File Name Generation: D-65 uses underscores in our file naming convention. Other software applications use all kinds of characters, including spaces, which are known as illegal characters in filenames. Use of illegal characters in filenames can cause applications to have difficulty reading the filename or substitute randomly generated characters in their place. Spaces are particularly notorious for causing problems between computers.

To ensure cross-platform compatibility, *Lightroom* provides some very cool options. Even if your filename contains illegal characters or spaces, *Lightroom* will substitute legal characters for the illegal ones. D-65 chooses to "Replace illegal filename characters with underscore" when a file name has a space or an illegal character. Without this powerful feature, you would have to manually rename all your files that had illegal characters. Now it can be done automatically for you upon import!

***Camera Raw* Cache Settings:** The *Camera Raw* Cache is used for caching RAW data for processing. Caching speeds up the Develop module.

Purging the cache. You may find that older camera profiles identified in the Calibrate panel may have displayed poor results at extreme ends of the temperature and tint ranges. There are new camera profiles for *Lightroom* and some of you may be using your own profiles created with X-Rite's Color Checker Passport (www.xritephoto.com/ph_product_overview.aspx?id=1257). Purging the *Camera Raw* Cache will clear any older profiles from the thumbnails. New thumbnails can then be generated using the latest version The *Camera Raw* Cache can be increased up to 200 GB. Whether this is a true benefit or not is debatable, but we will try to explain and then you can make your own judgment. The ACR Cache is really for an optimization process which will vary depending on the photographer's workflow.

The Previews.lrdata files in the *Lightroom* Catalog are *Lightroom* Previews stored in a JPEG format. These JPEGs are either 1:1, Standard or Thumbnail and are a user option set in Catalog Settings as well as under Import in the Library Module. These previews are used to display images in all of the modules of *Lightroom* with the exception of the Develop Module.

Develop scans the previews to initially render on screen, but then it reads the actual RAW data. After the RAW data is analyzed, Develop performs initial processing, frees up the sliders so you can start working, and then completes processing the RAW data to render everything properly. So the big difference is that the Develop Module is using true RAW data, not just the Previews. lrdata that the other modules use.

Now, here is where it gets a bit complicated. While *Lightroom* reads the RAW data, it also stores it in the *Camera Raw* Cache in a partially processed state, to save reading and reprocessing the full RAW data each time. That is particularly beneficial for speed, especially in Develop loading times, because part of the work has already been completed. If the data isn't in cache, as is the case with the same library but on a different computer (laptop for the road for example), it will just read the RAW data.

Once the cache reaches its limit, it becomes a temporary rolling cache, that is, the oldest images are removed to add the newest images. Images are added to the ACR Cache whenever the RAW data is read—for example, when building previews, updating previews, or loading into the Develop module.

NEW

Video Cache Settings: New in *Lightroom* 4 Default is not set but user has option of limiting the video cache. The maximum size can be adjusted up but the default setting if activated is 5.0 GB.

FIG 5.5
D-65's suggested setup for *Lightroom's* File Handling Preferences

I INTERFACE PREFERENCES

Panels: Feel free to play with the Interface preferences until you find a look that you like. These preferences allow you to customize the visual look and feel of *Lightroom*. You can see what engineers do for kicks late at night by trying some of the different Panel End Markers. For fun, try Yin Yang or Atom. And you thought that engineering was all work and no play!

Lights Out: Controls the color of the background in Lights Out mode. You can also control the dim level. 80% is the default and D-65 stays with the defaults.

Background: The color surrounding your image in Loupe View. Medium Gray is the default, although many people like to change this to black. You can also add pinstripes as texture.

Keyword Entry: You have a choice of commas or spaces for separating keywords, as well as the choice of auto completing text in the keyword tags field.

FIG 5.6
D-65's suggested setup for *Lightroom's* Interface Handling Preferences

Filmstrip: You You can choose "Show ratings and picks" as well as "Show badges." The other useful choices here are "Show photos in navigator on mouse-over" and "Show photo info tooltips and the ability to show stack counts in the Filmstrip (**Figure 5.7**).

FIG 5.7
Stack Count in Filmstrip

Tweaks: Some folks like the "Zoom clicked point to center" option. This option always centers the area that is zoomed. Choosing "Use typographic fractions" will display fractions in metadata fields using fraction characters, superscript or subscript.

| GENERAL CATALOG SETTINGS

Click on the General Preferences Window and click on "Go to Catalog Settings" on the bottom (**Figure 5.8**). You can also get to the Catalog Settings under *Lightroom's* Main Menu>Lightroom>Catalog Settings (**Figure 5.9**).

FIG 5.8
Go to Catalog Settings

FIG 5.9
Go to Catalog Settings
from Menu

FIG 5.10
D-65's suggested set up
for *Lightroom's* General
Catalog Settings

Information: This shows what catalog you are working on, and information on that specific catalog, such as the size, when it was created, backed up and optimized.

Backup: D-65 chooses to "Back up catalog:" Never.

Depending upon the preference you choose for backup, you might see a backup dialog box when *Lightroom* starts or exits. The only time you will not get this window is if you choose to "Back up Catalog:" Never.

The choice to "Backup every time *Lightroom* exits" is a desirable option for LR4, but we think that a better option is to use software like Super Duper or Retrospect to back up both the catalog and the images, which we do twice a day. **Understand that using the backup in *Lightroom* will back up the catalog but not the images themselves.**

I FILE HANDLING CATALOG SETTINGS

Preview Cache: Embedded previews, generated on the fly by the camera, are not correctly color-managed. These previews will not match *Lightroom's* interpretation of the proprietary RAW file. Previews rendered by *Lightroom* are fully color-managed.

Lightroom can create three types of Previews. It can create thumbnails, Standard and full 1:1 Previews. All of these previews are stored in the Lightroom_Catalog Previews.lrdata file. There is no right or wrong preview choice. The best choice depends on what works best with your workflow.

Previews are not the easiest thing in the world to understand, and in fact, just might be the most complicated concept in all of *Lightroom*. If you find it too complicated, many folks simply choose Standard and that should be fine for most needs. For those of you who zoom into 1:1 and don't like to wait, like us, you will probably want 1:1 previews.

Now, a more "geeky" explanation of preview technology for those geeks out there. For every RAW file, *Lightroom* needs several previews of different pixel dimensions called by engineering, a preview pyramid. The reason for this is that as you zoom in, *Lightroom* must be able to deliver a high-quality image. The first preview is set by the size you set for standard previews. If the RAW file is large, like one from a Canon 5D or 1DSM111 (e.g., 20 MP) and the standard size is down around 1440, you will initially have fewer previews for each image in this pyramid. If you render 1:1 previews, *Lightroom* will have rendered all the other previews required for each in the pyramid of the zoom levels up to 1:1. This makes the file quite large.

Standard Preview Size: Designates the maximum dimensions for the rendered preview. Ideally, you would choose a size appropriate for your monitor and camera pixel size. You have four choices: 1024, 1440, 1680 and 2048. If all you want is standard sized, then choose a size equal to or slightly less than your screen resolution. *Lightroom* will also build smaller versions at the same time. These versions are used for the thumbnail, 1:2, 1:3 and 1:4 zoom levels.

FIG 5.11
D-65's suggested
set up for Lightroom's
File Handling
Catalog Settings

The problem here is that many of you will use both a laptop and a desktop monitor. At some point in the future, it may be possible for *Lightroom* to build two different file sizes based on the size of the screen you are using. We use 30-inch monitors and as such we choose 2048 pixels.

Preview Quality: Designates the quality of the thumbnail. Low, medium and high, similar to the quality of the JPEG dialog box. You can see the image better with a high quality JPEG, although it will take up more space.

If you choose a Low resolution preview, it will take up very little space and will load very fast. However, should the file not be online, *Lightroom* will be unable to build very clear slideshows, web galleries or previews in the Library without them appearing jaggy.

Medium previews will work well for many people except that they display using the color space of Adobe 98 and if you need to zoom in to 1:1 to check focus, it will take a bit of time.

High Res 1:1 Previews have only one real downside, their size. 1:1 or full-size previews take up a large amount of hard disk space: ours consume almost 230 GB.

Some folks who like the benefits of the 1:1 previews build them on demand as an alternative to building them up front. They certainly take up a lot of space, and take time to build, but they allow for full-screen size images in the Library Module, Slideshow Module, and Web Module, even when the images are not online. High Res previews will also look exactly the same in the Library Module as in the Develop Module. If the High Res previews are saved and stored, you can even scroll through full screen images in your Library with rapid succession and zero wait time for any rendering. D-65 chooses High for our workflow.

Automatically Discard 1:1 Previews: The choice to discard previews depends on your workflow. For example, a photographer who shoots a job, works on it, delivers it, and never needs to go back to that job again probably never has any use to keep these high resolution previews. A photographer who is routinely moving between shoots would more likely want to keep the high resolution previews for an extended or indefinite period of time. A wedding photographer who works furiously on a wedding for three weeks straight and then hopes he or she never has to deal with that wedding again may want the 1:1 Previews for the three weeks that they were working on the wedding and then toss them. A photographer who shoots stock and is constantly going through images from different dates may find it more beneficial to never toss the 1:1 previews.

D-65 would never want to toss the 1:1 preview, and wait for them to be regenerated the next time we are in that folder in our Library. Let's discuss a couple of basic considerations depending upon your philosophy:

Lightroom grabs the smallest thumbnail it can in order to keep up speed. With a low-res preview, *Lightroom* will load the thumbnails very quickly, but when you scroll through the images they will take time to generate. If you choose a higher quality to begin with, the import process will slow down, but when it is done, the previews are fully generated.

Lightroom will start by loading the embedded or sidecar thumbnail. Nikon image files (NEF) are particularly slow because many of them have full resolution previews.

D-65's workflow sacrifices the time and speed up front in order to get the highest quality thumbnail preloaded. Processing power and RAM may play a significant role in your choice. If you're fortunate enough to have a powerful computer with lots of RAM, you will find that you can gain both speed and quality.

Import Sequence Numbers: This is the default first number of your sequence of images on import.

I METADATA CATALOG SETTINGS

Editing: The menu choice "Offer suggestions from recently entered values" is something of which we have grown very fond. *Lightroom* tries to auto complete what you are writing for keywords and captions.

For all of you who own an iPhone, you know that when you first got your phone, texting drove you nuts because the phone was entering values and text that you didn't want. Once you and the iPhone got used to the auto-complete behavior, it was fantastic! This is exactly the way *Lightroom* behaves with this feature. "Clear All Suggestion Lists" cleans out and restores the default values.

"Include Develop settings in metadata inside JPEG, TIFF and PSD files" is great idea as it allows us to move between *Lightroom* and *Camera Raw* without having to export a new file. Go to Lightroom>Catalog Settings>Metadata and include a check in the box to "Include Develop settings in metadata inside JPEG, TIFF, and PSD files." This is a great option.

Lightroom handles JPEG, TIFF and PSD in a non-destructive fashion. When you make changes to these files in the Develop module, you are only changing a preview of the image on screen. It looks like you're changing the photo permanently, but you're not. Just like a RAW file, if you ever want to get back to the original JPEG, just click the Reset button in the Develop module and it's like nothing ever happened at all. The file can retain all the settings just like copyright information in File Info. By checking this box, the changes are written as metadata to the file, which is really quite cool.

FIG 5.12
D-65's suggested set up
for *Lightroom's* Metadata
Catalog Settings

"Automatically write changes into XMP" is a subject of great debate. If you do not choose this, all changes to the XMP are written to the internal database only. This really allows *Lightroom* to fly. The problem with this is that if the database becomes corrupted, there is no way to extract this information. So in plain English, you might lose all the changes you have made to your images.

D65 advocates always saving an XMP file next to the original RAW file. We accomplish this by manually saving the metadata to the files, by choosing Save Metadata to File from the Metadata menu in the Library Module.

Automatically writing changes may sound great because you do not need to remember to save the XMP, but it is very taxing on the computer. Every time you make a change, the information is written to the internal database as well as to a sidecar XMP file. If the database ever crashes, you will not have lost any information.

Automatically writing XMP will also allow *Lightroom* and other programs like *Bridge* to work seamlessly by synchronizing the XMP settings. By doing this, the XMP files will always be located in the sidecar XMP with the RAW files.

To summarize, we feel it is safer to always write the XMP but *Lightroom* will take a speed hit to do it automatically. For those who want to write the XMP and not suffer a speed hit, uncheck

"Automatically write changes to XMP" and when you are done working on images, either select the individual images or the entire folder of images and choose Command-S or Lightroom>Metadata>Save Metadata to File. This means rather than saving each and every step, you wait to the end of your working session or part way through it and then write the XMP files all at once (Figure 5.13).

If you are the kind of person that can remember to manually save the XMP, you should uncheck the box to automatically save XMP but if you are the kind of person who will probably not remember to save the XMP you may want to check the box.

We prefer to manually save the XMP.

NEW

Reverse Geocoding Settings: New in *Lightroom 4*

Enable reverse geocoding of GPS locations to provide address suggestions.

Enable reverse geocoding suggestions whenever address fields are empty.

Geocoding is the process of finding associated geographic identifiers or coordinates (often expressed as longitude and latitude, or x and y) from text data, such as street addresses. With geographic coordinates the features can be mapped and embedded into media such as digital photographs. Reverse Geocoding is the opposite: finding an associated textual location such as a street address, from geographic coordinates. The idea is to permit the identification of nearby street addresses, places, such as neighborhoods, county, state, or country. Reverse geocoding is on by default. *Lightroom* will only perform reverse geocoding if all of the address fields that it affects (sublocation/ city/state/country) are blank. If you have hand-entered values for any of these fields *Lightroom* will leave them all alone and skip doing the lookup.

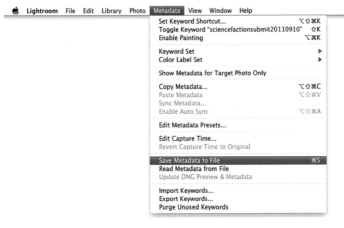

FIG 5.13
Manually Saving
Metadata to File

EXIF: Exchangeable image file format (EXIF) is a specification for the image file format used by digital cameras. "Write date or time changes into proprietary RAW files," the last option in this dialog box, is one we used to advocate as do not check but have since changed our minds. We theoretically would never want to change our proprietary RAW files. Choosing this option will write time or date changes directly to the file as opposed to writing them to the sidecar XMP file. The problem with this is that if you did change the time that a file was shot and you looked at the file outside of *Lightroom* with this option unchecked the change would not be present. In simple terms, if you flew on a plane to a different time zone and you didn't change the time in your camera, you could change it correctly in *Lightroom* but the change would only be present in *Lightroom* and not in the actual file. Because of this we now advocate to "Write date or time changes into the proprietary raw files."

I *LIGHTROOM* OPTIONS

Lightroom also has many configurable options as well as preferences.

I OPTIMIZE CATALOG

Catalog Optimization is improved in *Lightroom 4.0.* If your catalog is running extremely slowly and you are seeing a lot of spinning beach balls, or have any other problems, select Optimize Catalog. Even if you don't have lots of problems it is a good idea to optimize the Catalog on a regular basis.

FIG 5.14
Optimize Catalog

When you choose to Optimize Catalog, *Lightroom* will go through a series of corrective and preventative steps akin to an oil change for *Lightroom*.

FIG 5.15
Optimizing will indicate the last time you optimized the catalog.

FIG 5.16
Optimizing can take quite some time depending on size of catalog.

If optimization does find a problem, it will be corrected about 95% of the time. Should *Lightroom* be unable to repair the catalog, the application will be unable to launch the catalog. One of the most common problems causing a major *Lightroom* error is unplugging a drive containing a catalog or images before shutting down *Lightroom*. Because this is a common mistake and because it can produce a fatal *Lightroom* error, D-65 always suggests having a backup of your catalog. It's that 5% that falls under Murphy's Law, and will no doubt affect you if you do not have a backup.

FIG 5.17
One of the most common and potentially fatal conditions for *Lightroom* is disconnecting a drive containing images or a catalog before closing *Lightroom*.

FIG 5.18
When a catalog is launched after a problem is discovered, *Lightroom* will diagnose and attempt to fix the problem. 95% of the time the problem can and will be fixed and the catalog will be faster and more efficient. Unfortunately there is also a chance that the Catalog may be unable to be repaired.

| IDENTITY PLATE SETUP

Listed right under Preferences in *Lightroom's* Main Menu is the Identity Plate Setup.

FIG 5.19
Location of the Identity Plate Setup

Think of the *Lightroom* Identity Plate literally as a vanity license plate. You can create Custom Identity Plates which can be placed at the top left section of the *Lightroom* interface and in specific modules like Slideshow, Print and Web. In a Web Gallery the identity plate can be a live link. So for D-65 the logo is not only a vanity plate but it will also bring folks directly to D-65.com from a web gallery. This can be your logo or any graphic. You can save multiple identity plates. In our example below, we have saved an identity plate with the name D-65.

FIG 5.20
Identity Plate Editor dialog box.

| EDIT WATERMARKS

The Watermark Editor allows you to customize and identify any information you want to apply as a watermark to your images. There is control over font, opacity, position, size and you can embed watermark graphics into your images. The Watermark

Editor is available from the Library, Slideshow, Web, Print and Develop Modules as well as in the Export dialog box.

FIG 5.21
Selecting the Watermark Editor from the Library Module.

With the Watermark Editor, you can create a text-based watermark or utilize a graphic-based watermark created in another application like *Photoshop*. For a text based watermark, you simply enter the information for the watermark in the box below the image. In our case we typed "© 2012 Seth Resnick All Rights Reserved."

Under Text Options you can choose the font, style, alignment and color. Under the Shadow dialog box you can control the Opacity, Offset, Radius and Angle of a Shadow on the created text. Watermark Effects provides options for opacity, size, and positioning which is controlled by Inset, Anchor and Rotate.

FIG 5.22
Options for the
Watermark Editor.

I VIEW OPTIONS

One way to customize your Library is to display information over
your images for both Grid and Loupe Views. While these are
really options for the Library Module, we like to configure them in
advance of using the Library Module so it is appropriate to cover it
in this chapter on Preferences. The view options can be accessed
under the View Options in the View Menu of the Library Module.

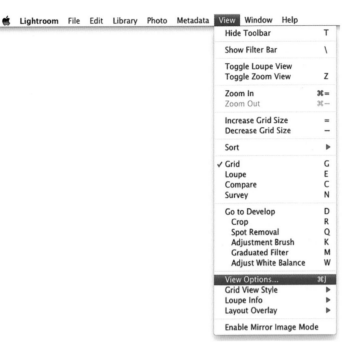

FIG 5.23
View Options Menu

Under Grid View in Library View Options (**Figure 5.24**), D-65 chooses Expanded Cells to display all of the available information on the thumbnails in the grid.

FIG 5.24
Library View Options

Under Options, we choose to uncheck "Show clickable items on mouse over only." With this checked, Rotation buttons and flags will only show when the pointer moves over the cell. Deselecting this option means that clickable items are always displayed.

"Tint grid cells with color labels" will display the color of a label (i.e., red) in the background of the cell. We find that this is incredibly hard on the eyes (**Figure 5.25**) and instead we uncheck this feature and check "Show Rating Footer, Include Color Label" (**Figure 5.26**).

FIG 5.25
Tint Grid Cells with
Color is hard on
the eyes.

Color Label in
Rating Footer is
much easier on
the eyes.

FIG 5.26
Show Rating Footer,
Include Labels is much
easier on the eyes.

"Show image info tooltips" will include a description of an item,
like a badge, or a pick flag, when the pointer is over the item.

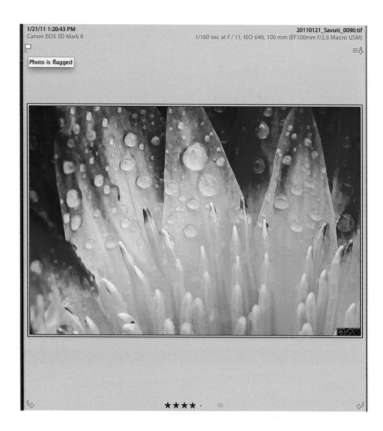

FIG 5.27
Image info tooltips

Under Cell Icons, "Flags" will display a Pick or Rejected icon in the upper-left corner of the thumbnail cell.

"Quick Collection Markers" shows the Quick Collection marker in the upper-right corner of the photo thumbnail. We turn this feature off and use the shortcut (B) to mark an image for a Quick Collection. We find it to easy to hit the marker by mistake.

"Thumbnail Badges" will reveal photos that have keywords, cropping applied, or image adjustments.

"Unsaved Metadata" is by default unchecked and we prefer to have it checked.

When you've added metadata to an image in *Lightroom* without saving the metadata to file, the "Metadata File Needs to Be Updated" icon will appear in the upper-right corner as a reminder.

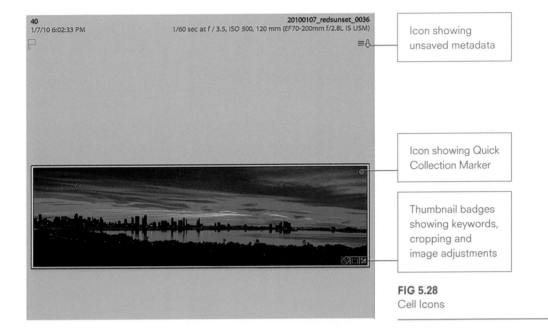

Icon showing
unsaved metadata

Icon showing Quick
Collection Marker

Thumbnail badges
showing keywords,
cropping and
image adjustments

FIG 5.28
Cell Icons

"Compact Cell Extras" can be chosen to show the Index
Number, which is the order number of the photo in Grid and
Rotation. "Index Number" shows the order number of the photo
in Grid view. "Rotation" makes rotation buttons available. "Top
Label" shows your choice of information from a menu as does
"Bottom Label."

FIG 5.29
Compact Cell Extras

"Expanded Cell Extras" offers "Show Header with Labels" which
can display up to four items that you choose from the menus.
"Show Rating Footer" shows the footer items you select. We like
to choose "Include Color Label" and "Include Rotation Buttons."

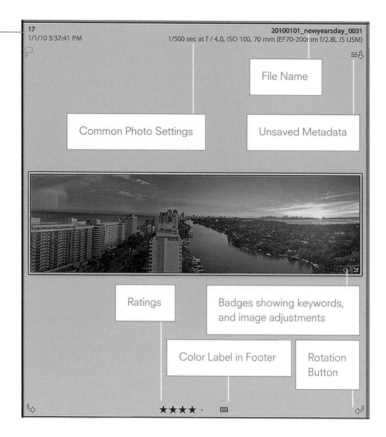

Index Number and Capture Date/Time

File Name

Common Photo Settings

Unsaved Metadata

Ratings

Badges showing keywords, and image adjustments

Color Label in Footer

Rotation Button

FIG 5.30
Expanded Cell Extras

17
1/1/10 5:37:41 PM

20100101_newyearsday_0031
1/500 sec at f / 4.0, ISO 100, 70 mm (EF70-200mm f/2.8L IS USM)

★★★★ ·

Under Library View Options Loupe View (Figure 5.31), D-65 chooses to show File Name, Capture Date/Time and Common Photo Settings. Whatever information is useful to you can be configured for your workflow.

- Info 1 displays the Info 1 Overlay.

- Info 2 displays the Info 2 Overlay.

- Cycle Info display cycles through the two Info Overlay sets.

- The letter I will toggle between the displays.

Library View Options

Grid View | Loupe View

☑ Show Info Overlay: Info 1 ▾

Loupe Info 1

File Name ▾ | Use Defaults
Capture Date/Time ▾
Common Photo Settings ▾
☐ Show briefly when photo changes

Loupe Info 2

File Name ▾ | Use Defaults
Exposure and ISO ▾
Lens Setting ▾
☐ Show briefly when photo changes

General

☑ Show message when loading or rendering photos
☑ Show frame number when displaying video time
☑ Play HD video at draft quality

FIG 5.31
Library View Options
Loupe View

20110121_Savuti_0062.CR2

FIG 5.32
Loupe View with File
Name, Capture Date/
Time and Common
Photo Settings. Using
the letter I you can
toggle between views.

| SUMMARY

- *Lightroom's* Preferences can be configured to streamline workflow.

- Using an External Editor in *Lightroom* allows for images to be worked on in another application and brought directly back into *Lightroom* without importing the images.

- The *Lightroom* Catalog also has settings to streamline workflow.

- If your *Lightroom* Catalog is running slowly, you can optimize and repair it.

- Choosing *Lightroom* preview quality really depends upon what your needs are as a photographer. D-65 chooses high quality previews all the time because it is the only preview that loads in the ProPhoto color space and allows for 1:1 previews.

- The Identity Plate in *Lightroom* is not only a vanity plate, but can also be used in slideshows and web galleries as a direct link to your website.

- The Watermark Editor allows you to customize and identify any information you want to apply as a watermark to your images.

- One way to enhance your Library is to customize the display information over your images for both Grid and Loupe Views.

CHAPTER 6
UNDERSTANDING *LIGHTROOM'S* CATALOG

I DIGITAL ASSET MANAGEMENT

Lightroom is a true digital asset management system, and much more powerful than a simple or even advanced browser. An image browser allows you to simply browse folder structures and see thumbnails, while *Lightroom* stores information directly into a database. One of the key differences here is that with *Lightroom*, all of your information about your images is available even if the image collection is not online or connected to your computer. This means that you can take *Lightroom* on a laptop and still see twenty years' worth of images and all the accompanying metadata, without physically having those images with you. You cannot do this with an image browser.

Let's make this really simple. Let's suppose that you have your images on an external hard drive. With *Adobe Bridge*, for example, in order to see those images, the hard drive has to be connected to your computer or the images will not be visible. With *Lightroom*, your external hard drive with the images can be a thousand miles away and you would still be able to see your images on your computer.

There are pros and cons to each of these approaches. The biggest pro for *Lightroom* is that the majority of the information about your images is available regardless of whether the images are with you or not (on- or off-line). The downside or the con to *Lightroom* is that in order to achieve the above, the images must be imported into *Lightroom's* database.

Looking at the biggest pro and con of *Bridge* in comparison to *Lightroom*, is that you do not have to import anything into *Bridge* to view it. You simply scroll through a hierarchy and can view your images. The downside is that anything you want to view must be connected to your computer or on your connected hard drive.

Lightroom will not replace *Bridge*. They are intended to complement each other. If you need to deal with files like PDFs, and you want to place files from one Adobe application into another, you will likely find that *Bridge* is good for your workflow needs. If you are a digital photographer and looking for a true digital asset management system, where you can even take your entire image collection on the road with you, then *Lightroom* is your answer.

I *LIGHTROOM* IS LIKE YOUR LOCAL PUBLIC LIBRARY

Let's explain the concept of the *Lightroom* Catalog using a visit to your local public library as an analogy (**Figure 6.1**). When you walk into your local public library, there are thousands of books, on many shelves and possibly on multiple floors. You've come to the library today to find one book. You can ask the librarian for help, or you can go to the card catalog (**Figure 6.1C**) for all kinds of specific information about every book in the library.

It would be possible but illogical to walk through the aisles looking at every book to find the title you are seeking. Instead, you go to the card catalog and find the location of your book and simply walk directly to the right location. Similarly, it is not efficient to browse through a million thumbnails to find one image. So *Lightroom* uses a catalog (*Lightroom* Catalog.lrcat) as its card catalog for your images, the same as the card catalog in your public library.

Now, let's add to this concept. Your public library doesn't exist with only a card catalog. There is a physical building that holds all the books within it, along with the card catalog. In *Lightroom*, your images are also stored in a physical place. D-65 prefers this image library to be an external drive, or a secondary internal hard drive. This hard drive is your "public library" and all the images that reside in it are your "books." You may have thousands of images, just like a library has thousands of books. These images become your *Lightroom* Library. To find a specific image, you will use the power of *Lightroom's* Catalog, exactly like the card catalog at your local public library.

FIG 6.1
Public Library

FIG 6.1A
Lightroom Library Hard Drive

FIG 6.1B
Folders of images & LR Catalog

FIG 6.1C
Public Library Card Catalog

FIG 6.1D
Lightroom Catalog

FIG 6.1E
Contents of *Lightroom* Catalog

I THE *LIGHTROOM* CATALOG

So how does *Lightroom* work? To fully understand how *Lightroom* works, we will need to examine its structure. *Lightroom* has some basic components:

1. There is the application itself, *Adobe Lightroom 4*, which resides in your application folder.

2. There is location where the images must live and the catalog must live. We use a dedicated hard drive for this and it is called Lightroom_Library.

3. There is also the actual catalog much like the card catalog in a public library. We create this catalog which lives on the hard drive that contains our images. We name that folder Lightroom_4_Catalog. This folder contains two very critical files: the Lightroom_4_Catalog.lrcat and the Lightroom_4_ Catalog Previews.lrdata. These two files are the heart of *Lightroom*. The default location for this *Lightroom* folder is in your User>Pictures folder.

    The Lightroom_4_ Catalog_Previews.lrdata file contains the thumbnail previews for each of your image files. There are several types of previews available to you, and we will cover them later.

    The Lightroom_4_ Catalog.lrcat file contains all of the database information related to your images.

    There is one more folder which is stored in your User>Library>Application Support>Adobe>Lightroom folder which contains all of the presets that come with *Lightroom*, as well as any custom presets that you may create. The Windows path for this information is Documents and Settings>[Username]>Application Data>Adobe>Lightroom.

4. The Develop Module in *Lightroom* uses the Preview cache only momentarily while it loads the actual RAW file. The Develop Module needs the full file in order to apply settings to the pixel data.

In order to optimize time spent switching between images in the Develop Module, *Adobe Camera Raw* stores some of the data it needs in a cache. This ACR Cache which is set as part of the preferences in *Lightroom* does not store previews, but stores processed image data that is used to give a boost to the Develop Module whenever it need rendering changes. The default location for the ACR Cache is Users>Library>Caches>*Adobe Camera Raw.*

FIG 6.2
Default Catalog Location

| *LIGHTROOM'S* CATALOG LOCATION

Here is the critical concept. The default location for the catalog created by *Lightroom* and your images is in your User>Pictures folder. For an amateur or even a professional who does not have a large collection of images, this default location is fine. But keep in mind that with today's cameras, like a Canon 1DS Mark III, each file can be close to 100 MB.

As your computer's internal hard drive becomes more than 50 percent full, it rapidly loses efficiency. Potentially, your catalog could easily become larger than the space on your main hard drive. For this reason, we prefer not to use the default location, and instead use large dedicated drives (internal or external) to hold our *Lightroom* Library and Lightroom_4_Catalog. D-65 is currently using a 2.0 terabyte 7200 RPM drive to hold the Lightroom_4_ Catalog and the *Lightroom* library.

To set up your new *Lightroom* Library and Catalog, we suggest using two large dedicated hard drives. One is for holding your *Lightroom* Library and Catalog, and one as a backup holding the exact same information. We name the drives Lightroom_Library, and Lightroom_Library_BK. Regardless of how many hard drives we have, we always know which one holds our images and catalog for *Lightroom.* Naming the hard drives in this way keeps things organized right from the start.

*TIP: A simplified approach for the hobbyist or for the
photographer who does not have thousands of images.*

The number one problem we encounter with folks using
Lightroom is that they end up with multiple catalogs on many
drives and they can't find their images. This problem is so
prevalent that we even did a video with Michael Reichman called,
"Where the #$@! Are My Pictures?"

Why the problem?

**If your *Lightroom* Catalog is on an external drive and is set
to be your default catalog in the preferences, everything will
work fine until one day when you start *Lightroom* and your
drive with the catalog is not plugged in or online.**

As soon as this happens *Lightroom* will start up from a new
catalog in the User>Pictures folder and it will appear that you
have lost all your images. We can't begin to tell you how many
times people have called us to say that *Lightroom* has lost their
images and 99% of the time this is the problem. **(Figure 6.3)**

FIG 6.3
Lightroom opened
up without the hard
drive that has the
catalog connected.

So, if you are not a technically inclined person or if you don't
have that many images, you may want to consider simply leaving
your catalog at the default location in the User>Pictures folder.
The benefit of this is that you will never misplace or "lose"
your catalog or your images. **If you are a power user or a
professional with thousands of images, we strongly
suggest that you maintain your catalog and images on a
dedicated drive.**

We use an internal drive to store our *Lightroom* Catalog and our RAW files. There is nothing else on this drive. It is dedicated to *Lightroom* only. By using an internal drive, we are able to have the fastest possible connection. We maintain an exact duplicate of this drive on a second drive just for safety and we call this drive Lightroom_Library_BK. The "BK" stands for backup.

Lightroom_Library

Lightroom_Library_bk

FIG 6.4
Lightroom_Library hard drive and backup drive

I WHAT IS THE *LIGHTROOM* CATALOG?

In order for *Lightroom's* Catalog to "see" or recognize an image, the file itself must be physically imported into *Lightroom*. The Lightroom_Library hard drive contains all of those imported files. In *Lightroom*, you can only have one catalog loaded at a time. We choose to use a 2.0 terabyte drive, so that we can hold all of our imported files and the Lightroom_Catalog on one dedicated hard drive that is always loaded as *Lightroom's* default.

D-65's *Lightroom* Library contains mostly RAW files and some finals that needed further work in *Photoshop*. These can be RAWs or DNGs. We try holding our RAW files in the *Lightroom* Library, and only a few processed files for one specific reason. *Lightroom* may slow down if more than 150,000 files are in the Library. Eventually, the goal is for *Lightroom* to be able to hold at least one million files.

D-65 has taken all of its RAW files going back to 1998, and imported them into the *Lightroom* Library. Our dedicated 2.0 terabyte drive contains folders of RAW files, each designated with a job name (year, month, day, underscore job name). Also on this 2.0 terabyte drive is our *Lightroom* Catalog folder. It is held within the Library. See **Figure 6.5** on the next page.

FIG 6.5
External Drive holding all the folders of RAW files, along with the catalog

As you can see, D-65's catalog folder is very large. This is our primary reason for a large, dedicated drive holding all of our *Lightroom* files. Most folks do not have the space necessary on their primary drives for this amount of data.

FIG 6.6
Lightroom Catalog.lrcat (the catalog that stores information on your images in the Library)

I PROCEDURE TO CREATE A NEW CATALOG ON NEW DRIVE

1. Start with a clean drive and name the drive Lightroom_ Library. From the *Lightroom* Library Module choose File>New Catalog or Start *Lightroom* while holding down the option key

2. The Select Catalog window will pop up with your catalog's location

3. Choose "Create New Catalog"

4. Choose the drive that you named Lightroom_Library

5. Under "Save As," type in Lightroom_4_Catalog

6. Choose Create

7. *Lightroom* will open with your new catalog loaded

FIG 6.7

The next time you start *Lightroom* with the option key down, you will see your new catalog listed. We suggest checking "Always load this catalog on startup" so that it will always load as your default catalog.

FIG 6.8
"Always load this catalog on startup" so that it will always load as your default catalog.

CATALOG TIPS:

- *If you ever lose your Library or Catalog, you have to physically choose the catalog file (.lrcat) within the Lightroom_Catalog folder.*

- *To create a new catalog, hold down the Option/Alt key on Windows or the Options Key on Mac when starting Lightroom.*

- *Lightroom's performance will decrease significantly if virus software is turned on.*

I USING MORE THAN ONE CATALOG IN *LIGHTROOM*

You can create more than one *Lightroom* Catalog in order to aid with organization and digital asset management. The downside is that you can only have one Library and one Catalog open at the same time.

There is no right or wrong answer as to how many catalogs you have in *Lightroom*. It is a matter of philosophy. A past *Adobe Lightroom* Evangelist, loved to have catalogs for every place he traveled. For him, this made total sense because he simply looked at the title of the catalog, and loaded the catalog he was trying to find. A photographer who shoots weddings, bar mitzvahs and social events may very well want a separate catalog for each type of event.

Since you can only view images from one catalog at a time, D-65 prefers to have one large catalog holding all the information on our images, and using extensive metadata and keywords to describe each image. In this way, we can drill down and find anything we want. For example, we will always have keywords or metadata describing the location we shot, so if we wanted to find all of our Miami Beach images, we would simply search the entire catalog for Miami Beach, and find those images.

| SUMMARY

- *Lightroom* is a digital asset management system, not just a browser.

- *Lightroom* needs a catalog to find images. It is just like the card catalog at the Public Library. Inside the *Lightroom* Catalog are two very important files, catalog.lrcat and Catalog Previews.lrdata.

- D-65 chooses to change the default location of the catalog because of its size.

- D-65 creates its own dedicated *Lightroom* Library drive that holds all RAW files and the *Lightroom* Catalog.

- You can create a new *Lightroom* Catalog.

- You can use just one catalog or more than one catalog, but only open one at a time.

CHAPTER 7
THE LIBRARY MODULE

Let's start by talking about *Lightroom's* first Module, the Library. The Library Module is "command central" for *Lightroom*. This is the heart of the digital asset management system. It is where you view, sort, search, manage, organize, rank, compare and browse through your images.

The *Lightroom* Library Module is a true database that catalogs all imported images so you can view previews and data whether the images are online or not. **All images must be imported into *Lightroom* to view them.** The import process imports the image and also creates a metadata record in *Lightroom's* Catalog. This record contains all the data about the image including location, editing instructions and previews. The catalog can be thought of as the authoritative source of information for *Lightroom*.

It is important to understand the distinction between the *Lightroom* Library Module, and the *Lightroom* Library hard drive that we create to hold image files and the *Lightroom* Catalog. The *Lightroom* Library hard drive is simply a physical place that holds yours images and *Lightroom's* catalog much like a public library. We've discussed the importance of this *Lightroom* Library hard drive in Chapter 4. Now, let's talk about the features of the *Lightroom* Library Module.

The *Lightroom* Library Module is one of *Lightroom's* seven modules and the module where all organization takes place.

There are many positive changes in *Lightroom 4* for the *Lightroom* Library. Here are a few of the cool ones:

NEW

New in *Lightroom 4*

I LIBRARY MODULE IMPROVEMENTS IN
  LIGHTROOM 4

- Email from directly within *Lightroom*

- New Zoom ratios (1:8 and 1:16)

- Mac version now includes a language selection option via preferences

- Move multiple folders from volume to volume (Previously only single folder workflow was enabled)

- Module picker can be customized via right-click option

- Additional Metadata controls on export

- "xmp has changed on disk" (i.e the up arrow) badges. This badge means you changed the XMP externally. This new badge should have always been showing, but LR didn't properly detect that condition in the past.

- "xmp conflict" (exclamation point) badges where you previously had "unsaved xmp" (down arrow) badges

- Enhanced output model for saving/storing settings applied in Web, Slideshow, Print and Book. Efforts are now clearly visible in Collections panel.

- Library Module walkthrough tips

| VIDEO

- Video playback directly within *Lightroom*

- Video trimming (In and Out points)

- Set Video poster frame. (This is the thumbnail that appears in the grid view)

| COLLECTIONS

- Flag status is now 'global' (One setting per image regardless of location in folder or collection)

- Stacking is now possible in collections

| THE LIBRARY FILTER

- Filter and search images by a saved or unsaved metadata property

- Metadata and filter options available for DNG file types

| PUBLISH COLLECTIONS

- Publish Collections can now include video publishing Export to Adobe Revel functionality

- Photos in publish collections that have been modified can be set to not re-publish

- Publish videos directly to Facebook or Flickr

I ENHANCED DNG OPTIONS

- Enhanced DNG options

- Embed Fast Load Data options dramatically improves image loading performance in the Develop module

- Lossy compression option provides significant file savings with minimal quality impact. (Ideal for archiving outtakes or reducing the size of time lapse projects without losing the flexibility of raw)

- Resolution reduction via export provides the ability to share lower resolution versions of the original raw file without losing the capabilities offered by raw.

Library Filter

Catalog Panel

Folders Panels

Collections Panel

Import and Export Buttons

Filmstrip

Toolbar

Grid View

Right hand side contains the Keywording Panel, Keyword List, and Metadata Panel, as well as the Histogram

FIG 7.1
The Library Module Main Window

Now, we'll go over how all the panels in the Library Module function. We'll start with the left-hand panels.

| NAVIGATOR PANEL

The Navigator is located on the top left. This gives you a preview of the selected image. Clicking on the image in the Navigator will go to Loupe Mode to display the image in a large view.

There are four views plus a drop-down menu in the Navigator. The drop-down menu contains 10 additional magnification choices ranging from 1:16 to 11:1.

A great shortcut for the Navigator is to use Command + and Command - to zoom in and zoom out. The spacebar also can be used to zoom as well as the Z key.

Move through the image using the Navigator.

FIG 7.2
The Navigator Window

Using the Navigator in Workflow

The Navigator is great for checking critical focus or pixel defects. Clicking on any of these choices will enlarge the image accordingly. One very neat feature is that you can move through the image using the Navigator (similar to *Photoshop*). Typically, you are going to want to see the entire image and then zoom in for a 1:1 view to check for sharpness. If you click on Fit and then click on 1:1, you will be able to cycle between those two views by using the space bar, or clicking on the image in Loupe View. **Figure 7.3** displays 1:1.

FIG 7.3
Cycle between two views by using the space bar or clicking on the image in Loupe View

The Catalog panel displays the number of photographs in your Library under All Photographs. When you highlight All Photographs, you will see all the images in your catalog displayed in the Grid. It also displays any Quick Collection you may have, as well as your previous import and previous export as a catalog or any missing files. Control-clicking on All Photographs will bring up the dialog Import Photos and Video and Import from another Catalog.

▽ Catalog	
All Photographs	**55877**
Quick Collection +	0
Previous Import	5805

FIG 7.4
The Catalog Panel

What are Quick Collections?

A Quick Collection is a temporary gathering of images. There are several ways to create a Quick Collection. Our favorite way is to simply use the keyboard shortcut B key. Use the B key while you have an image or images selected will automatically add it to the Quick Collection. To remove images from a Quick Collection, hit the B key again.

The default way to create a Quick Collection is to click on the circle on the top right of the cell around the image when browsing images. A dialog box will pop up and ask you if you'd like to add this image to a Quick Collection. Having the Quick Collection Marker turned on is controlled in View Options. We prefer to turn the marker off and use the B key instead (see View Options in Chapter 5).

A Quick Collection is not meant to be a permanent place to group images, just a temporary culling from a shoot to use in any module. You can only have one Quick Collection at a time. When you add an image to the Quick Collection, it does not move the image; it just adds a reference to the file's metadata. Think of a Quick Collection as a virtual shelf holding culled images temporarily.

Using Quick Collections in Workflow

Think about going through a group of folders to find your portfolio images. One way to do this is with a Quick Collection. As you browse through folders, you could add each potential portfolio image to a Quick Collection. When you have browsed all your folders, you may remove some images. Finally, when you have your selects for your portfolio, you may want to save the Quick Collection as a permanent Collection called Portfolio.

Quick Collections are great for making web galleries, slideshows, or books of selected images that do exist within the same folder. It is great as a temporary culling of your images. The advantage of having a Quick Collection is that you are not moving those images out of the folder(s) in which they exist. You are only adding pointers in the metadata that identifies those files.

You can export from a Quick Collection, even though it is just a virtual collection. You can always convert a Quick Collection to a permanent collection by choosing File>Save Quick Collection. You can clear a Quick Collection by choosing Clear Quick Collection from the File Menu. Additionally, if you Control-Click on the Quick Collection you can Save the Quick Collection or Clear the Quick Collection.

Click here to add to quick collection or just press the B key.

The dark circle shows that this image is part of a Quick Collection

FIG 7.5
Quick Collection Marker

Target Collections

There is a + next to Quick Collection. The + sign signifies that Quick Collection is designated as your Target Collection. Any collection can be deemed a Target Collection. A target is simply the location that the image(s) will be referenced to when using the B key. By default, Quick Collection is your Target Collection. You can only have one Target Collection at a time. To change your Target Collection, control- or right-click on the new collection you want deemed as your target, and choose Set as Target Collection.

In **Figure 7.6**, we have set our Antarctica 2011 Collection as our Target Collection, so anytime we hit the B key on an image, we are adding a metadata reference of that image to our Antarctica 2011 Collection.

FIG 7.6
Setting a
Target Collection

WORKFLOW TIPS FOR QUICK COLLECTIONS:

- *Command-B toggles you between the folder you
  are browsing and a Quick Collection you already
  have created*

- *D-65 prefers to use the B key to add/delete from the
  Quick Collection—it is too easy to accidentally click on
  the little circle when double-clicking on an image to go
  to Loupe View and inadvertently adding it to a Quick
  Collection—you can turn off the Quick Collection circle
  under View Options*

- *Control-Click on the Quick Collection to Save the Quick
  Collection or Clear the Quick Collection*

Previous Import in the Catalog Panel

Previous Import displays the number of images of your last
import. This is the field that will be selected first by default after
you import images into *Lightroom*. D-65 suggests moving off
Previous Import and going directly to the folder of images you
are working on. The main reason for this is some features that are
available at the folder level are not available in Previous Import.

I THE FOLDERS PANEL

When you import images into *Lightroom,* the folders containing
those images are displayed in the Folders Panel. The number of
imported images within that folder is shown to the right of the

folder name. The subfolders within the Folders Panel can also have subfolders for further organization. Simply click on the + icon next to Folders while you have a folder selected and it will prompt you to create a subfolder name. The Root Folder Display can show Folder Name Only, Path from Volume or Folder And Path.

FIG 7.7
Folder Panel showing
Folder Name Only

I THE VOLUME BROWSER

The Volume Browser (**Figure 7.8**) tells you where the images are and how much disk space is used/available (or photo count). Option/Alt clicking on the Volume Browser will select all the folders on that volume. Control-clicking on the volume browser (**Figure 7.9**) reveals available Disk Space, Photo Count, Get Info and Status.

FIG 7.8
The Volume Browser

FIG 7.9
Control Clicking on the
Volume Browser

Workflow in the Folders Panel

D-65 uses a specific file naming convention for all the imported folders of images, as well as for the images themselves. We import into a folder with a naming convention of Year, Month, Day, and Job Name. All of our image folders then line up in a hierarchical order based on year, month, and day, making it easy to browse through the jobs in a logical progression. The images inside those folders are also named using the same convention, with the addition of a sequence number. We will discuss this in more detail once we begin importing images.

The folders panel displays all the imported folders into *Lightroom*. Everything you import will show up in this panel in specific folders with the number of images included within each folder.

FIG 7.10
The Folders Panel

Click on the + icon to create a new folder or subfolder. Clicking on the – icon will remove a folder. You can also Add New Root Folder, display Folder Name Only, display Path from Volume and display Folder and Path

FIG 7.11
Click on the + icon to create folders

FIG 7.12
Control Click on a panel to display what panels will show or not show

You can move images within folders by dragging and dropping them. To move images, select the images you want to move in the Grid and drag them to the new folder location. Shift-select will select images in sequence and Command-select will select images out of sequence. You will see an icon, which looks like a stack of slides. The original location is shaded in light gray and the new location is shaded in light blue. **These are the actual images that are moving, not just reference files. The files will physically move on the hard drive where they reside as well.**

Moving Folders

You can move folders by dragging and dropping them. To move folders, select the folders you want to move in the Folders Panel and drag them to the new folder location. Shift-select will select folders in sequence and Command-select will select folders out of sequence. The original location is shaded in light gray and the new location is shaded in light blue.

New in *Lightroom 4* Move multiple folders from volume to volume, In *Lightroom 3* only single folder workflow was enabled.

FIG 7.13
Moving images between folders

Images we are moving from one folder into another folder. The original folder is shaded grey and the new location is shaded blue.

More Folder Panel Options

To rename a folder, Control-click or right-click on the folder and choose Rename. The folder name will be changed in the Folders Panel, and also in the physical location where the folder resides. You will also notice that you can create subfolders, Show in Finder, Get Info, Save Metadata, Synchronize, Update Folder Location, Export the Folder as a Catalog and Import into this Folder. Depending on where the folder is located, you can also add the parent folder or promote subfolders.

Synchronize Folders is useful as you have the option of adding files that have been added to the folder but not imported into the catalog, and removing files which have been deleted.

The Save Metadata option will update and save any changed metadata to either the catalog or to sidecar .XMP files as determined by your preferences. Lastly, Update Folder Location allows you to change the folder links without having to first remove the existing folder.

FIG 7.14
Options in the
Folders Panel

Lightroom as a DAM

Lightroom is a true digital asset management system (DAM) The catalog can display folders and images even if they are not currently physically present. In the example below, D-65 is on the road using a laptop computer. We have taken our Lightroom_Catalog with us but we have only taken a few folders of images from our *Lightroom* Library hard drive. We have taken these folders of images because we want to work on these files while we are on location. The folders in the light gray shade with the question mark (?) designate folders with images inside the folder that are not physically present on the external hard drive associated with our laptop's *Lightroom* Location Library. The folders shown in white are physically present on our external hard drive that we use as our *Lightroom* Location Library.

Shown in **Figure 7.15** are folders with question marks and a dark shade of gray. These files are not physically present. However, *Lightroom* still has the power to browse these files, search for these files, and perform other database activities, with the exclusion of actual developing.

The folders with the question marks are not physically on the laptop or the *Lightroom* Location Library hard drive. They are still "at home or at the studio." The folders of images in white are on the mobile external hard drive that we take on location for our *Lightroom* Location Library.

20100351_luci_pool	16	
20100402_beach	43	
20100403_south_beach	68	
20100404_luci	17	
20100414_d65_office	24	
20100419_rain	31	
20100419_underwater_pool	130	
20100423_jupiter	4	
20100425_kaly_luci	22	
20100426_gander	50	
20100427_NorthernLights	8	
20100427_reykjavik	220	
20100429_Hellisheidi	63	
20100429_Hvolsvollur	201	
20100430_Eldhraun	31	
20100430_lagoon	322	
20100501_volcano	647	
20100502_skogafoss_waterfall	39	
20100503_horses	82	
20100505_greenland	88	
20100508_bimini	391	

FIG 7.15
Images online and offline in the catalog

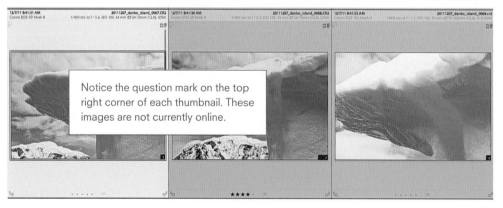

Notice the question mark on the top right corner of each thumbnail. These images are not currently online.

FIG 7.16
Images offline in the catalog marked with a question mark on the thumbnail

Using the Library Module in Workflow While "On the Road"

Because we have built high res 1:1 previews, we can even zoom in on these files without generating artifacts. This is one large plus for generating 1:1 previews. You can take the previews on the road without having the actual files and still make web galleries and slide shows and view the images at 100%. The only downside is that these previews do take up considerable space.

In **Figure 7.17**, we have a file that is offline, but has a high res preview. This allows us to zoom into 100%, and use the file for all purposes in *Lightroom* with the exception of the Develop Module, even without having the image physically with us. **Figure 7.18** is an example of an offline file which only has the low res preview generated. It reveals artifacts at 100%, rendering it useless for any purpose other than reference within *Lightroom*.

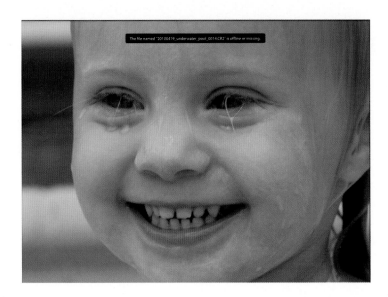

The file named "20100419_underwater_pool_0014.CR2" is offline or missing.

FIG 7.17
High res preview of an offline image

FIG 7.18
Low res preview of an offline image

I THE COLLECTIONS PANEL

The next panel on the left side is called Collections, and it is located under the Folders panel. There are both Smart Collections and regular Collections. Regular Collections are manually compiled, similar to Quick Collections, but they are permanent and you can have as many Collections as you would like. Smart Collections are automatically compiled based on a set of criteria that the user assembles.

Why Use a Collection?

Here is the real power of *Lightroom*. You have an image in one folder. You want to place this image with a group of other images called Portfolio and you also want to use this for a stock submission for your agency and maybe even for a gallery show. In the old days, you would have to duplicate the file and place it in different folders. If you changed something in the file, you would then have to change it in all the files. Because *Lightroom* is entirely based on metadata, you can create Collections based on the metadata.

In the example that follows, we created a collection called Nature Visions Keynote 2012 and placed 51 images into that folder. Many of these images are also in collections called Jewelbox and Portfolio. The beauty of *Lightroom* is that the master file remains in its original location. We do not need to duplicate the file. Instead, *Lightroom* creates a reference file that will go into one or more collections. While you will see the image in thumbnail and full size when you view a collection, the actual image never moves from its original location. How cool is that? You can even make changes to an image and export from a collection.

You can also create sub-collections within a collection. It is a great way of organizing your images. Any collection can also be set to be a Target Collection (**Figure 7.19**). A Target Collection will automatically send an image to a collection deemed to be a Target by using the commands for a Quick Collection. For example, if we wanted to make the collection Gallery Show a target, we would select the folder and Control-Click on it, choosing Set As Target Collection.

Each one of these images lives in a different folder, but they are all organized as "Gallery Show" collection based on the metadata

FIG 7.19
Example of a Collection

Smart Collections

Smart Collections are totally cool and they are automated so they work behind the scenes. They allow you to select criteria to automatically group your images into collections. For example, D-65 uses keywords to define images going to different stock agencies as well as color labels. We use both because the color labels are more visual in the Grid.

For the stock agency Science Faction we use the yellow label and we use a keyword called Science Faction. We like to keep track of all of our images at the many different agencies. In the past, we had to manually move them into their designated Collection which became tedious. Now we just build a Smart Collection that automatically moves any image with a yellow label and the keyword of Science Faction into its own special Smart Collection. The coolest part is that the next time we import images and they are keyworded with Science Faction and a yellow color label, they will automatically be grouped into the Science Faction Smart Collection.

FIG 7.20
Smart Collection

NEW

Collections can be organized and refined by building Collection Sets. We have created a Collection Set called Stock Agencies and in that set we have specialized Smart Collections for each agency. One welcome change **new in _Lightroom 4_** is the ability to target where a Collection or Collection Set will reside.

Create Collection Set

Name: STOCK AGENCIES

Placement

○ Next to Collection Set "Smart Collections"
◉ Inside a Collection Set:

Smart Collections ⇕

[Cancel] [Create]

FIG 7.21
Smart Collection Set

More on Smart Collections

Smart Collections can be edited as well. In fact they can be renamed, deleted and you can even import and export Smart Collections to another catalog.

FIG 7.22
Smart Collection Options

WORKFLOW TIPS FOR COLLECTIONS AND SMART COLLECTIONS:

- *Smart Collections can have very complex criteria. Hold down the Control key while clicking on the plus sign when making decisions. The plus sign will turn into a # sign and give you the added ability to make conditional rules (Figure 7.23) which are very cool. So you have the ability to add almost any criteria to determine your search results. Images that are in a collection have a badge on the thumbnail (Figure 7.24)*

FIG 7.23
Creating Smart
Collections with
Conditional Rules

FIG 7.24
Thumbnail badge
shows when photo is
in a Collection.

- ***New in Lightroom 4 Badge Enhanced output model for
saving/storing settings applied in Web, Slideshow,
Print and Book. Efforts are now clearly visible in
Collections panel.***

- *New in Lightroom 4 Flag status is now 'global' (One setting per image regardless of location in folder or collection)*

NEW

- *New in Lightroom 4 Stacking is now possible in collections*

NEW

| PUBLISH SERVICES

Publish Services allows you to publish photos to popular online photo management sites directly from within the *Lightroom* Library. Facebook, and Flickr come with *Lightroom 4* but others will be available by using the Find More Services Online button below Publish Services. We will specifically look at the Facebook plug-in but all work in a similar fashion.

Hold down the Control key while clicking on the plus sign to the right of Publish Services to open the Publishing Manger (**Figure 7.25**).

FIG 7.25
Control Clicking opens *Lightroom* Publishing Manager

From here you can set up your preferences and account information for Facebook (**Figure 7.26**) to *Lightroom*. (If you do not have a Facebook account you will have to create one first.

123

FIG 7.26
Configure Facebook
Settings and
account information
with *Lightroom*
Publishing Manager

To publish your images to Facebook, simply drag them on to
the Photostream directly beneath Facebook. (**Figure 7.27**) then
press the Publish button or click on the Photostream. *Lightroom*
will automatically begin the process of uploading the photos
to Facebook.

FIG 7.27
Drag image(s) to
the Photostream

Once published, *Lightroom* will show the images as Published
Photos. (**Figure 7.28**)

FIG 7.28
Photostream showing
published photos
in Lightroom

Control-clicking on the Photostream allows you to create a
Collection, Set as Target Collection, Edit Collection, Rename,
Delete,Publish Now, Mark to Republish, Show Album in Facebook
and Smart Collection Settings.

it may take more than 400 keywords to accurately describe an image without actually looking at the thumbnail. Building a Keyword Hierarchy can be a tedious and painful task, but it is essential to digital asset management.

Keywords help in identifying and searching for images in a catalog. Keyword tags are stored either in the image files or in XMP sidecar files or in *Lightroom* Catalog. The XMP can be read by any application that supports XMP metadata.

Keywording Images

To keyword your images, think globally first and then go for local. Think of keywording the same way you would classify an animal. A Spider Monkey would first be a Mammal then an Ape, then a monkey and finally a spider monkey. For example, to classify Miami Beach, you would start with a parent called Continent and a child called North America. A second Parent Inside North America would be called Countries, with a child keyword of United States. A third Parent might be called States, with a child keyword of Florida and finally a parent called Cities with a child called Miami Beach. You could even add sub categories like South Florida and South Beach. So the hierarchy might look like this: North America > United States > Florida > South Florida > Miami > Miami Beach > South Beach. So it might take 7 keywords just to classify South Beach. Most images that D65 prepares have about 50 keywords which really isn't all that much when you consider the concept of hierarchies.

Below is an example of an image of a green iceberg from Antarctica, with proper keywording. The top level Parent Keywords are in CAPS but they are private metadata and act as a placeholder and do not export with the image. All the child levels have the first letter of each word capitalized.

Location is an obvious keyword but there are many keywords that aren't as obvious that make finding and organizing images a breeze. We have a Parent called Technique, for example (**Figure 7.35**) whose Children include items like Blur, Reflections, Macro, Motion, Silhouette, and Time Exposure.. This really helps when looking for certain types of images. We have another Parent called View (**Figure 7.36**) with Children like Aerial, Eye Contact, Fisheye, Panorama, and Underwater. Again, the more specific the keyword, list the easier it becomes to find images that you seek.

FIG 7.34
An image with extensive keywords applied

FIG 7.35
Keyword Technique

FIG 7.36
Keyword View

Creating and Managing Keywords

Keywords can be generated by clicking on the + sign to the left of Keyword List. Keywords can be removed by highlighting the keyword and clicking on the – sign to the left of Keyword List. Keywords can also be created by typing in a keyword in the "Click here to add keywords" box under Enter Keywords in the Keywording Panel.

The top level parents are in capitals and are private meaning that they do not export. They are placeholders only.

Click the + icon to create a new keyword tag

The first letter of each child is capitalized

The number of images that contain a given keyword are displayed to the right of the keyword.

By clicking on the number adjacent to any keyword tag, you will go to those images that contain that keyword.

FIG 7.37
Adding Keywords to the Keyword List

FIG 7.38
Parents and Children in Keyword List.

Creating Keyword Tags with Synonyms and Export Options

When creating keywords, you can add synonyms and export options. Synonyms are similar or related terms for keyword tags. Synonyms allow you to apply one keyword and automatically apply additional synonyms. For those of you keywording animals, for example, one very useful tidbit is to use the Latin name or scientific name of the animal as a synonym.

Creating Private Metadata

You can also choose to include keywords or exclude keywords on export. This too is a very valuable feature. D-65 uses keywords for jobs, portfolio images, stock agencies and for names of folks we know. We put this type of information into a Parent Keyword called Private Metadata and exclude it on export. This way the information becomes useful in searching within *Lightroom* but it isn't included in the images on export.

Keyword tags can be created as children of parent keyword tags. For example, a parent tag might be "Weather" and the child could be "Hurricane" and you could apply a group of synonyms at the same time.

Create Keyword Tag

Keyword Name: Hurricane

Synonyms: Storm, Violent, Destruction, Wind, Rain, Catastrophic

Keyword Tag Options
☑ Include on Export
☑ Export Containing Keywords
☑ Export Synonyms

Creation Options
☑ Put inside "Environmental Issues"
☐ Add to selected photos

Cancel Create

FIG 7.39
Creating Keywords with
Synonyms and Options

The Keyword Filter

The Keyword Filter is a very useful tool. In our Keyword List, we have over 6000 keywords all listed in a hierarchy. One of the problems of working with keywords in a hierarchy is locating a particular keyword. The Keyword Filter makes this easy. Simply type in the keyword you are looking for in the filter and it locates it for you in the hierarchy. In **Figure 7.40** we searched for the keyword "Leopard" and the filter traced it to the parent Animals and the full hierarchy leading to Leopard. It also conveniently displays the number of images with this keyword.

Keywording also utilizes autofill. The application tries to fill in the remainder of a word before you finish typing. While most folks find this useful, if you want to turn this off, open Catalog Settings — Metadata tab then deactivate "Offer suggestions from recently entered values."

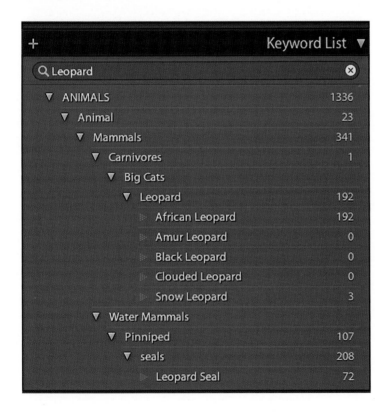

FIG 7.40
Keyword Filter

KEYWORDING TIPS:

- *If an asterisk appears next to a keyword that means that this keyword is present in some but not in all of the selected images.*

If the keyword has an asterisk next to it, that means that the keyword is present in some, but not all of the images selected.

FIG 7.41
Asterisk in Keyword Tags

- *In the Grid mode, you can see that an image has keywords with the keyword badge. Clicking on this badge will bring you to the Keywords panel and display the keywords in the image.*

In the Grid mode, you can see that an image has keywords with the keyword badge. Clicking on this badge will bring you to the Keywords panel and display the keywords in the image.

FIG 7.42
Keyword Badge

- *Clicking on the number of keywords for a keyword will bring up all of those images in the Grid. In Figure 7.43, we clicked on the number 311 next to Neon Light and all 311 related images appear in the Grid. It is an awesome way to cull images and create collections of specific types of images. Every time you add a keyword to an image, the Keywords Tags panel will keep track of how many images in your entire Library have that specific keyword.*

FIG 7.43
Clicking on the number of keywords for a given keyword will bring up all of those images in the Grid.

Keyword Sets

Keyword tags can also be organized into categories called keyword sets. We might create a keyword set for "Lightning," for example, which includes words like Electrical Storm, Lightning, Thunder, Thunderstorm, Ominous, and Downpour. Every time lightning is photographed, you could choose this set and apply each keyword. Unfortunately you can't apply the entire set with one click.

To create a Keyword Set, go to the Keyword Set Panel and click on drop-down menu, choosing "Save current settings as a new preset."

	Edit Keyword Set	
Preset: Save Current Settings as New Preset...		
Keywords		
Electrical Storm	Lightning	Lightning Bolt
Thunderstorm	Thunder	Rain
Dark	Ominous	Downpour

Cancel   Change

FIG 7.44
Keyword Sets

Organizing Keywords in Workflow

Keywording, while very powerful, can quickly get out of hand if the keywords aren't organized. In order to keep your keywords organized, we suggest creating keywords in the Keywording Tags panel and to regularly arrange Parents and Children in the Keyword List. Do not wait until you have several hundred keywords to begin the organization. D-65's advice is to organize on a regular basis.

Creating and Applying Keywords

You can create and apply keywords in various ways in the Library Module. We'll demonstrate them all below, even though a few of the tools haven't been covered yet in this chapter.

1. **Keywording Panel:** The Keywording Panel is located on the right-hand side of the Library Module. To use it, select one or more images in the Grid and start typing the keyword(s) you want to insert in the keyword tags panel. Hit Return and the keywords will be placed in the image(s). **Note:** To create parent-child relationship hierarchies, use the pipe key (|) between the keywords or drag keywords from the keyword list into other keywords.

Select one or more images and then type into the Keywording panel the keyword(s) you want to add to the image(s)

FIG 7.45
Enter Keywords

2. **Copy and Paste Keywords:** Select one image, keyword it, and then copy and paste the keywords from one image to another.

3. **Sync Keywords:** Select one image, keyword it, then select the other images you want to contain those keywords and choose Sync Metadata. Scroll down and place a checkmark in Keywords.

Synchronize Metadata

▶ ☐ **Basic Info**

▶ ☐ **Camera Info**

▶ ☐ **IPTC Content**

▶ ☐ **IPTC Copyright**

▶ ☐ **IPTC Creator**

▶ ☐ **IPTC Image**

▶ ☐ **IPTC Status**

▶ ☐ **IPTC Extension Administrative**

▼ ☐ **IPTC Extension Artwork**

Artwork or Object in the Image   0 items   Replace ⬍ ☐

▶ ☐ **IPTC Extension Description**

▶ ☐ **IPTC Extension Models**

▶ ☐ **IPTC Extension Rights**

▶ ☐ **Video**

▼ ☑ **Keywords**

Keywords | Air Pollution, Air Traffic, Billow, Billowing, Cataclysm, Cauldron, Crater, Danger, Dangerous, Deadly, Devastation, Ecosystem, Environmental Hazard, | ☑

[Check All]   [Check None]   [Check Filled]   [Cancel]   [Synchronize]

FIG 7.46
Sync Keywords

4. **Drag Keywords:** Select one image or a group of images and either drag the image(s) to the keyword as in **Fig 7.47** or drag the keyword to the image(s) as in **Fig 7.48**.

FIG 7.47
Drag image to Keyword

FIG 7.48
Drag Keyword to image

5. **Painter Tool:** Click on the Painter Tool in the Toolbar and add keywords to the field in the Toolbar. After the keyword(s) are added, hit Return to save them. The Painter Tool can then be used to apply these keywords to other images. Click on the image(s) that you want keyworded with the Painter Tool. Once you click on the image(s) you will see the assigned keywords on your screen and that the keywords have been applied.

FIG 7.49
Painter Tool to
paint keywords

After clicking on
the Painter Tool,
add keywords in
the field. Then use
the Painter Tool
to applythose
keywords to
other images.

FIG 7.50
Painting Keywords using
the Painter Tool

PAINTER TOOL WORKFLOW TIPS:

- *Using the Option key will turn the Painter Tool into an Eraser Tool—in Lightroom 2 the Painter automatically became an eraser after applying the Painter—the use of the Option key to toggle the Painter Tool to an Eraser Tool is a welcome change for 3.0*

- *Remember to click off the Painter Tool when you are done with it, or you will continue to "paint" all your images*

- *If the Painter Tool has a keyword associated with it, the shortcut Shift-K will apply the keyword—this is totally cool because you can be in full screen view and use the shortcut Shift-K to apply keywords*

6. **Check Box in the Keyword List Panel:** Select one image or a group of images and click on the check box next to the keyword you want to apply as in **Figure 7.51**.

FIG 7.51
Using the checkbox to apply keywords

7. **Keyword Suggestions and Keyword Set:** One feature that is truly fantastic is Keyword Suggestions in the Keywording panel. The concept is that if you apply a keyword to a specific image, that keyword will become a suggested keyword for any other images that share a close enough capture time. This feature is great most of the time and should allow a faster way to generate and apply keywords, but just because the capture times are similar does not always mean that the images are similar. To apply both keywords from the Keyword Set and or from the Keyword Suggestions, simply select your image(s) and click on the keyword(s) in the set or in the suggestions.

FIG 7.52
To apply both keywords
from the Keyword
Set and or from the
Keyword Suggestions
simply select your
image(s) and click on
the keyword(s) in the set
or in the suggestion.

| METADATA PANEL

The Metadata Panel is on the right side of the Library under the
Keyword List. The metadata panel displays all the metadata in the
image. You can apply metadata to one image and sync to other
images. You can also create metadata templates, save them,
and apply them using the drop down arrow next to Preset in the
Metadata Panel. You can delete, add, or change metadata to any
single image or group of images. The list of metadata can be a
long list, so the panel is configurable to show different subsets
of available metadata. While D-65 prefers to show EXIF and IPTC
Metadata, there are several views available as shown below in
Figure 7.53.

FIG 7.53
The Metadata Panel

Quick Describe View

While D-65 prefers to show all metadata, one view that is very popular is Quick Describe which is shown in **Figure 7.54** below.

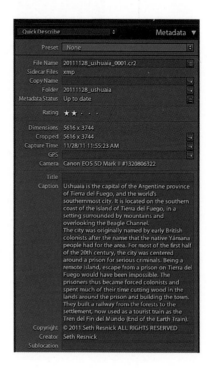

FIG 7.54
Quick Describe View in the Metadata Panel

IPTC Extension has many new fields for "objects shown," "model name," "model's age," "release contract" and such and conforms with the PLUS Coalition Standards. PLUS has established universal standards for communicating image rights metadata.

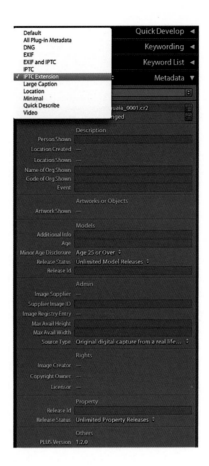

FIG 7.55
IPTC Extension Metadata

Using the Metadata Panel in Workflow

Now, and certainly in the future, all searching will be based on metadata. All the fields are important to fill out but particularly important are keywords and the Caption Field. A good caption and an image maintain a symbiotic relationship. A caption describes the unseen. The caption brings totality to the image by providing context and adding depth. The image draws attention to the caption, and the caption helps to provide the complete picture. The caption should provide the "who, what, when and where" as well as information that can't necessarily be derived by simply looking at the image.

All of this information is searchable, which means that a good caption can be the difference between finding an image or not finding it. This is crucial for photographers looking at licensing stock. A good caption and proper keywording can give you an edge on your competition. D-65 applies a basic metadata template including copyright and contact information on import, and then uses the metadata panel to apply selective metadata once the images are in the Library.

You can copy Metadata from one image and paste it into other images. For example, if you didn't apply metadata such as IPTC on import, then you could write it to one file and copy and paste it into the rest of your shoot. The Sync Metadata Button works in the same way and overwrites any existing metadata in the selected images.

You can also edit the Capture Time if your camera was incorrectly set.

FIG 7.56
EXIF and IPTC Metadata Template filled out with Caption information

Sample Caption for Image

The shadow of an African painted reed frog from the underside of a leaf in Vumbra Plains, Botswana. Painted reed frogs have tiny suckers on their "fingers". These enable them to cling to reeds and other plants. Painted reed frogs spend most of their time on land and in the sun where they are at risk of drying out. They are able to conserve water by, sitting motionless for hours and slowing down their metabolism. They can also turn white to reflect sunlight and are able to store water in their bladders that they then release through their skin. The adult color pattern is extremely variable and has led to many classification uncertainties about this species. The pattern varies from distinct stripes through dots and splotches, and the colors of the patterns vary from dark brown or black through to yellow and peppermint green. The adults aestivate during the dry season, and have been found sheltering some distance from their breeding sites in vegetation or under logs and stones. Although males will call after rain at any time of the year, breeding normally takes place from October to February. During the day, adults usually move into the canopy of surrounding trees or bask in the sun on emergent vegetation at the edge of the breeding site. They utilize a wide variety of breeding sites, ranging from temporary ponds, marshes, reedbeds, to permanent bodies of water. At dusk they descend to the pond where males take up specific call sites which they return to on consecutive nights and call consistently from dusk to just after midnight. Where present, tall emergent plants such as reeds and sedges are favored as call sites, but males will also call from trees, grasses, bushes, floating vegetation or even bare soil at the water's edge. On average, males only call for a few nights in a row, returning to the breeding chorus after a period of about 10 days. Between 150 and 650 eggs are laid in flattened clumps of about 20, on the surface of submerged leaves, stalks or stones or amongst the roots of aquatic plants The major threat to this species is habitat loss through drainage of wetlands and afforestation. In several areas of prime habitat the planting of exotic Eucalyptus forests has lowered the water table to such a degree that many ponds within the coastal dune forest have completely disappeared.

FIG 7.57
Sample Caption for Image

METADATA TIPS:

- *There is a drop-down menu next to Preset which allows you to apply a metadata preset that you have already created, or edit a preset and save a new one*

- *There is an icon to the right of File Name, which allows you to Batch Rename an individual photo, or groups of photos*

- *To the right of Copy Name (when you are working on metadata on a virtual copy) there is an arrow that will bring you to the master file*

- *To the right of Folder, there is an arrow that will display the folder from the selected image (good for use in Collections)*

- *Clicking on the arrow to the right of Date/Time Original will filter based on the exact date of the selected image—all of your images shot on that date will appear in the Grid*

- *Under Email, Website and Copyright Info URL, you can go directly to the URL or create an email by clicking on the arrow on the right*

- *If an image has been cropped, it will show crop dimensions and you can go directly to crop overlay*

- *Images with GPS data (open in Google Maps)*

- *Images with WAV files attached will play the audio*

FIG 7.58
Metadata drop-down menu next to Preset allows you to apply a metadata preset

- *When metadata has been changed or is not up to date, a badge in the image will show in the Grid mode (**Figure 7.59**) if Unsaved Metadata is checked in Lightroom Library View Options*

- *Clicking on the badge will update the metadata in the selected images (**Figure 7.60**)*

When metadata has been changed or is not up to date, a badge in the image will show in the Grid mode. By clicking on the badge the metadata can be updated in the selected images

FIG 7.59
Metadata Badge showing update is needed

The metadata for this photo has been changed in Lightroom. Save the changes to disk?

☐ Don't show again   Cancel   Save

FIG 7.60
Updating Metadata in image

NEW

In *Lightroom 3* the application did not detect external metadata changes when just the XMP sidecar had changed. In *Lightroom 4* this has been corrected, and as a consequence, you may notice a bunch of new metadata status badges on thumbnails in grid view. "xmp has changed on disk" (i.e the up arrow) badges. This badge means you changed the XMP externally. This new badge should have always been showing, but LR didn't properly detect that condition in the past.

"xmp conflict" (exclamation point) badges where you previously had "unsaved xmp" (down arrow) badges. Like the missing changed on disk badges, these new conflict badges should have always been showing. In earlier versions of LR, the conflict would eventually show up, but only if you tried to save XMP that was only modified in LR. You would get a conflict warning dialog and then the conflict badge would show if you canceled the dialog. This change will only apply to customers with RAW plus xmp and really only affect those that tend to change the XMP in external applications like *Bridge*.

Adding Metadata to Images

Adding metadata to one or more images is done in a manner similar to keywording and can be accomplished in several ways.

1. **Metadata Panel:** Select one or more images in the Grid and start typing the metadata into the fields you want to insert in the metadata panel. Hit Return and the metadata will be placed in the image(s).

Select one or more images and then type into the field in the metadata panel to add selective metadata the image(s)

FIG 7.61
Inserting Metadata

2. Sync Metadata Button:

FIG 7.62
Sync Metadata

a) Add metadata to the Metadata Panel and hit Return. Select the other images to which you would like to apply this metadata.

b) Click on the Sync Metadata button to the right of the Toolbar.

c) The Synchronize Metadata window will appear.

d) You can choose what fields you would like to synchronize by checking the boxes on the right.

e) You can also change the information in any field in this window and apply it.

f) Click on Synchronize when you are ready to apply the metadata to your images.

FIG 7.63
Sync Metadata between images using Sync Metadata Button and Synchronize

3. **Copy and Paste Metadata:** You can also select one image, add metadata to a field, and then copy and paste the metadata from one image to another.

4. **Spraying Metadata with the Painter Tool**

   a) Click on the Painter Tool and choose to paint Metadata from the drop-down menu. Choose a template that you have created and hit return.

   b) The Painter Tool can then be used to apply this metadata to other images. Click on the image(s) to which you want to add metadata with the Painter Tool. Once you click on the image(s) you will see the newly assigned metadata that has been applied on your screen.

FIG 7.64
Painter Tool for Metadata

Creating a new Metadata Preset

You can create a metadata preset and choose it at any time or apply it during import. A template is useful if it is something you are going to use over and over again. D-65 creates a basic copyright metadata preset which contains copyright information and creator information. Filling out metadata creator information can aid in a defense against the pending Orphan Works Act which is a proposed change to current copyright law.

To create a new metadata preset:

1. Mouse down on the metadata preset drop-down menu (**Figure 7.65**) and choose Edit Presets (**Figure 7.66**). An old preset can be edited and updated or a new preset can be created and saved with a preset name. You can also edit a Metadata Preset by going to Library Main Menu>Metadata> Edit Metadata Presets.

Mouse down on drop down menu and choose Edit Presets

FIG 7.65

FIG 7.66
Edit Metadata Preset

FIG 7.67
Creating or Editing a
Metadata Presets

| THE LIBRARY FILTER

The Library Filter is located above the Grid. The Library Filter contains search criteria based on Text, Attribute and Metadata.

Text can be searched for in File Name, Copy Name, Title, Caption, Keywords, Searchable Metadata, Searchable IPTC Metadata or Searchable EXIF Metadata.

Attribute (we're not so fond of this name) provides the ability to search based on Stars, Flags, Color Labels, Master Photo, Virtual Copies or Video.

Metadata can be searched by Date, File Type, Keyword, Label, Camera, Camera Serial Number, Lens, Focal Length, Shutter Speed, Aperture, ISO, Flash State, GPS Data, GPS Location, Location, City, State, Country, Creator, Copyright Status, Job, Aspect Ratio, Treatment and Develop Presets and saved or unsaved metadata status.

NEW

New in *Lightroom 4* Filter and search images by saved or unsaved metadata status.

When someone asks you what your favorite F-stop or shutter speed is, you can now accurately give them an answer. The Filter uses the Boolean operators "and" between the columns and "or" within the columns. You can even add more columns by pressing down on the drop-down menu at the far right of the Library Filter.

All these features gathered under one roof makes this a pretty strong searching mechanism. Of course, after the search has been performed, the images can be viewed in the Grid, and you can make the selection into a Quick Collection, Collection, or even a Smart Collection.

Library Filter Keyboard Shortcut

The left-slash (\) key will hide or open the Library Filter.

Using the Library Filter

Starting with **Figure 7.68**, we demonstrate the power of the Library Filter. We have selected our entire Library and hit the \ key to open the Library Filter. We mouse down on the Text menu and select Keywords from the drop-down menu. We choose Contain and type in the keyword Graphic. By the time we finish typing "g-r-a-p-h, there are 1389 images matching that criteria.

FIG 7.68
Library Filter

In **Figure 7.69** we choose to show images with Changed Metadata. This refines the matching selection down to 846 images.

FIG 7.69
Refining the selection

In **Figure 7.70**, we click on the drop-down menu at the far right next to Label and choose Add Column.

FIG 7.70

We add Camera Serial Number in **Figure 7.71**.

FIG 7.71

This narrows our search down to 158 images (**Figure 7.72**). We could, of course, save this final selection as a Quick Collection or Collection if we choose.

FIG 7.72
Our search criteria narrowed our choice to 158 images

We can even save this set of search criteria as a preset to use in the future as demonstrated in **Figure 7.73**. The Library Filter is truly an amazing new tool for *Lightroom*.

FIG 7.73
Saving Filtered Results as a Preset

LIBRARY FILTER TIP:

- *Click any mode name to show and hide its options. The mode label is white when those options are open. One, two, or all three filter modes can be open at once.*

- *Shift-click a second or third label to open multiple modes at once.*

- *Click None to hide and turn off all filter modes.*

- *Contains Searches for the specified alphanumeric sequence(s), including partial words. For example, performing a Contains search for Miami Beach returns results that include the word Miami.*

- *Contains All Searches for text that contains all specified alphanumeric sequences. For example, you have a folder of photos and each photo is tagged with the names of the cats in the shot. You could perform a Contains All search on Cassie and Cleo to find all photos that contain both Cassie and Cleo.*

- *Contains Words Searches for text that contains all specified alphanumeric sequences as whole words. To find photos with the keyword Miami Beach using a Contains Word search, for example, type Miami Beach.*

- *Doesn't Contain Searches for text that does not contain any specified sequence.*

- *Starts With Searches for text that begins with the specified alphanumeric sequence.*

- *Ends With Searches for text that ends with the specified alphanumeric sequence.*

| IMPORT

We've finished the Panels and Library Filter, and now are moving back to the left-hand side to cover the import and export buttons.

Import and Export Buttons

FIG 7.74
Import and Export
buttons in
Library Module

In order to work on any image in *Lightroom*, it must first be imported into the *Lightroom* Library. You can choose to import by either moving, copying or referencing the files into the Library. After the specified files have been imported, *Lightroom* will begin building previews, which will appear in the Grid and Filmstrip views. We demonstrate the steps for import in Chapter 15.

Lightroom 4 can import the following file formats, and supports up to 65,000 pixels long or wide. Files are supported in RGB as well as CMYK.

The supported file formats are:

- RAW

- DNG

- TIFF

- PSD

- JPEG

- Video files captured by newer DSLR cameras

I VIDEO FORMAT SUPPORT

New in *Lightroom 4*

- **Video playback directly within *Lightroom***

- **Video trimming (In and Out points)**

- **Set Video poster frame. (This is the thumbnail that appears in the grid view)**

NEW

- **Extract a single frame from a video as a JPEG file**

- **Most popular DSLR, compact camera and smart phone video formats supported including AVCHD (AVCHD is the native format for Sony DSLRs and many new Mirrorless Interchangeable Lens, MIL, cameras)**

- **Videos can be adjusted with a subset of the same controls we use for images including White Balance (JPEG Equivalent), Basic Tone, Exposure, Contrast, White Clipping, Black Clipping, Saturation, Vibrance, Tone Curve , Color Treatment (HSL) , Black and White ,Split Toning, Process Version and Calibration**

Lightroom 4 now supports video playback directly with the Library loupe window. This should prove very popular with photographers who shoot both still and video. Even more popular will be the fact that *Lightroom* now supports a wide range of video formats including AVCHD (i.e. the native format for Sony DSLRs and mirrorless cameras such as those from Panasonic). Tagging, rating, filtering, Collection and Smart Collection features are available for organizing video content. Video filter will help narrow down your collection to just your video files instantly. In the Grid and Loupe views of *Lightroom,* the duration of a video file is displayed on the preview.

FIG 7.75
Video Support in Library

Lightroom 4 provides support for extracting a single frame as a JPEG file as well as the ability to set the Posters Frame and Trim videos. These features are accessed through the controller that appears in the lower section of the Library loupe window. The controller can be expanded by either end and dragging. The trimming controls are located at either end of the controller.

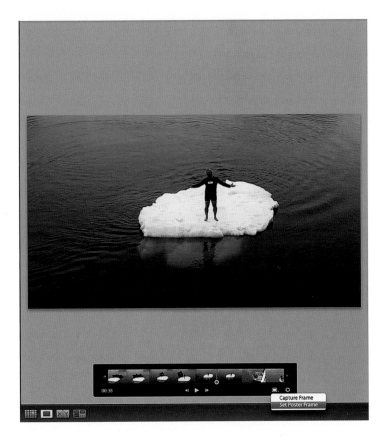

FIG 7.76
Video Controller can be used to extract JPEG file, set the Posters Frame and Trim videos.

Lightroom 4 provides the ability to not only view videos but now videos can be adjusted with a subset of the same controls we use for images in Quick Develop.

FIG 7.77
Basic tone adjustments
for video

Lightroom 4 caches video in a dedicated folder, and the size of is cache can be limited from within the File Handling panel of *Lightroom* preferences.

Finally, for video, *Lightroom 4* provides support for exporting to DPX files. DPX is a lossless, folder-based format intended for Adobe Premiere Pro.

LIBRARY VIDEO SUPPORT TIPS:

- *Videos can be rated, filtered, tagged, added to Collections, saved in Smart Collections, and managed*

- *The video camera icon identifies the image as a video and shows its length*

- *The video controller can be expanded by either end and dragging.*

I EXPORT

Lightroom allows you to export single or multiple images from the Library or Develop Modules to the location of your choice. D-65 uses the Export button after we have tweaked our files in the Develop Module. The files can be up-sized, down-sized or processed in really any way you need them.

One very cool feature is that exporting works in the background, allowing you to perform multiple exports at the same time. We could even create an Action in *Photoshop* and turn that Action into a Droplet and have that Droplet executed automatically by *Lightroom,* which is really cool. We will discuss exporting completely in Chapter 15.

Exporting formats include:

- JPEG

- PSD

- TIFF

- VIDEO

- DNG

- Original

I THE LIBRARY TOOLBAR

The Toolbar is located under the Grid and to the right of the Export button. The Toolbar is turned on and off with the letter T key. There are several buttons on the Toolbar that come as a default. Clicking on each tool will add additional buttons to the Toolbar that are associated with that specific tool. The default Toolbar buttons in the Grid View are:

- Grid View, which displays the images like a light table

- Loupe View, which allows you to zoom in on an image up to 11:1 ratio

- Compare View

- Survey Mode

These change the views in the Library.

Additionally, there are other options that you can add to the Toolbar. There is a drop-down arrow on the far right of the Toolbar, to the left of the Sync Settings button. Clicking on that drop-down menu will give you the options to add to the Toolbar and customize it for your needs. Simply place a check next to the field that you'd like to show. Anything checked in the drop-down menu will appear on the Toolbar. Your screen size will affect how many options you can have showing on your Toolbar.

FIG 7.78
The Library Toolbar with drop-down menu

Survey and Compare Modes

When you are editing your images in *Lightroom,* you can select combinations of images and use the Compare or Survey buttons to help cull your edit. Once in either Compare or Survey mode, you can zoom in and check detail by using the zoom slider. You can collapse both the left and right side panels to view the images even larger by clicking on the Tab Key or using the arrows on the side of the panels. To exit Compare mode, press the C key.

FIG 7.79
Survey and Compare Mode Buttons

Compare Mode

The Compare Mode cycles through a group of images to find the best picture within that group. When you click done, you can rank your select or add it to a Quick Collection if you are using Quick Collections for editing.

To use this feature, first highlight an image from the Filmstrip. This will be your "select." Using the arrow key on the Toolbar (or your keyboard arrow keys) move through your images. When you find another candidate that you like better than the original select, click on the XY Make Select button. That takes your original select out, and tags the new image as your select and you can move through and compare all of the images to that select.

Next to the Compare Button in the Toolbar is an icon that looks like a lock. It is called the Link Focus Icon. Locking the Link Focus Icon allows you to zoom in simultaneously on both images using the zoom slider. Unlocking the Link Focus Icon allows you to zoom in on the selected image. Using the Sync button next to the zoom slider can synchronize the zoom ratios between images. This is a great tool for editing and checking sharpness between images.

TIP: The spacebar can also be used to toggle between Fit and 1:1 View

FIG 7.80
Compare Mode

In **Figure 7.80** we compare two images. In **Figure 7.81**, we lock the zoom and check focus and can see that the Select is sharper than the Candidate.

FIG 7.81
Zoom is locked and focus checked in Compare Mode

Survey Mode

Survey Mode displays the active photo (the one you clicked on first is denoted with a white box around it) and then one or more selected photos to compare it to (images with an x). If you want to compare more than two images at one time, it works great. You can change the orientation of the images, and zoom in and rate the images too.

FIG 7.82
Survey Mode

Painter Tool

By clicking on the spray can icon, you have the ability to "paint" in Keywords, Labels, Flags, Ratings, Metadata, Settings, Rotation and Target Collection. A field opens next to the spray can and you insert the information you want to spray into the image.

Click the Painter Tool icon on an image or images in the Grid view and the information will be inserted. The spray can becomes an eraser with the Option Key after you apply it to the image.

FIG 7.83
Painter Tool

Choose what you'd like to paint in the image

FIG 7.84
Choosing options for the Painter Tool

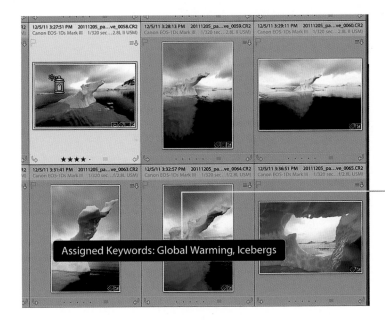

After clicking the Painter Tool on an image, you will see what has been assigned

FIG 7.85
Spraying on the option with the Painter Tool

I SORT DIRECTION AND SORT CRITERIA

FIG 7.86
Sort Direction

Next to the Painter is Sort Direction. This allows you to choose between ascending and descending order for your images to appear. There is a drop-down menu located next to the icon, which further allows you to define your sort criteria. You can even choose "User Order" and organize the images yourself by moving them into any order you prefer in the Grid view. It is important to note that "User Order" is only an option if you are on a folder. If you are on your entire catalog, user order is not an option.

I STARS, FLAGS AND LABELS

Ranking and editing in *Lightroom* works in much the same way that a film-based photographer works on a light table. First, we click on an image and use the navigator tool with an appropriate zoom level to move through the image and check focus. After checking focus, a photographer typically used a star or a dot to mark a select, two stars to mark second tier selects and three or four stars to mark and cull "keepers."

You can do exactly this within *Lightroom*. You can add and remove stars from an image by using the Toolbar, or by using the number keys 1 thru 5, or by using the left ([) and right (]) bracket keys. You can also add color labels via the Toolbar, and by using the numbers 6 through 9. You can also rate and color label using the Photo Menu and then choosing Set Rating, Set Color Label or Set Flag. Additionally, you can select an image in *Lightroom* and manually add or subtract stars by clicking on the dots immediately below the thumbnail.

In short, there are quite a few ways to rate and color label your images. These rankings and color labels will stay with the image, in its metadata, even after you process the files.

Why would you use both rankings and labels? There is always going to be a best image from a shoot and that image might get 4 stars. However, just because it is the best image from a shoot doesn't necessarily mean that it is a portfolio image. You could give 4 stars plus a color label to define an image that is the best from a shoot and a portfolio image.

FIG 7.87
Toolbar for flags, ratings and labels

FIG 7.88
Ranking with Stars and Color Labels

You can rank by either using the numbers 1-5 or by using the] key to increase the rating or the [key to decrease it. You can apply a color label by using the numbers 6-9

Color Label Sets

You can enhance labels even further by creating a Color Label Set. D-65 creates a custom label set using different colors for different stock agencies and to label an image as a portfolio image.

FIG 7.89
Color Label Edit Menu

FIG 7.90
Creating Custom Color
Label Sets

RATING SHORTCUT TIPS TO SPEED UP WORKFLOW:

- *You can use the] key to increase the rating and the [key to lower the rating and Command-Z will undo a rating*

- *Having CAPS LOCK on while you are rating images automatically moves to the next image after you rate one image*

- *You can also Set a Flag as a Pick, instead of rating and color labeling. For our workflow, we use ratings and color labels for our choice images and the X Key and U*

Key for marking images for deletion. We do not typically use the P key but P is a Pick, the X key is a reject and the U key removes the flag.

- *It is extremely useful to go through a group of images using the X Key to flag for deletion and delete them when you are done editing with Lightroom>Library>Photo> Delete Rejected Photos*

FIG 7.91
Deleting Rejected Photos using the X Key to Flag for deletion

I ROTATE AND ADVANCE

You can manually rotate your images, counter clockwise with the left rotate icon, and clockwise with the right rotate icon, or by Control-[on a PC and Command-[on a Mac rotates the photo. You can also select the next photo or previous photo with the left and right arrow keys.

FIG 7.92
Rotate and Advance Buttons on the Toolbar

I IMPROMPTU SLIDESHOW

At any time you can select a folder or group of images and build a slideshow on the fly by clicking on the slideshow icon. The slideshow will start playing almost immediately. Pressing the Escape button gets you out of the slideshow. The spacebar pauses and resumes playing the slideshow. The show automatically advances, but you can also use your arrow keys to go back and forth.

FIG 7.93
Impromptu
Slideshow Button

I THUMBNAIL SLIDER

In the Grid View Toolbar, you can scale your thumbnails with the Thumbnail Slider. The thumbnail size in the Filmstrip is also scalable. To change the Thumbnail preview size in the Filmstrip, move your mouse between the Grid and the Filmstrip and then drag the Filmstrip larger or smaller.

FIG 7.94
Thumbnail Slider

I THE FILMSTRIP AND FILMSTRIP SOURCE

Located below the Toolbar is the Filmstrip. The Filmstrip displays your most current selection of images, based on either a folder, collection, keyword set or Quick Collection. You can move through the Filmstrip using the arrow keys.

On top of the images in the Filmstrip is your Filmstrip Source. This shows the folder, search, or collection that you have selected, the number of images in that selection, as well as any active image name. At the top left of the Filmstrip is the ability to turn on a second monitor and to go backward or forward in your browsing history. Filtering tools are located at the far right of the Filmstrip Source.

FIG 7.95
Filmstrip and Filmstrip Source

I MULTIPLE MONITORS

Using dual displays or multiple monitors in *Lightroom* rocks. This is fantastic for editing and culling images and once you try a second monitor you will never want to work on just one monitor again.

FIG 7.96
Multiple Monitors in Filmstrip Source above Filmstrip

Grid, Loupe, Compare, Survey and Slideshow are all available to use on either the first, second or on both monitors. This enables you, for example, to see the Grid of all your images as thumbnails on one monitor and the Loupe of a specific image on the second monitor at the same time. This is very useful indeed. If you don't have a second display, the new window will appear as a second window on your main display.

There are three views available for the Loupe View on the second monitor:

Normal mode, Live mode and Locked mode. With Normal mode, the image on the second monitor is the same image as on the main monitor but you can use a different zoom ratio, which is fantastic for checking sharpness on the fly. With Live mode, the second monitor is continually updated showing the image that the mouse is over on the main display. With Locked mode, the image on the second monitor is fixed which allows you to really compare two images in full screen on two monitors.

FIG 7.97
Multiple monitors in Normal View with Grid on one screen and loupe on second

FIG 7.98
Multiple monitors in Locked Mode. One image locked on the left monitor in Loupe View and another image in Loupe View on the right monitor. This really makes details like checking eyes for sharpness between two similar images a breeze.

Keyboard Shortcuts for Multiple Monitors:

- Grid (Shift-G)

- Loupe (Shift-E)

- Compare (Shift-C)

- Survey (Shift-N)

- Click and hold shows the Multiple Monitor list

- Slideshow Command-Shift-Option-Return

| GRID AND GO FORWARD AND GO BACKWARD BUTTONS

One very cool feature that has always been in *Lightroom* but few people seem to know about is the ability to move forward and backward in your workflow. This is especially useful when you leave a folder to accomplish a different task and then want to get back to that folder. The figures below demonstrate leaving a folder to go to a specific set of keywords and then use the Go Back button to get back to the original folder.

FIG 7.99
Grid and Go Forward and Go Backward Buttons in Filmstrip Source above Filmstrip

In **FIG 7.100**, In FIG 7.100, we are on a folder of images called 20110123_vumbura_plains. As we browse this folder, we see that there are images with lions and we decide we want to see how many other images in the entire catalog have lions.

FIG 7.100
Folder of images called 20110123_vumbura_plains with lions

Since all of our images are keyworded, we go to the keyword list (**Figure 7.101**) and click on the number 208 next to the keyword "Lion."

FIG 7.101
Clicking on the number 208 next to Lion in our Keyword list on the right side panel will bring up all of the images of lions

After we click on the number 208 next to "Lion," we are now in the entire Catalog showing all the images that contain the keyword "Lion." We might consider making a collection of Lion or we might want to go back to our Vumbura Plains images. Most folks end up navigating through the hierarchy of folders and this can be tedious and time consuming.

FIG 7.102
Catalog showing all photographs with Lion. No longer in Vumbura Plains Folder

Instead, clicking on the "Go Back" button in the Filmstrip, we can return to our original Vumbura Plains folder (**Figure 7.103**). While we only went back once in this demonstration, the Go Back and Go Forward Buttons allow you to go back or forward to ten, twenty or even a hundred locations if you so desire.

FIG 7.103
Using the Go Back Button to move back to our original folder 20110123_vumbura_plains

| FILTERING IN FILM STRIP SOURCE |

The Filmstrip also contains filters in addition to the Library Filter covered earlier. The Film Strip Source Filter contains Attribute from the Library Filter and is sort of the "lite" version of filtering. At the very end of the Film Strip Source is the filter on/off switch. Finding your rated and color labeled images is easy in *Lightroom*. Go to the Filters and select how you want to filter. **Filtering can be based on:**

- Flag status: Picks, Picks Only, Picks and Unflagged Photos, or Any Flag

- Star rating

- Color label

- Or a combination of color label and rating

Filtering can be further defined by including the Boolean operators greater than or equal to (≥), less than or equal to (≤), or equal to (=).

The last button on the Filmstrip Source next to the color labels is Filter On/Off.

FIG 7.104
Filtering for Attribute of four or more stars in multiple folders in Film Strip Source

Filter on/off button

This selection is filtered based on greater than four stars.

The Library Filter Source has some very cool added features including the ability to add favorites to the Filmstrip drop-down menu to the immediate right of the file name. (**Figure 7.105**)

FIG 7.105

I THE MAIN MENU IN THE LIBRARY MODULE

The majority of your workflow can be accomplished in the window of the Library Module, but there are also some very important features that can be located from the menu bar. We'll cover each menu one by one below, pointing out the basics.

Lightroom   File   Edit   Library   Photo   Metadata   View   Window   Help

FIG 7.106
Lightroom Library Main Menu

The File Menu allows you to Optimize the catalog, import, export, Tethered Capture, work with Quick Collections and Filter. It also allows you to export catalogs, and create new catalogs. We'll talk more about exporting as a catalog later on in Chapter 17. **New in *Lightroom 4*** is direct email from within *Lightroom*. This has been a very popular feature request from the days of the very first public back in 2006.

NEW

🍎	Lightroom	**File**	Edit	Library	Photo	Metadata	View	Window	Help

New Catalog...
Open Catalog...   ⇧⌘O

Open Recent   ▶

Optimize Catalog...

Import Photos and Video...   ⇧⌘I
Import from Another Catalog...
Tethered Capture   ▶
Import from Application...
Auto Import   ▶

Export...   ⇧⌘E
Export with Previous   ⌥⇧⌘E
Export with Preset   ▶
Export as Catalog...

Email Photo...   ⇧⌘M

Plug-in Manager...   ⌥⇧⌘,
Plug-in Extras   ▶

Show Quick Collection   ⌘B
Save Quick Collection...   ⌥⌘B
Clear Quick Collection   ⇧⌘B
Set Quick Collection as Target   ⌥⇧⌘B

Library Filters   ▶

Page Setup...   ⇧⌘P
Print...   ⌘P

FIG 7.107
Lightroom Library
File Menu

| EMAIL FROM THE FILE MENU

The Preset drop-down menu opens the normal Export dialog window, which then allows you specify the size, format, etc for the file. The address button opens a self contained Address Book, which is only accessible by *Lightroom*. It's unfortunately not possible to use the address book within your default email application.

FIG 7.108
Email from the *Lightroom* File Menu

I TETHERED CAPTURE FROM THE FILE MENU

Simply plug in your Nikon or Canon camera via USB or Firewire, start a tethered session and view important camera settings, control the shutter release or apply metadata and develop settings to incoming images.

There is no longer any need for camera manufacturer or third party software or "watched" folders. If your camera isn't supported, think twice before you scream at Adobe. Support is directly related to the camera makers' willingness to supply a software development kit (SDK) to Adobe.

To use Tethered Capture, go to the Library File Menu and choose Tethered Capture>Start Tethered Capture (**Figure 7.109**).

FIG 7.109
Tethered Capture from
the Lightroom Library
File Menu

The Tethered Capture Settings Dialog Box will open. Configure
the Session Name, Choose a naming template, the destination
where the images will reside and any metadata template. When
complete, press OK at the bottom of the dialog box.

FIG 7.110
Starting
Tethered Capture

The Tethered Capture Control Panel will open. As long as the camera is connected, the model number of the camera will be displayed. You can shoot directly from the camera or you can use the Capture Button on the bottom right to trigger the camera.

New in *Lightroom* Collapse the tether toolbar down to the shutter button by Option or Alt clicking the close button.

NEW

FIG 7.111
Tethered Capture
Control Panel

TETHERED CAPTURE SETTINGS TIPS:

• *The Develop Settings menu allows you to choose any Camera Raw profiles that are installed*

• *The X button on the top right of the control panel will close the panel*

• *The panel can be hidden by using Command-T on a MAC or Control-T on a PC*

I EDIT MENU

The Edit Menu handles selections. In *Lightroom,* images that are selected will appear in both the Filmstrip and the Library Grid. You can change your ratings, flags and color labels here, as well as checking your spelling.

FIG 7.112
Library Edit Menu

185

Active Photos

While you can select multiple images, only one image at a time is considered Active. The Active image's cell color is lighter and more opaque and is also the image that appears in the Navigator (**Figure 7.113**).

This is the **active image**, designated by a lighter cell color.

These are the **additionally selected images**, not quite as light as the Active Image.

FIG 7.113
Active and Additionally Selected Images

I LIBRARY MENU

It is in the Library Menu that you create new collections and folders, find images and turn filtering on and off.

Refine Photos causes any unflagged images in the folder to be marked as rejected and will set any picks back to unflagged. The rejected images will not go anywhere until you choose Delete Rejected Photos (from the Photo Menu). It is a way of editing. You can find Missing Photos to locate offline or missing photos and Find Previous Process Photos to locate photos first processed in an earlier version of *Lightroom*.

You can also rename your images and convert to DNG, define preview quality and move through your selected images. D-65 renames its images here for the second time after editing if necessary (the first rename is on import).

You can change the quality of previously rendered previews here by selecting the folder of images, individual images, or even your entire Library. While 1:1 Previews may be desirable, they do take up a lot of space and it can take a long time to generate a Library of high res previews. One tip that we like is to check Show Photos in Subfolders. Doing this keeps the count correct on the parent folders in the Library. With this unchecked, the parent folder shows 0 images and only the subfolders show the correct count.

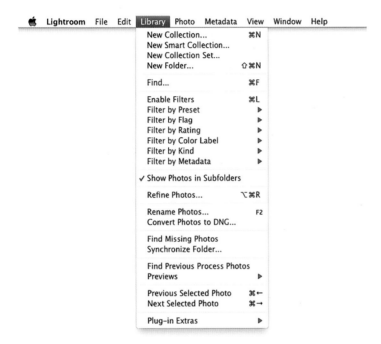

FIG 7.114
Lightroom Library Menu

| PHOTO MENU

The Photo Menu has some Library basics such as Set Rating, Set Flag, Delete, Open in Loupe and Rotations. It is from the Photo Menu that we can also directly Edit in *Photoshop* and then save the edits back into *Lightroom*. This will be covered later. In Develop Settings you can Match Total Exposures. There are also some very cool features in the Photo Menu demonstrated below like Stacking and Virtual Copies.

FIG 7.115
Lightroom Library
Photo Menu

Stacking

NEW

New in *Lightroom 4* is the ability to Stack in collections.

Stacking allows you to group images together, so there is one top image, and similar images that are nested below the top image or select. To create a stack, select the images that you want together and then from the Photo Menu, drop down to Stacking and fly out to Group into Stack or use the keyboard shortcut, Command-G.

You can open or close stacks by clicking on the stack icon in the top left of the image or through the menu or via the Photo Menu or by pressing the S key. You can move through stacks and even Auto Stack by Capture Time.

Note: When applying changes to a stack, such as Renaming Photos, only the top image in the stack will be affected. If you want to apply a change to all the images in a stack, you will need to unstack them first. Also stacks can't contain images from different folders.

FIG 7.116
Choosing Group into Stack in Lightroom Library Photo Men

FIG 7.117
Group into Stack in
Lightroom Library

FIG 7.118
Stack Badges can be toggled on and off in the Filmstrip

GROUP INTO STACK TIPS:

- *Double-clicking on stack count badge now expands the stack with all photos selected*

- *Stack Badges can be toggled on and off in the Filmstrip.*

Virtual Copy

Virtual Copy may just be one of the coolest features in *Lightroom*. A virtual copy is a copy of the metadata in the *Lightroom* Library, which acts like a duplicate of the image. You would use this when you want have multiple versions of one image with different adjustments. You are not physically duplicating the image. You still only have one image, but with multiple sets of metadata. You can export a "real" file from any virtual copy. The metadata on the virtual copy becomes an actual image on export only. Now, that's cool!

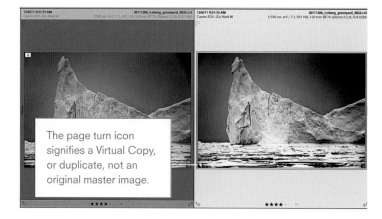

FIG 7.119
Virtual Copy Created from *Lightroom* Library Photo Menu

The page turn icon signifies a Virtual Copy, or duplicate, not an original master image.

VIRTUAL COPY TIP:

By default, Lightroom only stores information about Virtual Copies in the catalog. It is NOT stored in the XMP metadata, so this is a real potential problem if your catalog becomes corrupt. But there is a pretty good workaround: when you are done working on your Virtual Copy, save a Snapshot. When you go back to the original image, you'll notice that the Snapshot is also available next to the original.

Match Total Exposures

It is accessible in the Library module from Library>Photo> Develop Settings>Match Total Exposure. If you highlight an individual image in the series and select "Match Total Exposure," the other images in that selection will auto correct the exposure value to match the exposure of the primary selected image. It is looking to match the values calculated by combining shutter speed, ISO, aperture, and exposure compensation. The more common usage would be to even out the results from a set of related shots.

| METADATA MENU

There are many useful features in the Metadata Menu. Many of them have been covered earlier in the chapter like Set Keyword Shortcut, Color Label Set, Edit Metadata Presets, and Save Metadata to File. Under the Metadata Menu is where you can Import and Export Keywords, Purge Unused Keywords and a totally cool feature which allows you to Edit Capture Time.

FIG 7.120
Lightroom Library
Metadata Menu

Edit Capture Time

The ability to edit capture time is a noteworthy feature in this menu. Ideally, you would want to have your camera date and time set correctly, but many times, this is not the case especially when crossing time zones. *Lightroom* offers a solution allowing you to adjust camera-generated time and date by adjusting to a specified date and time or by shifting by set number of hours or by changing the file's creation date.

FIG 7.121
Lightroom Library
Metadata Menu Edit
Capture Time

| VIEW MENU

The View Menu contains lots of good shortcuts to help customize your workflow. They include Hide Toolbar, Show Filter Bar, Toggle Loupe View and Zoom View, Zoom In and Zoom Out, Increase and Decrease Grid Size, Sort Options, Grid, Loupe, Compare, Survey, Go to Develop, Crop, Spot Removal, Adjustment Brush, Graduated Filter, Adjust White Balance, View Options, Grid View Style, Loupe Info, The Spot Removal and Adjustment Brush and Enable Mirror Image Mode.

View Options, Grid View Style and Loupe information were covered when we set up *Lightroom's* Preferences.

Choosing Enable Mirror Image Mode will flip all the images **in your entire library** as if viewed in a mirror. This may be useful when showing someone portraits of himself or herself. Remember, when most people see themselves, they see themselves in a mirror and are not used to looking at themselves straight on. This is one feature where we understand the explanation, but that we would never use.

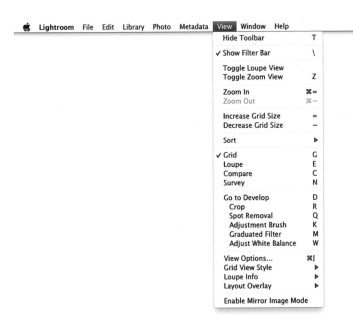

FIG 7.122
Lightroom Library
View Menu

| WINDOW MENU

The Window menu brings you through the modules, determines screen mode and Lights Out. Lights Out, keyboard shortcut L, has three modes. The first is Dim Lights, which darkens everything in your screen, including a second monitor, except the images. The second is Full Lights Out Mode, which completely blacks out everything on the screen except the image(s). You can cycle through the various modes using the L key. Additionally, you can control options for a Secondary Display in the Window menu.

NEW

New in *Lightroom 4* Module picker can be customized via right-click option

FIG 7.123
Lightroom Library
View Menu

I HELP MENU

Lightroom's online help is terrific. You can also check for updates and find keyboard shortcuts for each module in the Help Menu.

FIG 7.124
Lightroom Library
Help Menu

Library Shortcuts

View Shortcuts

Esc	Return to previous view
Return	Enter Loupe or 1:1 view
G	Enter Grid Mode
E	Enter Loupe view
C	Enter Compare mode
N	Enter Survey mode
Command + Return	Enter Impromptu Slideshow mode
F	Cycle to next Screen Mode
Command + Option + F	Return to Normal Screen Mode
L	Cycle through Lights Out modes
Command + J	Grid View Options
J	Cycle Grid Views
\	Hide/Show the Filter Bar

Rating Shortcuts

1-5	Set ratings
Shift + 1-5	Set ratings and move to next photo
6-9	Set color labels
Shift + 6-9	Set color labels and move to next photo
0	Reset ratings to none
[	Decrease the rating
]	Increase the rating

Flagging Shortcuts

`	Toggle Flagged Status
Command + Up Arrow	Increase Flag Status
Command + Down Arrow	Decrease Flag Status
X	Set Reject Flag
P	Set Pick Flag

Target Collection Shortcuts

B	Add to Target Collection
Command + B	Show Target Collection
Command + Shift + B	Clear Quick Collection

Photo Shortcuts

Command + Shift + I	Import photos and videos
Command + Shift + E	Export
Command + [	Rotate left
Command +]	Rotate right
Command + E	Edit in Photoshop
Command + S	Save Metadata to File
Command + -	Zoom out
Command + =	Zoom in
Z	Zoom to 100%
Command + G	Stack photos
Command + Shift + G	Unstack photos
Command + R	Reveal in Finder
Delete	Remove from Library
F2	Rename File
Command + Shift + C	Copy Develop Settings
Command + Shift + V	Paste Develop Settings
Command + Left Arrow	Previous selected photo
Command + Right Arrow	Next selected photo
Command + L	Enable/Disable Library Filters
Command + Shift + M	Mail selected photos

Panel Shortcuts

Tab	Hide/Show the side panels
Shift + Tab	Hide/Show all the panels
T	Hide/Show the toolbar
Command + F	Activate the search field
Command + K	Activate the keyword entry field
Command + Option + Up Arrow	Return to the previous module

FIG 7.125

Lightroom
Library Shortcuts

SUMMARY

- The Library Module is "command central" for *Lightroom*. This is your digital asset management system. It is where you view, sort, search, manage, organize, rank, compare and browse through your images.

- The *Lightroom* Library Module is a true database that catalogs all imported images so that you can view previews and data whether the images are online or not.

- The left panel holds the Navigator, Catalog, Folders, Collections and Publish Services panels as well as the Import and Export buttons.

- The right-hand panel holds Histogram, Quick Develop, Keywording, Keyword List, Metadata and Comments as well as the Sync Settings and Sync Metadata buttons.

- The Library Filter is located above the Grid, which resides in the middle of the main window and displays your images.

- At the bottom of the Grid is the Toolbar.

- The Filmstrip is located underneath the Toolbar.

THE DEVELOP MODULE

The Develop Module holds all the controls that you need to adjust images. It is D-65's "tweaking command central." The image processing engine used in *Lightroom* is *Adobe Photoshop Camera Raw*, which ensures that digital RAW images processed in *Lightroom* are fully compatible with *Camera Raw* and vice versa.

Lightroom 3 introduced some major improvements to the product's image processing capabilities (officially known as "Process Version 2010"), and *Lightroom 4* has taken this even further with the new Process Version 2012 and associated controls:

I DEVELOP MODULE IMPROVEMENTS IN *LIGHTROOM 4*

Here is a list of some of the changes occurring in the *Lightroom 4* Develop Module:

NEW

New in *Lightroom 4*

I PROCESS VERSION

The process version specifies which version of *Camera Raw* image processing technology should be used when rendering and editing files. Because the processing engine has been so improved, there is a substantial difference in images processed in *Lightroom 3* and in *Lightroom 4*. A "process version" has been introduced to differentiate between the old process and new process and to allow you to choose how you want to process your images. The process version allows *Lightroom* to maintain virtually identical representation of images you've edited in the past, but will also allow you to take advantage of updating the image to the latest processing version. All images edited prior to *Lightroom 4* are associated with Process Version 2010. All images newly imported into *Lightroom 4* have are associated with Process Version 2012.

- Process Versions have been named 2010 and 2012, relating to the year that each process version was introduced

- Any images with existing settings will be set to the old Process Version 2010

- Any new images imported into *Lightroom 4* will be assigned the new Process Version 2012

- There's a warning exclamation mark in the lower right of the image if it's set to the old Process Version 2010 which you can click if you want to update to the Process Version 2012

- Process Version is under the Settings menu, in the Calibration panel and the Sync dialog box

- By clicking on the Process Version graphic you have the ability to see a before/after view of the old and new Process

Versions and have the ability to update all the selected images or all of the images in the filmstrip at the same time

The New Process Version 2012 :

- Implements a new tone mapping algorithm, for easy yet powerful contrast management.

- More intuitive to new users and less confusion over what slider to use. For example, in Process Version 2010 there were three ways to adjust the overall image brightness: Exposure, Brightness, and Fill Light. They affect the highlights and shadows in different ways, but they all affect the mid-tones. In Process Version 2012, there is one way to adjust the overall image brightness: Exposure.

- Clean subset for mobile and tablet applications, where user interface real estate is at a premium.

- Easy to synchronize between RAW and JPEG. In Process Version 2010, it was hard to synchronize RAW and JPEG because there were different baseline settings. Brightness, Contrast, Blacks, and Point Curve had different default settings. In 2012, tone controls have the same default settings and the same math for RAW and & JPEG. This help facilitate mixed RAW/JPEG workflows and means that tone presets can be applied effectively to both RAW and JPEG images.

- Is available to utilize with both global and local tools, with the same behavior for both.

- Reduces the need for parametric and point curves when performing common tonal adjustments (because curves are less intuitive to new users).

I BASIC PANEL

- Simplified controls in the Basic panel for Exposure, Contrast, Highlights, Shadows, Whites, Blacks (no more Fill Light, Brightness or Recovery).

- Image content aware Shadow and Highlight controls extract greater dynamic range from a single image.

- Updated Clarity adjustment for superior results without causing artifacts.

- Updated Chromatic Aberration correction solution.

I TONE CURVE PANEL

- Per channel curves adjustments.

I LENS CORRECTIONS

- *Lightroom* will now only look for lens profiles inside the application folder/package. *Lightroom* will continue to look for lens profiles in the user specific lens profiles folder for profiles that were created by the Adobe Lens Profile Creator or download via Adobe Lens Profile Downloader or *Photoshop*. If you have copied your own custom lens profiles into the shared lens profiles folder previously, those lens profiles will not show up in the new *Lightroom 4*. Please move your custom lens profiles to your user specific lens profiles.

I LOCALIZED ADJUSTMENTS

- White balance brush to apply localized color temperature and tint corrections

- Localized controls to reduce noise and remove moire´

- Localized controls for shadows and highlights

I SOFT PROOFING

- Paper and ink simulation

- Choose between perceptual and relative intent

- Intuitive virtual copy creation for profile-specific adjustments

- Profile and monitor gamut warnings and print module brightness/contrast option to address differences between monitor and paper characteristics

A non-destructive edit doesn't alter the original pixels in your image. The big advantage of non-destructive editing is that you can undo any edit at any time, and in any order. You can go back and change the parameters of any edit at any time, keeping the history of a file even after the file is closed. *Lightroom* also allows all of the controls to be used not only for RAW and DNG files but also for JPG, TIF and PSD files and It is completely non-destructive on RAW files, and non-destructive on other files until you export the file. This is a major breakthrough for adjusting images.

The editing data is stored inside the *Lightroom* Catalog, whether you choose to import your images into the Library or leave them in their original locations and import them as references. If you're working with RAW files, you can also choose to have the edits and metadata changes stored in the sidecar XMP files, which D-65 strongly suggests.

WORKFLOW TIP:

*Decide in advance if you are the type of person who can remember to manually save metadata after adjustments. If you can remember this, then simply Choose Command-S every now and then and save the metadata to file manually. If you are the type of person who is going to forget this critical step, then choose to activate the metadata auto save feature by going to Lightroom>Catalog Settings>Metadata, and checking the "Automatically write changes into XMP sidecar files" option. This second option **does slow down performance**, but if you are going to have a tough time remembering to do it manually, it alleviates potential issues with regards to losing the XMP sidecar files. More on this later.*

While RAW files don't have an embedded color profile, the Develop Module assumes a very wide color space based on the values of ProPhoto RGB. Technically, it is Melissa RGB ProPhoto with a gamma of 1.0. ProPhoto is a color space that contains all of the colors that your camera is able to capture. Since ProPhoto is really a 16-bit space, *Lightroom* uses a native bit-depth of 16 bits per channel. *Lightroom* is capable of 32,000 levels of tonal information, which surpasses the amount from any digital camera today. Quite simply, in English, *Lightroom* can safely contain all the tone and color information from any camera.

Lightroom manages color internally by using a gamma of 1.0 instead of 1.8. A gamma of 1.0 matches the native gamma of RAW camera files. But here is where it gets a bit complicated. To provide useful information in displaying the Histogram and corresponding RGB values, *Lightroom* utilizes a gamma value of 2.2.

I FEATURES IN DEVELOP

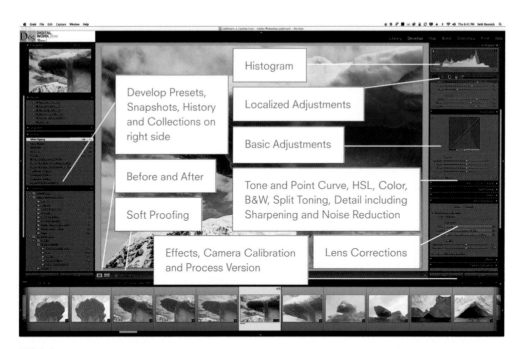

FIG 8.1
The Develop Module Main Window

I TOOLBAR IN DEVELOP MODULE

We'll start off with the Toolbar, and then move to the left-side and right-side panels in the Develop Module. The letter T key always opens and closes the Toolbar, so if you suddenly think your version did not ship with a Toolbar, try the letter T key to solve the problem.

FIG 8.2
The Toolbar in the
Develop Module

Loupe View

The first button is Loupe View, which offers you the ability to zoom in on an image, same as in the Library.

Before and After View

The next button to the right is Before & After View, which is a very handy feature. This allows you to compare an image before and after you have made adjustments. You can view either side by side, or top and bottom. The down arrow next to the Before & After view allows you to choose the orientation. The backslash key (\) will also act as a Before & After view toggle.

Flag as Pick or Rejected

You can flag an image as a Pick or as Rejected in the Develop Toolbar.

Ranking and Labels

You can rank an image and/or apply a color label in the Develop Toolbar.

Move Forward or Backward

You can move forward or backward through the Filmstrip with these buttons.

Impromptu Slideshow

This button lets you create a slideshow on the fly.

Zoom Fit

With this button you can go from Fit all the way to 11:1.

NEW

New In *Lightroom 4* Soft Proofing

This is command central for Soft Proofing which we will address later in the chapter.

Select Toolbar Contents

At the far right is the Select Toolbar Contents drop-down arrow. You can use this button to select what features you want to see in the Toolbar.

I DEVELOP MODULE PANELS

Now let's move to the right-side panels.

Histogram

The *Lightroom* Histogram appears in the top right-hand corner of both the Develop and the Library Modules. A histogram is a visual representation of the tonal range in your image and how much of any given tone exists. The Histogram shows three layers of color representing the red, green and blue data channels. The left side of the Histogram represents pixels with 0% luminance (black) while the right side represents pixels with 100% luminance (white).

The highlighted area of the histogram portrays the corresponding values in Exposure, Contrast, Highlights, Shadows, Whites and Blacks

FIG 8.3
The Develop Module Histogram Panel

ISO 100   35 mm   f / 6.3   ¹/₄₀₀ sec

This box/arrow will display highlight clipping and the box/arrow on the left will show shadow clipping.

The Histogram panel in *Lightroom's* Develop Module becomes a tool. You can adjust an image by adjusting the Histogram itself. Exposure, Highlights, Shadows, Whites and Blacks, all shown in the Histogram, directly relate to the tone sliders below the histogram. You can physically make adjustments to an image by dragging the tone sliders or in the Histogram itself.

The Histogram also allows you to preview the image with a clipping warning for both Shadows and Highlights by clicking on the Shadow and Highlight buttons in the upper left-hand and right-hand corners. A color overlay with blue indicates shadow clipping and a color overlay with red indicates highlight clipping (shown in **Figure 8.4**).

Blue indicates shadow clipping.

In this image, red shows highlight clipping

FIG 8.4
Image showing clipping in Shadows (blue) and Highlights (Red)

Localized Adjustments

Lightroom 4 introduces some major positive changes for localized corrections.

New In *Lightroom 4*

- White balance brush to apply localized color temperature and tint corrections

- Localized controls to reduce noise and remove moire´

- Localized controls for shadows and highlights

NEW

- The **Local Adjustment** tools have been updated to reflect the new Process Version 2012 settings. Both the Graduated Filter and the Adjustment Brush panels reflect the new controls. If the photo being edited has Process Version 2010 then the panels will open with the old sliders from *Lightroom 3* rather than the new ones from *Lightroom 4.*

The adjustments are done using masks or gradients. You create a gradient or you paint a mask and fill it with one of the adjustments listed below. And the best thing of all is that: it is non-destructive.

You can "paint" or use a "Graduated Filter"using the following adjustments:

- Temperature

- Tint

- Exposure

- Contrast

- Highlights

- Shadows

- Clarity

- Saturation

- Sharpness

- Noise

- Moiré

- Color

Cropping, Spot Removal and Red Eye Reduction are also located in the Tool Strip. Clicking on each one then opens its own tool drawer. We'll explain how these work in the order that they appear from left to right.

FIG 8.5
Localized
Adjustment Panel

THE DEVELOP MODULE

Crop Overlay and Straighten Tool

When you click on the Crop Tool or press the R key, the Tool Strip expands and offers more options, including the Crop Frame Tool, Lock, drop-down menu with crop presets, the Straighten Tool and Constrain to Warp. The Reset button on the bottom of the panel clears the settings you apply in this panel.

Clicking on the Crop Overlay Tool will present a crop bounding box that allows you to crop your image. You can choose to constrain the image by locking the lock button and by using the handles on the crop overlay or by moving the image behind it.

You can also choose from a drop-down menu of aspect ratio presets next to the Lock. You can also enter and save custom presets.

FIG 8.6
Crop Panel

New in *Lightroom 4*

NEW

- The list of crop ratios includes default screen-shaped ratios – 3:4 1280×1024, 16×9 1920×1080, 16×10 1280×800

- Increased the maximum value allowed to be entered in the custom aspect ratio dialog from 999.99 to 9999.99 so the user can enter in a screen resolution to get its ratio. Whenever the user enters large numbers (greater than 20) for a custom crop aspect ratio, the decimal place shifts over to the left to reinforce these are only ratios, not exact dimensions. (ex: Typing in 1024×768 results in a ratio of 10.24 x 7.68)

FIG 8.7
The List of crop ratios

The Tool Overlay choices are: Always, Never or Auto depending on your preference

FIG 8.8
Crop Overlay with Tool Overlay on

The Filmstrip will display the crop you applied to an image.

Straighten Tool and the Straighten Tool Slider

This tool is great for straightening a horizon line.

Using the Straighten Tool and Straighten Tool Slider

You can straighten an image in two ways:

1. Mousing down on the Straighten Slider, and dragging it to the right or left will straighten out your image in live time using a grid to align the horizontal or vertical access.

2. The Straighten Tool (the ruler) works by grabbing it from the Toolbar, mousing down, dragging the tool into the image and drawing a line along the path you want to straighten, as demonstrated in **Figures 8.10** through **8.14**.

Use the Straighten Ruler or Slider to correct your image.

FIG 8.9
Straighten Tool

FIG 8.10
Image needs gate straightened with horizon line.

FIG 8.11
Grab the Straighten Tool and Mouse down in the image.

Straighten Tool dragged parallel to crooked horizon line

FIG 8.12
Drag the tool along the line of the path you want to straighten.

FIG 8.13
The image with the cropping guides showing after using the Straighten Tool.

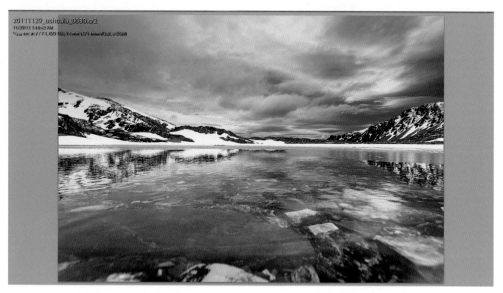

FIG 8.14
Hit Return and set the crop and the final image is cropped and skyline is straight.

Red Eye Correction Tool

The Red Eye Correction Tool does exactly what its name implies, that is, it reduces and/or corrects red eye.

FIG 8.15
Red Eye Correction Tool

Click on a red eye to see the slider. Make a selection around the red eye using the Pupil Size slider, which increases the size of the selected area (**Figure 8.16**).

FIG 8.16
Make a selection around the red eye using the Pupil Size slider, which increases the size of the selected area.

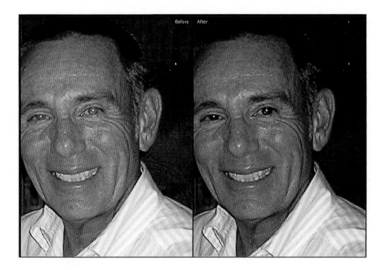

Before   After

FIG 8.17
Before and after using
Red Eye Reduction and
the White Balance tool

Cloning and Healing

There is a difference between the Cloning and Healing tools. Cloning applies the same sampled area to a different area—it is an exact duplicate of what you are selecting. Healing matches texture, lighting and shading from the sampled area to the selected area you are correcting.

Generally the Cloning tool is a better choice when removing a spot close to an edge, and the Healing Tool a better choice when you are away from a defined edge.

Let's look at an example. There are some dust spots on the sensor in the upper right-hand corner of **Figure 8.18**. The spot is in the sky, so the Spot Healing Tool would be fine, but we are going to demonstrate both methods.

Using the Spot Removal Tool

Click on the Spot Removal Tool to open the menu (**see Figure 8.19**).

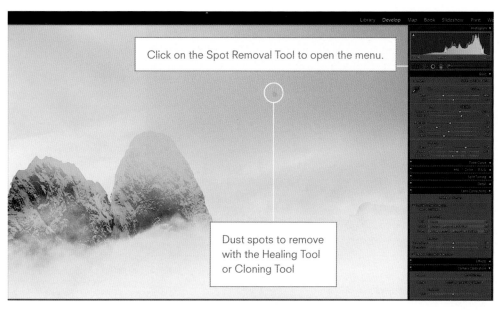

FIG 8.18
Dust spots on sensor need to be removed with Spot Removal Tool.

FIG 8.19
Spot Removal includes
Clone Brush and
Heal Brush.

Using the Navigator, navigate to the dust spot using the little
rectangle and zoom in to at least 1:1 to see the dust spot. In this
case we are zooming to 2:1.

FIG 8.20
Zooming to 2:1 using
the Navigator to see the
dust spot.

To Clone: Choose Clone and a brush size the same size or a bit larger than the object you want to clone. Mouse down and move the circle to the area you want to clone. Note that the left bracket key ([) will make the selection area smaller and the right bracket key (]) will make the selection area larger. The scroll wheel on the mouse will also adjust the size of the selection.

FIG 8.21
Pick Clone and a brush
size the same size or a
bit larger than the object
you want to clone.

Mouse Down and drag the circle to the Clone Source or the location from which you want to clone.

THE DEVELOP MODULE

FIG 8.22
Mouse Down and
drag the circle to the
Clone Source.

Release the mouse and the cloned object will appear. Both the
size of the selection circle and the Opacity can be adjusted
further after you release the mouse.

FIG 8.23
Release the mouse
and the cloned object
will appear.

To Heal: Select the Healing Brush and size it a little larger than
what you want healed. Mouse down on what you want healed
and bingo!

FIG 8.24
To heal, select the
Healing Brush and
mouse down on what
you want healed.

The Heal Brush will automatically make a selection matching
the texture, lighting and shading of the sampled adjacent
area. This will remove the dust or spot quite easily. D-65 uses
Healing for most dust and spot removal on our RAW files. It is an
awesome tool!

FIG 8.25
The Heal Brush will
automatically make a
selection matching the
texture, lighting and
shading of the sampled
adjacent area.

SPOT REMOVAL TOOL WORKFLOW TIP:

- *The H key toggles the Spot Removal Tool–we use the H
  key a lot to hide the Spot Removal Tool so that we can
  see if there's another spot close by, then H again to
  reveal the Spot Removal Tool*

- *The letter Q key is the Keyboard Shortcut for entering Spot Removal Mode*

- *Spotting can be synchronized like other Develop tools, but be mindful that if the dust spot on the sensor is in the sky in one image and on a building in a second image, the sync probably won't work well*

Localized Corrections Graduated Filter

Localized corrections appeared in *Lightroom 2* and they are still one of the coolest features in the Develop Module. First we will cover the Graduated Filter Tool. To activate the Graduated Filter, click on the gradient icon or use the keyboard shortcut, the M key.

FIG 8.26
The Graduated
Filter Tool

The Graduated Filter panel offers many choices:

- Temp &Tint White apply localized color temperature and tint corrections

- Exposure corresponds to F stops with a range of minus 4.00 to plus 4.00

- Contrast increases or decreases contrast by adjusting the white and black points simultaneously

- Highlight and Shadow controls are content aware offering a greater dynamic range from a single image.

- Clarity is mid-tone contrast and it works like sharpening–it needs edges:

  ✓ More clarity is adding sharpness but in a tonal way

  ✓ Less clarity is like smoothing and is great for skin tones

- Saturation will saturate all colors

  ✓ Add saturation by moving the slider towards the plus side

  ✓ Desaturate by moving the slider towards the minus side

- Sharpness adjusts overall sharpness of an image

- Noise allows for local control of noise reduction

  NEW

  ✓ More Noise Reduction is applied moving the slider to the right and less Noise Reduction when moving the slider to the left.

  ✓ If you have a plus noise reduction brush applied, adding another negative noise reduction brush would cut down on the amount of the plus noise reduction brush.

- Moiré removes rainbow like patterns

  NEW

  ✓ More Moiré Reduction is applied moving the slider to the right and less Moiré when moving the slider to the left.

  ✓ If you have a plus Moiré reduction brush applied, adding another negative Moiré reduction brush would cut down on the amount of the plus Moiré reduction brush.

- Sharpness adjusts overall sharpness of an image

- Color allows you to create a tint within an image

FIG 8.27
The Graduated
Filter Panel

FIG 8.28
The Panel can be reset
by holding down Option
and Clicking on Effect.

Effect becomes Reset
when holding down the
Option Key and Clicking

FIG 8.29
Show/Hide pins in
the Toolbar

Using the Graduated Filter

The image in **Figure 8.32** would be more pleasing to the eye in multiple ways by using *Lightroom's* Graduated Filter. When talking about adjusting images, I love a comment I heard from friend and business partner Jeff Schewe. Jeff said that when he adjusts images, he starts by letting the image talk to him and tell him what needs to be done. In this case the image is telling me that the sky needs to come down and it could use some color and the front area needs to be opened up and it too could use a little color.

The adjustment panel comes with some presets and you can even create your own or we can go about these adjustments in a totally customized fashion.

FIG 8.30
Mouse down on Exposure to open Presets

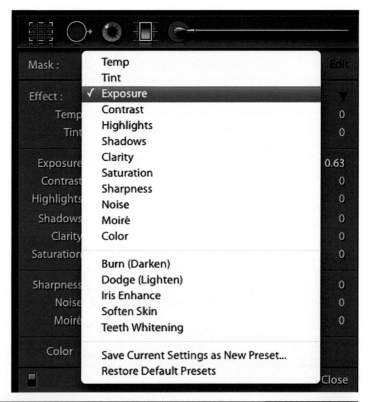

FIG 8.31
Drop-down menu accessed by clicking on Exposure.

Mask :

Effect :

Temp	
Tint	
✓ Exposure	
Contrast	
Highlights	
Shadows	
Clarity	
Saturation	
Sharpness	
Noise	
Moirė	
Color	
Burn (Darken)	
Dodge (Lighten)	
Iris Enhance	
Soften Skin	
Teeth Whitening	
Save Current Settings as New Preset...	
Restore Default Presets	

Edit

Temp 0
Tint 0

Exposure 0.63
Contrast 0
Highlights 0
Shadows 0
Clarity 0
Saturation 0

Sharpness 0
Noise 0
Moirė 0

Color

Close

FIG 8.32
The Graduated Filter can help make this image more pleasing.

For starters, we could bring down the sky, add a little saturation and add a little blue. We can always change the settings after the fact, but let's approximate what we want to do first. Let's set exposure to about 1/2 stops down and saturation to 17 and the color temperature down to -15. To do this, we mouse down and drag the slider tool from the top down to the horizon line to apply the Graduated Filter.

***GRADUATED FILTER WORKFLOW TIP:** Hold the Shift key down when you drag down the Graduated Filter, and it will be applied perfectly level. This is an ideal tool for this image. If you do not hold the Shift Key down the Graduated Filter can be applied at an angle.*

FIG 8.33
Gradient applied and now it can be further edited.

After we make our basic adjustment, we can refine the Graduated Filter and see the effects in live time. In **Figure 8.34**, we open up the Color Floating Panel, keep the mouse button depressed and go into the image to sample color from the image, which is very cool.

FIG 8.34
Color sampled from the image by depressing the mouse button and holding it down on the Color Floating Panel and dragging the sample into the image.

We make some further changes to the image and get the first gradient to look the way we want and we hit Return to set the gradient. We can always edit it later by clicking on the pin which will allow us to edit the gradient. The pin is the name for the place holder or marker for the gradient. The letter H will toggle the pin on and off. Notice the pin in **Figure 8.35**.

FIG 8.35
Additional edits are done on the gradient. The pin for the gradient is in the center of the image. It can be toggled on and off with the letter H.

Now it is time to apply our second gradient. This time we will apply a gradient from the bottom of the image, opening up the foreground and adding a little color sampled from the warm sky.

FIG 8.36
New gradient is applied from the bottom of the image up. We add a little color from the sky and open up Exposure to 1.62, Highlights -47, Shadows 92, Clarity-9, Saturation to 48.

FIG 8.37
A third gradient is applied at the top just to darken the upper part of the image.

FIG 8.38
A before and after comparison. The sky has been successfully darkened and warmed up and the foreground has been lightened. All of this is non-destructive and relatively easy to apply.

GRADUATED FILTER TIPS:

- *The letter M key opens the Gradient Tool*

- *The letter H key will hide and reveal the pin*

- *Using Auto next to Show Edit Pins will reveal the pin when the mouse is over the image*

- *Constrain gradient to vertical—hold down the Shift key while dragging mouse*

- *Invert gradient—Apostrophe key (')*

- *Set a gradient—Enter key*

- *Delete selected pin—Delete key*

- *Holding down the Option/Alt keys activates Erase mode*

Localized Corrections Adjustment Brush

In addition to the Graduated Filter, there is a Localized Adjustment Brush which is also totally cool.

FIG 8.39
Adjustment Brush

This adjustment brush just plain rocks, providing a simple painting tool to locally and non-destructively adjust Temperature, Tint, Exposure, Contrast, Highlights, Shadows, Clarity, Saturation, Sharpness, Noise Moiré and Color. There is an Effect drop down menu that defines the initial setting for the Brush. You can also create two preset brushes (A and B). Each preset brush can be adjusted for Size, Feather, Flow and Density. There even is an Auto Mask capability which confines the brush strokes to areas of similar color.

Using the Adjustment Brush

To define a brush tint value click the Color Picker on the palette.

FIG 8.40
Adjustment Brush Panel

FIG 8.41
Adjustment Brush
Color Picker

The Localized Corrections Adjustment Brush controls work in the following ways:

- **Temp** corresponds to color temperature

- **Tint** corresponds to the tinting from green to magenta of the color temperature

- **Exposure** corresponds to F stops with a range of minus 4.00 to plus 4.00

- **Contrast** increases or decreases contrast by adjusting the white and black points simultaneously

NEW
- **Highlights** increases or decreases mid range highlights

NEW
- **Shadows** increases or decreases mid range shadows

- **Clarity** is midtone contrast and it is like sharpening—it needs edges: more clarity is adding sharpness but in a tonal way; less clarity is like smoothing and is great for skin tones

- **Saturation** increases saturation when it is on the plus side and decreases saturation when it is on the minus side

NEW
- **Sharpness** Selectively and locally adjusts sharpness

NEW
- **Noise** Noise Reduction is applied moving the slider to the right and less Noise Reduction when moving the slider to the left

NEW
- **Moiré** Reduction is applied moving the slider to the right and less Moiré Reduction when moving the slider to the left

- **Color** allows you to create a tint.

- **Size** controls the diameter of the brush.

- **Feather** creates a soft-edged transition: the larger the feather, the softer the gradation

- **Flow** is the strength at which the tool is working, somewhat like opacity

- **Density** controls the amount of transparency in the stroke

For example, setting the Density to less than 100 will cause brush strokes applied with the lower setting to be some percentage of the Amount specified. This means that you can have an Exposure -4, but if some brush strokes are applied with a density setting of 50, those strokes will only have 50% strength, or -2. The individual strokes can be varied in their density, but still be part of the same pin, which can have its overall strength controlled with the Amount slider.

LOCALIZED ADJUSTMENT BRUSH TIPS:

- *The letter K key will open the Adjustment Brush*

- *The lette H will Show and Hide the Pin*

- *Holding down the Option/Alt key will allow you to subtract from the mask*

- *Enter will commit a brush stroke*

- *Delete selected pin with Delete key*

- *To paint a new adjustment, click New and then change a value, such as Brightness—when you click on it after you have made the adjustment, you can see this is like the ultimate dodge and burn*

- *Auto Sync only syncs global corrections; it does not sync local corrections—Regular Sync will sync everything selected*

- *Increase/decrease brush size with right bracket (]) and left bracket ([)*

- *Increase/decrease feathering with Shift+] and Shift+[*

- *The letter A key will Toggle Auto Mask on and off*

- *The letter O key will toggle the Overlay on and off*

- *Shift+O cycles through additional colors for Overlay*

Using the Localized Adjustment Brush

Figure 8.42 could certainly benefit from contrast in the iceberg, selectively lightening the water and the underside of the iceberg and adding some saturation and selectively cooling parts of the image.

FIG 8.42
Adjustment Brush Color Picker

We select a brush of Exposure, +1.36, Contrast, +52, and Clarity +68, then paint the underside of the iceberg and the iceberg below the water.

FIG 8.43
Paint strokes to lighten iceberg and water and build contrast

LOCALIZED ADJUSTMENT WORKFLOW TIP:

When we complete the task, we can either hover over the pin and check the mask or use the letter O key to toggle the mask on and off, or use Show Selected Mask Overlay with Adjustment Brush in the Toolbar.

We can then use the Option/Alt key to subtract from the mask and clean up some of the edges.

FIG 8.44
Show Selected Mask is on and we can use the Option/Alt key to subtract or erase from the mask.

The process is continued as we darken the sky, lighten and darken parts of the iceberg and adjust Color Temperature to make the image more dramatic.

FIG 8.45
Each Pin reveals a place that was edited in this image.

We do a few more minor adjustments on the various pins and voila! we are done. We compare the two images using the Y key for before/after or the backslash key. All of this took only a few minutes to complete. Wow!

FIG 8.46
Compare before and after with Y key or Backslash Key

I THE BASIC PANEL

The basic panel holds all of our basic adjustments including Temperature, Tint, White Balance, Exposure, Contrast, Highlights, Shadows, Whites, Blacks ,Clarity, Vibrance and Saturation. It's not so basic, after all. The panel is organized under Treatment, Tone and Presence.

WORKFLOW TIP: *Double-click on any slider to reset it to the default.*

Treatment

The treatment panel holds the White Balance, Temperature and Tint sliders. You can also convert an image to Black and White in this panel.

Black and
White Converter

There are nine choices
for RAW files in the
drop-down menu for
White Balance including:
As Shot, Auto, Daylight
(5500K), Cloudy (6500K),
Shade (7500K), Tungsten
(2850K), Fluorescent
(3800K), Flash (5500K)
and Custom (your White
Balance setting).

FIG 8.47
Basic Panel in the
Develop Module

White Balance

The first slider controls the White Balance. The numbers on
the slider 2000 to 50,000 refer to the temperature measured in
degrees Kelvin. White balance indicates the color of the light
under which the image was captured. The default value is the
white balance at which the image was captured ("As Shot").

The white balance of an image can be adjusted in three ways:

- Choosing a value from the White Balance drop-down menu

- Sliding the Temperature slider and the Tint slider

- Using the White Balance Selector tool to click on a neutral
  white or gray area in the image

Temperature

The Temperature slider allows you to fine-tune the white balance to a precise color temperature using a Kelvin color temperature scale. Moving the slider to the left produces a correction for images taken with a lower temperature. The slider adds blue to the image to compensate for yellow of lower temperature values. Moving the slider to the right produces a correction for images taken with a higher color temperature. The slider adds yellow to the image to compensate for the blue of higher temperature values.

Moving the slider to the left makes the images appear cooler, while moving the slider to the right makes the images appear warmer. When working with JPEG, TIFF and PSD files, the scale is -100 to +100, rather than in degrees Kelvin.

Tint

The Tint slider allows you to fine-tune the white balance to compensate for green or magenta tints in images. Moving the slider to the left adds green while moving the slider to the right adds magenta. Think of Tint as a personal adjustment slider. If you think your images from your camera are slightly green or magenta, you can correct that cast here.

***TINT WORKFLOW TIP:** If the cast appears in the shadows, refer to the Shadow Tint Slider in the Camera Calibration Panel.*

White Balance Selector Tool

The white balance selector tool is located in the top left of the Basic panel. It looks like an eye dropper. To white balance an image, pick an area that is neutral light gray or close to the second white patch on an X-Rite ColorChecker card. While you are working with this tool, the navigator will display a preview of the color balance as you move the tool around the image.

White Balance Toolbar Options

- **Show Loupe:** Displays a close-up view with the corresponding RGB values

- **Scale Slider:** This zooms the close-up view of the Loupe

- **Auto Dismiss:** This dismisses the White Balance Selector Tool after one click

- D-65 chooses not to have this checked in our workflow

- **Done:** Dismisses the White Balance Selector Tool, changing it to the Hand or Zoom Tool

Workflow Shortcuts in the Basic Panel

- **Command U:** Auto Tone

- **Command-Shift U:** Auto White Balance

- **Letter W Key:** White Balance Selector Tool

White Balance Demonstration

Let's go ahead and white balance the image in **Figure 8.48**.

FIG 8.48
Image before being white balanced

We select the White Balance Selector Tool (**Figure 8.49**).

When the White Balance Selector Tool is activated, the Toolbar for it opens up under the image. The Toolbar can be toggled on and off with the letter T key.

Next, we go to the Navigator and zoom in to a section of the image that has white with detail. In this case, the white of the eye is perfect.

We choose to uncheck Auto Dismiss in the Toolbar so that we can make multiple selections with the White Balance Tool if we so desire. We also choose to Show Loupe which displays a close-up view and the RGB values of the pixel.

Then we set the Scale Slider so that we get a close-up view in the Loupe.

Next, we move the White Balance Selector Tool to the white of the eye and click (**Figures 8.50 and 8.51**).

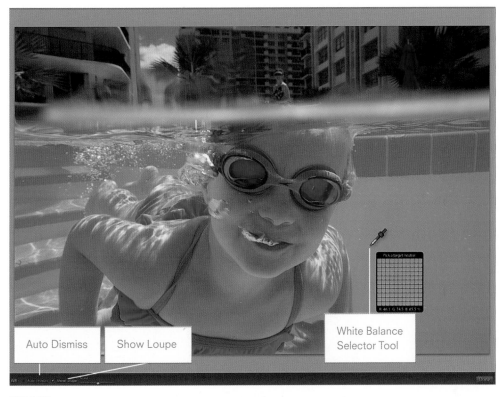

Auto Dismiss

Show Loupe

White Balance Selector Tool

FIG 8.50
Sampling White Balance from eye and checking color in the Navigator.

The Loupe can tell us quite a bit about our image: for instance, the RGB values based on luminance and percentages. White with no detail would thus be 100, 100, 100 and black with no detail would be 0, 0, 0. Neutral is 50, 50, 50. If you wanted to check to see if there was detail in the balconies, you could put the White Balance Selector Tool there and read the value, which is pretty cool. In our case, we see the white of the pool wall is 46.1, 74.5, 65.5. (**Figure 8.51**).

FIG 8.51
Sampling White Balance
checking the RGB
values in the Loupe.

We can keep sampling and checking the Navigator window as we go, which gives us a live time view. Once we have a pleasing result, we hit Return to set the White Balance (**Figure 8.52**). In many situations, this technique will work well, assuming you have some area where there is white with detail.

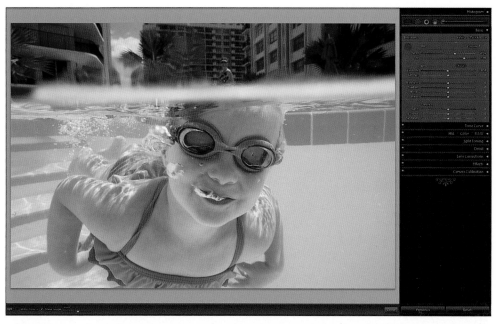

FIG 8.52
Image after being white-balanced

Using an X-Rite ColorChecker Passport to Achieve Critical White Balance

Another way to achieve a more accurate white balance would be to place an X-Rite ColorChecker Passport into the scene. Using the White Balance Selector Tool, click on the second patch from the bottom right on the checker. This will provide the correct white balance. The corrected image can be synced to a group of other images, which we will cover later.

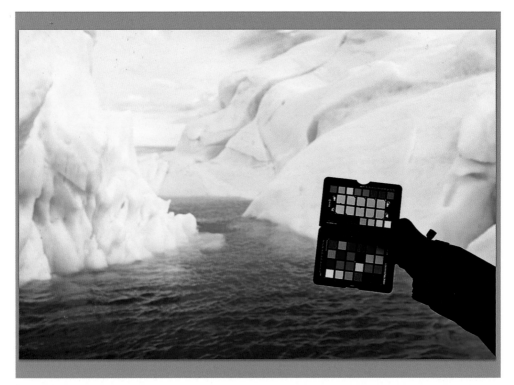

FIG 8.53
X-Rite ColorChecker Passport photographed on location. Use the second patch from the right to white balance.

If you use the ColorChecker Passport, simply use the White Balance Selector Tool and click on the second patch from the left on the bottom as indicated in Figure 8.53. Using the X-Rite ColorChecker Passport, you can build a custom camera profile for even more accuracy. This will allow you to use a very accurate calibration each and every time the camera is used at a particular ISO. To do this, select the image of the ColorChecker Passport (Figure 8.53) in the *Lightroom* Library and choose Export. You will export to the Passport Plug-in (Figure 8.54).

FIG 8.54
Export from the
Lightroom Library to
the X-Rite ColorChecker
Passport Plug-in.

The Passport will create a custom profile that will be available
under Camera Calibration in the Develop Module. You can even
warm this up or cool this down further to customize it using
the image of the ColorChecker Passport Enhancement Target.
You can then set this as a default for a particular camera serial
number and ISO so that you can achieve critically accurate color.

FIG 8.55
Profile is available under
Camera Calibration

FIG 8.56
Camera Calibration
Tab showing the list of
available profiles for a
particular camera by
serial number and ISO.

FIG 8.57
By choosing the
calibration desired from
the Calibration Panel
and then pressing the
Option Key, *Lightroom*
can re-set the default
calibration based on
serial number and ISO.
So every time this
camera is used at this
ISO, this calibration can
be automatically applied
to the processing.

Now that is totally,
totally cool.

| THE TONE PANEL

The Tone Panel holds the Exposure, Contrast, Highlights, Shadows, Whites, and Blacks. There is also an Auto button.

New in *Lightroom 4*

- Removed controls for Recovery, Brightness, and Fill Light.

- Exposure in Process Version 2012 is a combination of PV2010's Exposure and PV2010's Brightness.

- Added controls for Highlights, Shadows, and Whites.

- Image content aware Shadow and Highlight controls extract greater dynamic range from a single image.

- Clarity is integrated with Highlights and Shadows. The three controls are based on a new adaptive tone mapping algorithm, which is edge-preserving (meaning: reduced halos).The positive direction of Clarity is now integrated with the new tone mapping logic. Hence the appearance and effect are different than before.

- The minus direction of Clarity is unchanged (same behavior in all process versions).

- Highlights and Shadows are the new tone mapping controls.

- Whites and Blacks are the highlight & shadow clipping controls. They are useful for adjusting how much of the highlights and shadows are clipped off, while preserving the overall tonal relationships in the image.

- Contrast is essentially the same in 2010 and 2012.

The sliders in this panel ideally should be used in the order they appear.

Exposure Slider

The Exposure Slider is the main control for setting the overall image brightness. It is actually a combination of Process

Version's 2010 Exposure and Process Version 2010 Brightness. The values shown on the right of the slider (+1.00) are equivalent to roughly opening up one stop. The slider works in the same way for the negative values. As the Exposure Slider is moved to the left, the overall image will become darker and, as the Exposure Slider is moved to the right the overall image will become lighter as shown in **Figures 8.58** and **8.59**.

Using the Exposure Slider to See highlight and shadow clipping

The Exposure Slider provides yet another incredibly valuable tool for a photographer using *Lightroom*. Pressing down the Option key while moving the slider will locate the technically correct white point. The technically correct white point is at the point when you first begin to see detail. This is very similar to the Levels Dialogue in *Photoshop*. The "unclipped" areas of the image are black, and the "clipped" areas appear as white. Move the slider just to the point that an image begins to become clipped.

Underexposing to hold highlights when using digital capture is generally a bad idea. You will lose dynamic range, and there will be a tendency to induce posterization when the image is lightened. An ideal exposure has specular highlights just at the point of clipping. One of *Lightroom's* most remarkable features is its extended highlight recovery logic. If you have a choice during capture, it's better to choose overexposure than underexposure.

FIG 8.58
Moving the Exposure Slider to the Left will make the overall image darker.

FIG 8.59
Moving the Exposure Slider to the Right will make the overall image lighter.

Contrast

The Contrast Slider increases or decreases contrast in an image. Its greatest effect is on the midtones, like Brightness. As the Contrast Slider is moved to the right, the darker areas of an image will become darker and the lighter areas will become lighter, as shown in **Figures 8.60** and **8.61**.

FIG 8.60
The image before adjusting the contrast

FIG 8.61
As the Contrast Slider is moved to the right, the darker areas of an image will become darker and the lighter areas will become lighter.

Highlights

The Highlights Slider increases or decreases midrange highlights in the image. Adjust highlights to recover blown out highlights or to darken. As the Highlights Slider is moved to the left, the highlights will become darker and as the Highlights Slider is moved to the right the highlights will become lighter, as shown in **Figures 8.62** and **8.63**.

FIG 8.62
As the Highlights Slider is moved to the left highlight detail is recovered.

FIG 8.63
As the Highlight Slider is moved to the right the highlights are opening up and eventually blowing out the detail.

Shadows

The Shadows Slider increases or decreases midrange shadows in the image. Adjust shadows to recover shadow detail or to darken. As the Shadow Slider is moved to the right, the shadows will become lighter and as the Shadow Slider is moved to the left the shadows will become darker, as shown in **Figures 8.64** and **8.65**.

FIG 8.64
As the Shadow Slider is moved to the right, the shadows will become lighter.

FIG 8.65
As the Shadow Slider is moved to the left, the shadows will become darker.

Whites

The Whites Slider increases or decreases high range highlights in the image. Adjust the brightest highlights to recover highlight detail or to darken. As the Whites Slider is moved to the right, the brightest highlights will become lighter and as the Whites Slider is moved to the left the brightest highlights will become darker, as shown in **Figures 8.66** and **8.67**.

FIG 8.66
As the Whites Slider is moved to the right, the brightest highlights will become lighter.

FIG 8.67
As the Whites Slider is moved to the left, the brightest highlights will become darker.

Blacks

The Blacks Slider increases or decreases high range shadows in the image. Adjust the darkest shadows to recover deep shadow detail or to darken. As the Blacks Slider is moved to the right, the darkest shadows will become lighter and as the Blacks Slider is moved to the left the darkest shadows will become darker, as shown in **Figures 8.68** and **8.69**.

FIG 8.68
As the Blacks Slider is moved to the right, the darkest shadows will become lighter.

FIG 8.69
As the Blacks Slider is moved to the left, the darkest shadows will become darker.

Auto

The Auto button will analyze an image creating a custom tone map based on the individual characteristics of the image. Auto will often produce excellent results. Auto is a very good starting point when correcting images, allowing the user to see how *Lightroom* would want to correct a particular image.

WORKFLOW TIPS FOR THE TONE PANEL:

D65 general cautions:

- *Blacks control is translated conservatively from Process Version 2010 to Process Version 2012. So in general, if you applied a strong amount of Blacks in 2003/2010, then updating to 2012 will result in a much weaker amount of black clipping. This means the resulting image will be lighter. Some images will be "converted" to an initial appearance in 2012 that is very different from 2003/2010.*

- *There will be minimal black clipping (by default) if using the new profiles. Of course, you can choose to increase black clipping by dragging the Blacks slider to the left.*

D65 general tips:

- *Command U autocorrects all of the Tone Panel Slider*

- *You can set any slider to its default by double-clicking on it*

- *You Using the Option/Alt Key will show highlight clipping for Exposure, Highlights and Whites, and shadow clipping for Shadows and Blacks*

D65 general workflow guidelines on using the new controls are:

- *Don't try to relate the new controls to the old controls. It's an understandable urge, but totally an unproductive one. The more you think of the new control set in terms of the old control set, the harder the new controls will be to use.*

- *Work with controls in successive pairs. For example: at first, limit yourself to the first two controls, Exposure and Contrast, and don't touch the others. Do the most you can with just these two. You may not get all the nuances you're after, but you should get pretty darn close. Then, allow yourself to touch two more controls: Highlights & Shadows. At this point you're editing with only the top 4 controls (Exposure thru Shadows). See how far that takes you because you should be able to accomplish almost everything you are setting out to achieve. Finally,*

*add in the last pair (Whites and Blacks) and you have
total perfection.*

- *Don't be afraid the full range (i.e. values as high/low as
+100/-100)*

D65 recommended workflow use:

- *Use Exposure first. Doesn't matter whether it's a high-
key, low-key, high-contrast, low-contrast, overexposed,
or underexposed image. Using the other controls will
be a lot easier if you've first "normalized" the image
brightness using Exposure.*

- *Adjust contrast for overall punch which may requires a
readjustment of the Exposure Slider*

- *Adjust highlights to recover blown out highlights or
to darken*

- *Use Highlights & Shadows gently (esp. Highlights).
They have a lot of power, but not all images need the full
power. If you're used to cranking Recovery to 50 or 100,
realize that Highlights is not like that. A little bit goes a
long way.*

- *If endpoints are still too bright/dark, adjust whites, blacks.*

I THE PRESENCE PANEL

There are three sliders in the Presence panel: Clarity, Vibrance,
and Saturation.

Clarity

New in *Lightroom 4* **Updated Clarity adjustment for superior
results without causing artifacts.**

NEW

Clarity is a midtone contrast adjustment tool. The Clarity
adjustment is one that can usefully be applied to a great many
kinds of photographs. It boosts the midtone contrast to bring out
crisper detail. Most photographs can gain from adding a small

clarity adjustment. It is akin to high pass filtering, increasing the contrast of large details without adding noise. Most importantly Clarity will give your images extra punch. It adds depth to an image by increasing local contrast Clarity is one of the most popular and photographer-friendly features in *Lightroom*. In **Figure 8.70**, Clarity is set to 0 and in **Figure 8.71** it is set to 85. Look at the incredible difference!

FIG 8.70
Clarity set to 0

FIG 8.71
Clarity set to 85

While many photographers typically just set Clarity to around 50 because it makes their images look more crisp, they rarely think about negative clarity which is also very cool to use. It softens skin and has a very mystical quality on landscapes. In **Figure 8.72** we have Clarity set to 25 and in **Figure 8.73** we use negative Clarity, setting it to -30. Look at how much nicer the skin looks with negative Clarity.

FIG 8.72
Clarity set to 25

FIG 8.73
Clarity set to -30

Vibrance

Vibrance increases the saturation in a nonlinear or non-equal manner, meaning the lower saturation values are increased more than high saturation values. This differs from Saturation in that Saturation does an across-the-board saturation increase regardless of the current value.

Vibrance is particularly useful in adjusting colors that would otherwise be clipped as they become fully saturated. It constrains the colors that would come out of gamut with printing. It is excellent for adjusting skin tones because it creates saturation without the skin tones going magenta. In **Figure 8.74**, Vibrance is set to 0 on the left and on the right it is set to 20. Notice that on the right the reds are popping in the background and blond hair and skin are more pleasing without being overly saturated.

FIG 8.74
Adjusting Vibrance: 0 on the left and 20 on the right

Saturation

Many photographers have always been attracted to the saturated colors of Kodachrome or Velvia. Think of Saturation as your Kodachrome or Velvia adjustment tool. The Saturation slider gives you the option of reproducing that look and feel. Moving the slider to a value of -100 makes a monochrome image. Moving the slider to a value of +100 doubles the saturation. Be aware, however, that too much saturation can be a bad thing. If you increase the saturation value to a very high number, you are likely to create out-of-gamut colors.

FIG 8.75
Adjusting Saturation: 0 on the left and 17 on the right

| THE TONE CURVE PANEL

New in *Lightroom 4* Per channel curves adjustments.

NEW

In Process Version 2012, the default point curve for raw files is Linear. In Process Version 2010 the default was Medium Contrast. The actual internal default tone curve for raw files is unchanged. In simple terms Process Version 2010's "Medium Contrast" default curve in is Tone Curve now includes the ability to correct tone and color on a per channel basis. Fixing color casts via Curves gives you more options than using White Balance alone.

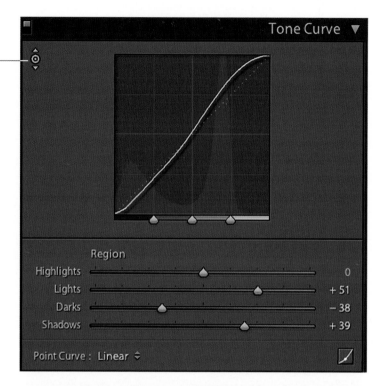

Targeted
Adjustment Tool

FIG 8.76
Traditional
Parametric Curve

Click to toggle
between Point
Curve and
Parametric Curve

RGB Point
Curve

FIG 8.77
RGB Point Curve

Tone Curve

The Tone Curve tool is a very powerful and flexible image manipulation tool in *Lightroom*. The Tone Curve affects tones and contrast. Similar to the Levels feature in *Photoshop*, curves can take input tones and selectively stretch or compress them. Unlike Levels, which only has black, white and midpoint control, a tonal curve is controlled using any number of anchor points. The key concept with Tone Curve is that you can redistribute contrast. This is controlled with Highlights, Lights, Darks and Shadows.

- **Highlights:** The brightest points of the image

- **Lights:** From the midtones to the highlights

- **Darks:** From the midtones to the shadows

- **Shadows:** The darkest points of the image

So, if I want to bring down or control the brightest tones in an image, I would concentrate my efforts on the Highlight slider. Being able to work on essentially four different tonal ranges of the image independently gives you a tremendous amount of versatility and control. Each of the controls in the Tone Curve panel is contributing to the shape of the final curve applied to your image.

The histogram in the Tone Curve panel represents the range of values you define when you set your black and white point.

Under the Histogram, you will find three sliders, which give even more control over the range of the area that you are working on. You can narrow or broaden the range of tones affected by the curve by expanding or contracting the area of the curve. As you mouse through the Tone Curve, you will see the corresponding parts of the image made active in the panel. The coolest thing in the Tone Curve panel is the Targeted Adjustment Tool. Click on the Targeted Adjustment Tool and move it into the area(s) of the image you want to adjust. Then click down and use the up and down arrow keys to open up or close down that area of the image. This will be reflected in the Tone Curve. In **Figure 8.78** we have selectively toned down the Highlights and the Darks. **Figure 8.79** shows the before and after.

The original parametric curve uses essentially the same concept as the Tone Curve and you can use the Targeted Adjustment Tool or the sliders. The advantage of this approach is that the adjustment of the curve is constrained to predefined limits, which have been optimized to prevent detrimental adjustments to the shadow, midtone and highlight regions. However, these constraints on occasion may not allow for precise adjustments, meaning it is off to *Photoshop*.

With the Point Curve, very fine adjustments to specific parts of the curve are possible because you can set locks and adjust the curve within them. By using the Option/Alt key you get exceptionally precise control.

Using the Targeted Adjustment Tool, mouse down on the area of your image and use your up or down arrow key to lighten or darken. Here we are using the down arrow key with the Targeted Adustment Tool to darken our sky which correlate to the Darks on the curve.

FIG 8.78
Using the Targeted Adjustment Tool to adjust a parametric Tone Curve

TONE CURVE WORKFLOW TIP: Drag the curve and points in the histogram to make adjustments.

FIG 8.79
Before and after comparison of a Parametric Curve adjustment

I HSL /COLOR / B & W

At first glance, the color adjustment panel seems a bit intimidating, but it actually makes a lot of sense after you play with it for a little while. This panel fine-tunes Hue, Saturation and Luminance on individual channels. Hue changes the color of the chosen channel. Saturation intensifies or reduces the color. Luminance changes the brightness of the color channel.

This panel also has a Targeted Adjustment Tool so that you can click down on any area of an image and using your up and down arrow keys, adjust that specific area in the specific channels that are being affected in Hue, Saturation or Luminance.

FIG 8.80
The Color Adjustment
Panel, HSL / Color /
B & W

Hue

The Hue sliders control color balance. There are six sliders and each slider will produce an effect on that particular hue. There are separate sliders for altering the hue, saturation and luminance of the red, orange, yellow, green, aqua, blue, purple, and magentas in your image. As an example, if you use the Yellow slider, moving it to the right will make the yellows greener and moving it to the left will make the yellows redder.

One little interesting tidbit I can share is that people sometimes ask, "Why aqua?" Well, the truth is that a group of us have gone to Antarctica a few times and one of the crew was Thomas Knolls (check the *Lightroom* or *Photoshop* credits) and ice in Antarctica is an iridescent-like blue. Thomas needed the color aqua for adjusting his Antarctica images. Hence "aqua" was born.

Saturation

The Saturation sliders control the amount of saturation for each hue. Moving them to the right increases saturation and moving them to the left decreases saturation.

Luminance

The Luminance sliders will darken or lighten colors. Moving them to the right will lighten and moving them to the left will darken.

HSL and Color do the same thing, but just have a different display. Color does not have a Targeted Adjustment Tool.

HSL / Color Demonstration

In **Figure 8.81** we wanted to create the look of a Polarizing Filter on the sky. We increase the hue of the blue sky, increase the saturation of the sky, and lower the luminance of the sky.

FIG 8.81
Using HSL to create the effects of a Polarizing Filter

We will use HSL to create the effects of a Polarizing Filter in **FIG 8.81** through **8.85**. We start by putting the Targeted Adjustment Tool on an area of the blue sky. *Lightroom* chooses Blue Hue and bumps it up to plus 8 and aqua to plus 2. We accomplish this by using the up arrow tool.

Steps:

1. Change to Hue and increase Blue Hue to +8 and Aqua Hue to +2.

2. Change to Saturation and increase Blue Saturation to +75 and Aqua Saturation to +15.

3. Change to Luminance and decrease Blue to -66 and Aqua Luminance to –14.

4. Comparing the two, we can see that the effect is very similar to using a Polarizing Filter.

Use the up and down arrow Keys to increase or decrease The Targeted Adjustment Tool

FIG 8.82
Increase Blue Hue to +8 and Aqua Hue to +2

FIG 8.83
Change to Saturation and increase Blue Saturation to +75 and Aqua Saturation to +15

FIG 8.84
Change to Luminance and decrease Blue to -66 and Aqua Luminance to –14

FIG 8.85
Comparing the two, we can see that the effect is very similar to using a Polarizing Filter

| B & W

Selecting B & W activates the B & W Panel which in prior versions
was called the Grayscale Panel. The default B & W setting applies

an Auto adjustment that is based on the current White Balance and Tint settings. This default setting is a good starting point to work from, as shown in **Figures 8.86** and **8.87**.

Once you get familiar with the Black & White Mix panel, you will be able to create custom black and white conversions by having access to all the color channels using these sliders. This panel also has a Targeted Adjustment Tool, which works great! You can create any black and white effect imaginable. If you can't imagine anything, you will notice a whole bunch of *Lightroom* Presets for different B & W effects on the left side of the Develop Module under Presets (**Figure 8.88**).

FIG 8.86
To convert to B & W we choose B & W in the Color Adjustment Panel

FIG 8.87
Converting to B & W using Auto and then refining the image using some of the sliders

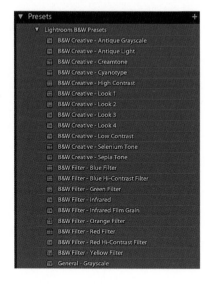

FIG 8.88
Presets for B&W available from the Develop Presets Panel.

I THE SPLIT TONING PANEL

Using the Split Toning controls on images after they have been converted to black and white allows you to add some color to the image. You can independently control the Hue shift and saturation of Highlights and Shadows. The Hue sliders adjust the hue and the Saturation sliders can be used to apply varying degrees of color tone. The Balance Slider balances the effect between the Highlights and the Shadows. A positive number on the balance slider increases the effect of the Highlights Slider, while a negative number increases the effect of the Shadows Slider.

This tool is useful for creating black and white effects such as Sepia, Brown Tone, Warm Tone, or Cool Tone. These adjustments can be saved as a Custom Preset and used again later. You can create your own "look" to use over and over again. Of course, you can do this on color images as well, warming highlights and cooling shadows.

FIG 8.89

Split Toning Panel

To Use Split Toning

You will not see results by simply shifting the Hue slider. You must hold the Option/Alt key down, and click down on Hue and then if you drag the slider back and forth, you will see the hue change. Find a hue you like for the highlights and release the mouse.

Now go to the Saturation slider, starting at 0. Do not hold the Option/Alt key down for this step.
Drag the slider to the right until you have the appropriate saturation of the hue. Do the same thing for the shadows.

The Balance slider can then be used to mix both results together weighting one more than the other.

FIG 8.90
Comparison of before and after Split Toning an image

I THE DETAIL PANEL

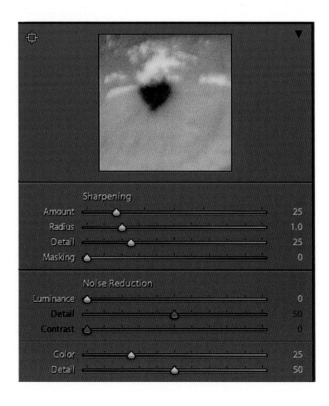

FIG 8.91
Detail Panel

Sharpening

The Detail Panel in *Lightroom* allows you to sharpen using Amount, Radius, Detail and Masking with the use of sliders. The detail panel also incorporates Noise Reduction.

The Sharpening Panel has a default set for RAW file processing because most RAW files need some degree of sharpening. We'll explain why.

When photons are digitized to pixels, sharpness is lost. Regardless of how large the camera sensor is, pixels are sampled as a fixed grid of gray tones. These gray tones mimic the continuous graduations of color perceived by the human eye and are used to shape specific pixels.

Digitization is accomplished by reconstructing data at a "frequency" that produces aliasing or non-alignment. Out of necessity, most cameras today deploy an anti-aliasing filter that eliminates the highest frequency detail. The net effect is that the detail rendered appears soft. Therefore, digital photographs look soft because of the very nature of how the pixel is constructed. For this reason, we typically want to capture and sharpen, defining basic focus to restore any sharpness that was lost in the capture process.

The Sharpening Default for *Lightroom* is:

- Amount 25

- Radius 1.0

- Detail 25

- Masking 0

When sharpening, it is critical to set the zoom level to 100% or greater in order to view the effects of the sharpening controls. A general rule when sharpening is to sharpen pixels without adding any ugly artifacting. There is a magnification window right in the sharpening panel. You can click on the button in the upper left hand corner and wherever your cursor moves, that area will be magnified in the window. A click locks the focus on a specific point (**Figure 8.92**).

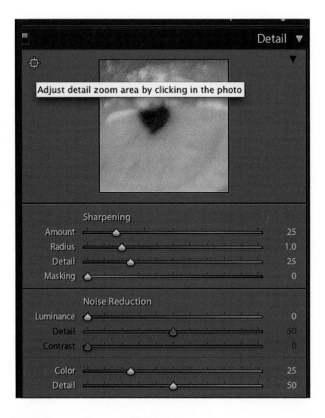

FIG 8.92
Magnification Window
in Detail Panel

Sharpening Different Types of Images

Most images tend to be either high frequency or low frequency. High frequency images are highly textured and detailed, and low frequency images have less texture and detail. A close-up of text on a soda can would be a good example of high frequency detail and most faces are a good example of low frequency detail.

There are two Sharpening presets that come with *Lightroom* in the Presets Panel. One is a preset for Wide Edges (Faces) and one is a preset for Narrow Edges (Scenics). These are both very good starting points. You may find them satisfactory, or you may want to create your own sharpening custom preset.

Wide Edges (Faces) Preset Applied

Notice in the image below that the skin is smooth while the eyes are sharp with Faces preset. When the Landscape Preset is applied to the same image (**Figures 8.92** and **8.93**), there is a noticeable difference. You can see the eyelash in detail across the eye, and blemishes are emphasized. Everything is very sharp, too sharp for this type of image.

FIG 8.93
Wide Edges (Faces) Preset applied

FIG 8.94
Narrow Edges (Scenics) Preset applied

How to Sharpen

When we view an image, we see the whole image, but the digital image is really comprised of individual pixels each with a distinct shape. When enlarged, they can be viewed as blocks. The edges of these blocks are both light and dark. Sharpening essentially makes the edge of the lighter block a lighter value and the edge of a darker block a darker value.

FIG 8.95
Sharpening makes the edge of the lighter block a lighter value and the edge of a darker block a darker value.

Amount: The Amount regulates how aggressive the sharpening will be by controlling edge definition. With the Amount set to 0 (0 turns off sharpening) the edges will be less prominent and as the Amount is increased, the edges will get more exaggerated. The light lines will get lighter and the dark lines will get darker. This adjustment locates pixels at the transition point that differ from the surrounding pixels, and increases their contrast.

AMOUNT WORKFLOW TIP: Press Alt (Windows) or Option/Alt (Mac OS) while dragging this slider to view the sharpening on a grayscale preview which may make it easier to see.

FIG 8.96
Amount slider set to 0 with Option/Alt depressed and zoomed in to 11:1 to see detail.

FIG 8.97
Amount slider set to 0 with Option/Alt depressed and zoomed in to 1:1 to see detail.

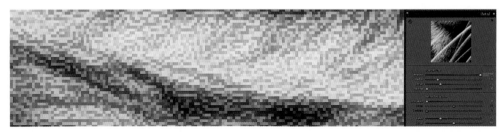

FIG 8.98
Amount slider set to 150 with Option/Alt depressed and zoomed in to 1:1 to see detail.

FIG 8.99
Amount slider set to 150 with Option/Alt depressed and zoomed in to 1:1 to see detail.

Radius: The Radius determines how wide an area is affected by the sharpening. An amount between .8 and 1.8 is generally the effective range. Using a higher radius may cause halos at the edges. Landscapes generally use more radius and portraits generally use less. The amount really depends on the detail of the image. Very fine details need a smaller radius. Using too large a radius will generally produce unnatural looking results.

RADIUS WORKFLOW TIP: *Press Alt (Windows) or Option/Alt (Mac OS) while dragging this slider to preview the radius effect in grayscale on edge definition.*

FIG 8.100
Radius slider set to 0

FIG 8.101
Radius slider set to 3

Detail: The Detail slider adjusts the quantity of high-frequency information sharpened and how much suppression is applied to the edges to counteract halos. Lower settings primarily sharpen edges to remove blurring. Higher values are useful for making the textures in the image more pronounced. When Detail is at 100 there is no halo suppression, and when it is at 0 there is total halo suppression.

DETAIL WORKFLOW TIP: Press Alt (Windows) or Option/Alt (Mac OS) while dragging this slider to view the sharpening on a grayscale preview which can make it easier to see.

FIG 8.102
Detail slider set to 0

FIG 8.103
Detail slider set to 100

Masking: Masking sets how much of a mask will be applied to the edges. The Edge Masking amount (which you can preview by holding the Option/Alt key) goes from 0 where it's hitting only edges to 100 where there is no edge preservation at all. At zero, everything in the image receives the same degree of sharpening. At 100, sharpening is mostly restricted to the areas near the strongest edges.

MASKING WORKFLOW TIP: When you hold down the Option/Alt key and drag the slider, the white areas will be sharpened and the black areas will be masked.

FIG 8.104
Masking slider set to 9

FIG 8.105
Masking slider set to 81

D-65's Suggested Starting Point for Sharpening

D-65 has found that as a general rule for all images, a medium ground starting point is:

- Amount between 25-50

- Radius between .8 and 1.8

- Detail between 25-65

- Masking between 15-30

- Landscapes: less masking; portraits: more masking

Noise Reduction

Noise is an inherent issue with digital cameras, long exposures and high ISOs. Noise can only be eliminated at the sensor level. After capture noise can be masked to be less noticeable but it cannot be eliminated because it is inherent in the capture. The way the camera processes the signal will determine how the noise appears in the final image. There are two types of noise which photographers need to address.

Chrominance Noise or Color Noise: is visible as random red and blue speckled pixels you sometimes see upon close inspection in darker midtones and shadow areas. While the reasons for chrominance noise are quite complex, the simple answer is that with a 12-bit capture, your shadow areas have 1/64 the information of your highlight areas. With less information, there is a greater chance for noise to occur. Chrominance noise is usually very unnatural and obvious on close inspection and can render images unusable if not kept under control. This noise has far less impact than luminance noise on fine details of your subjects, so it can often be reduced without appearing to blur or soften your images.

Luminance Noise: Luminance noise makes an image look grainy and monochromatic on screen. It is typical in high ISO images and in low ISO images where the brightness has been severely edited. It can appear as jaggy edges especially on diagonal lines. Fine detail is a component of luminance noise, so you have to pay careful attention that you do not remove it altogether. It's very easy to blur the noise to a point where you end up with an image that's totally lacking subject detail.

Removing luminance noise reduces the sharpness and removing the chrominance noise damages color. So noise reduction is a balance between how much softness and color damage you are willing to accept.

The need to adjust Luminance and Color Noise Reduction depends on the specific camera model. Shooting at the optimum ISO may eliminate the need to adjust these values for many cameras. Also, some of the new Canon and Nikon cameras really do a phenomenal job of reducing or eliminating noise at the sensor level. As the ISO increases, noise is inevitable. New models from both Canon and Nikon claim usable images from ISO's above 10,000 but lower ISO's still produce better quality.

Digital noise tends to be most noticeable in plain, solid areas of a subject, especially if they're midtone or dark areas. A photographer shooting high ISO in a basketball arena will likely see much less noise in the images than a photographer shooting ballet at the same ISO in a dim theatre. You will also see much more noise in the file if it is underexposed.

Noise is not grain and the two should not be confused. Grain can be beautiful, but an image filled with noise is usually not that pleasing to the eye. Noise reduction can present a bit of a dilemma. Removing luminance noise reduces the sharpness of the image and removing the color noise damages some of the correct color. There is no perfect noise reduction. Something is always sacrificed so noise reduction becomes a balance between how much softness and color damage you can tolerate, and how much noise you want to remove.

Luminance reduces noise in the darker tones, which usually result from shooting at a high ISO. To reduce luminance noise, slide the Luminance Slider to a higher value. Be aware that adjusting the Luminance Slider may impact image sharpness. To reduce color noise, slide the Color Noise Reduction slider until the noise is eliminated from the image.

Lightroom's Noise Reduction masks the effects of noise, while maintaining image detail. To judge noise, you typically want to look at the shadows and make sure that you are at 100%. Some images may contain both color noise and luminance noise. When working on the Luminance channel, you can quickly compromise image detail, so remember the trick is to reduce noise without losing too much image detail.

Luminance: Controls the amount of luminance noise reduction. A value of 0 does not apply any luminance noise reduction. If

Luminance is set to 0, the Detail and Contrast sliders will be grayed out and disabled.

Luminance Detail: Sets the noise threshold. Dragging the slider to right will preserve more detail. The one danger in doing this is that as you move to the right, you may also cause noise to be perceived as detail and therefore not corrected with smoothing. Dragging to the left will increase smoothing. The danger here is that you may cause needed detail to be incorrectly detected as noise that has been smoothed. The key here is to find a balance that works. This slider will be disabled when the Luminance slider is set to 0. The results of this slider are more noticeable with higher ISO images. The default value is 50.

Luminance Contrast: Dragging this slider preserves contrast and texture. Be careful, because high ISO images can produce wacky results that look like globs of noise. Dragging the slider to the left enhances fine grain smoothing, but you may sacrifice contrast and texture. This slider will be disabled when the Luminance slider is set to 0. The results of this slider are more noticeable with higher ISO images. The default value is 0.

Luminance Color: The default setting of 25 isn't bad, but D-65 tends to set it to 20 if we are shooting at optimum ISO (ISO 100 on a Canon). The key to this slider is to reduce color noise while still maintaining edge detail. Setting the slider to 0 means that no color noise reduction will be applied at all. As the slider is moved the right, the amount of color noise reduction is increased. More than 25 is pretty aggressive and eventually it will cause color bleeding around the edges.

Luminance Color Detail: This slider is really designed for very noisy images. It allows users to refine color noise reduction for detailed edges. As the slider is moved to the right, it aims to retain color detail in the edges but this can cause those red and green speckles to remain obvious in the image. As the slider is moved to the left, color speckled noise is suppressed but edge features can easily become desaturated. Adobe suggests that you try zooming to 400% pixel view to get a clearer understanding of the effect. This slider will be disabled when the Luminance slider is set to 0. The results of this slider are more noticeable with higher ISO images. The default value is 50.

In **Figure 8.106** we have a good image to test the efficiency of noise reduction in *Lightroom 4*. The shot was taken in Mendocino, California and it is a 45-second exposure at ISO 1600 showing the Milky Way. The camera used for the shot was a Canon 5D Mark II.

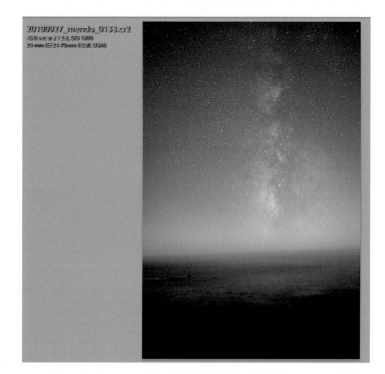

FIG 8.106
45 second exposure at ISO 1600 showing the Milky Way.

FIG 8.107
When we zoom in
on this image, we
can clearly see both
Luminance noise and
Chrominance Noise
and a lot of it!

FIG 8.108
By moving the Color
Noise Reduction slider
to 45 and the Detail
slider to 15, we have
almost completely
eliminated the
Chrominance Noise,
leaving the Luminance
Noise very visible.

FIG 8.109
By moving the Luminance Slider to 50, the Detail slider to 30 and the Contrast slider to 12, we have greatly reduced Luminance Noise.

FIG 8.110
A side by side comparison of the Before and After show astounding results

I THE LENS CORRECTIONS PANEL

NEW

New in *Lightroom 4* Updated Chromatic Aberration correction solution.

With the introduction new automated Chromatic Aberration algorithms the old sliders are gone and have been replaced with a checkbox. This new correction solution can even correct Chromatic Aberration present in images shot with a Tilt Shift lens, something the previous methods weren't able to accomplish. Chromatic aberration adjustments in profiles are now ignored but are left there for earlier Process Versions. Many lens profiles have been updated to include crop factor metadata.

Chromatic Aberration: Chromatic Aberration is caused from the lens focusing colors of light as different frequencies. Each color is in focus but at a slightly different size, and that results in color fringing. The results of these lens defects are enhanced in digital cameras. In the long term, we need better lenses manufactured.

Lens Corrections provide totally non-destructive editing technology designed to address lens correction via two methods: Lens Profiles and Manual Correction.

The easiest way to use Lens Corrections is to automatically apply the lens profile technology, which incorporates geometric distortion (barrel and pincushion distortion), and lens vignetting characteristics. For full manual use, and to build your own profiles, a Lens Profile Creator Utility is posted on Adobe Labs at http://labs.adobe.com/technologies/lensprofile_creator/

Lens Corrections also contains manual distortion corrections that extend beyond traditional geometric distortion and provide horizontal and vertical transformation adjustments

FIG 8.111
Lens Corrections Panel
set to Auto

FIG 8.112
Lens Corrections Panel
in Manual

Automatic Correction

Automatic Correction uses lens profiles to automatically apply
corrections which generally work very well. Further, Automatic
Corrections can be tweaked for specific effect. For example, you
can reduce the amount of Vignetting correction applied by the
profile by moving the slider to a value less than 100.

Automatic has three settings:

Default: Will check to see if the user specified a default for the lens and if so will use that.

Auto: Uses computer algorithms for finding what *Lightroom* thinks is the best available profile for your lens.

Custom: Custom will be displayed if you choose different settings from the Make/Model/Profile pop-up menus.

When a profile can't be found, there is a warning message. The user can also save customized settings as well as new lens profile defaults.

FIG 8.113
An iceberg in Antarctica with Chromatic Aberration

FIG 8.114
When we zoom in on the iceberg we can see Chromatic Aberration causing pretty severe magenta fringing at the top of this iceberg. Long lens images with light objects against a dark background will sometimes show this kind of fringing especially on the highlight edges.

FIG 8.115
Using the new Remove Chromatic Aberration Checkbox, the image is quickly corrected.

Lens Corrections in Manual

One of the first questions that arises when folks start to play with the Lens Correction Panel is, "What about what camera body I am using?" Camera body variations are much less important than factors like f-stop, focal length and focus distance.

For example, the Canon 85 f/1.2 lens has almost zero lateral chromatic aberration when focused at infinity, but has a lot of lateral chromatic aberration when focused at 1 meter. This difference—between infinity and 1 meter focus–is much bigger than what you'd see when comparing shooting the same lens on other Canon full-frame bodies. The lens is really the issue, much more than the camera body.

Transform

Distortion: Moving the slider to the right will bend the image in with a concave-like effect. Moving the slider to the left will bend the image out with a co nvex-like effect.

FIG 8.116
Moving the Distortion slider to the right

FIG 8.117
Moving the Distortion slider to the left

Vertical: This slider is for vertical perspective transformation, for example, to correct for keystoning in architectural photography.

FIG 8.118
Moving the Vertical slider to the right

FIG 8.119
Moving the Vertical slider to the left

Horizontal: This slider is for Horizontal perspective transformation. Both the Horizontal and Vertical sliders use calculations that correct perspective and are dependent upon the focal length of the lens in use, specifically, the angle of view. They enable the user to get converging lines to become parallel without strange aspect ratio problems.

FIG 8.120
Moving Horizontal slider to the right

FIG 8.121
Moving Horizontal slider to the left

Rotate: Rotate is effective for dealing with perspective adjustments like keystoning.

FIG 8.122
Moving Rotate slider to the right

FIG 8.123
Moving Rotate slider to the left

Scale: Applying a distortion or perspective adjustment can push pictorial elements out of a frame, making an image no longer a clean rectangle but rather a very weird shape. Scale recovers elements that get pushed out of the frame.

FIG 8.124
Moving Scale slider to the right

FIG 8.125
Moving Scale slider to the left

Lens Vignetting

Amount: Lens Vignetting is fairly common with many wide angle lenses. Lens Vignetting in the Lens Correction panel is different from Lens Vignetting in the Effects Panel. In the Lens Correction panel, Lens Vignetting is used to correct any unwanted light fall-off you might have in one or more corners of your image. Moving the Amount Slider to the right lightens the corners of the image and moving the slider to the left darkens the corners of the image. So negative numbers darken, and positive numbers lighten.

Midpoint: The Midpoint controls how far from the edge the effect begins.

Red/Cyan: Adjusts the size of the red channel relative to the green channel. This compensates for red/cyan color fringing.

Blue/Yellow: Adjusts the size of the blue channel relative to the green channel. This compensates for blue/yellow color fringing.

Defringe: You can choose Highlight Edges, All Edges or Off.

I THE EFFECTS PANEL

FIG 8.126
The Effects Panel

I POST-CROP VIGNETTING

There are choices of three separate vignette styles: Highlight Priority, Color Priority and Paint Overlay.

The first thing to address here is the confusion that exists between Lens Vignetting and Post Crop Vignette. Lens Vignetting is fall-off that occurs on the sides of some lenses which is fairly common with many wide angle lenses. This type of vignetting should be and can be corrected in the Lens Corrections Panel.

Post-Crop Vignette is really designed as a creative tool. To apply a dark or light vignette for artistic effect to a photo, use the Post-Crop Vignetting options in the Effects panel. A Post Crop Vignette can be applied to a cropped or uncropped photo.

Post-Crop Vignettes adjust the exposure of the cropped image, preserving the original image contrast and creating a more natural effect.

For optimal results, you will want to remove any Lens Vignetting prior to Post-Crop Vignetting.

In the Post-Crop Vignetting area of the Effects panel of the Develop module, choose an option from the Style menu:

Highlight Priority: Enables highlight recovery but can lead to color shifts in darkened areas of an image.

Color Priority: Minimizes color shifts in darkened areas of an image.

Paint Overlay: Paints white or black into the corners.

Amount: Moving the Amount Slider to the right lightens the corners of the image and moving the slider to the left darkens the corners of the image. So negative numbers darken, positive lighten.

Midpoint: The midpoint controls how far from the edge the effect begins. Moving the slider to the left applies the Amount adjustment to a larger area away from the corners. Moving the slider to the right restricts the adjustment to an area closer to the corners.

Roundness: Moving the slider to the left makes the vignette effect more oval. Moving the slider to the right makes the vignette effect more circular.

Feather: Moving the slider to the left reduces softening between the vignette and its surrounding pixels. Moving the slider to the right increases the softening.

Highlights: Controls the degree of highlight contrast preserved. Suitable for images with small highlights, such as candles and lamps.

FIG 8.127
Before and after with Post-Crop Vignetting applied. The amount was set to +100, Midpoint +31, Roundness -85 and Feather +100.

| GRAIN

A traditional film-style grain slider provides a very natural looking grain. Grain is not noise. It would be pretty rare to look at an image with noise and say to yourself, "Wow! That looks great!" Grain, on the other hand, can be a really beautiful effect. Many photographers in fact have a style with their traditional images that capitalize on a very grainy look. Grain is sort of like a layer of texture but it can create a dramatic effect.
There are three sliders to add Grain.

Amount: Amount controls the visibility of the grain effect.

Size: Size controls the diameter of the grain.

Roughness: Roughness defines how the even the grain appears.

FIG 8.128
Before and after with Grain applied

| THE CAMERA CALIBRATION PANEL

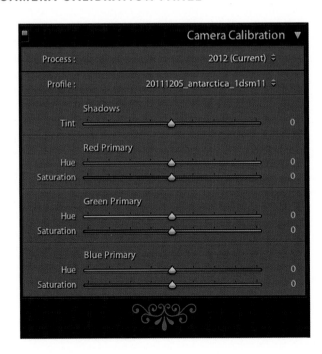

FIG 8.129
Camera Calibration
Panel showing a custom
profile and Process
Version 2012

Camera calibration is probably one of the most misunderstood, yet cool functions of the Develop Module. Many folks will never use this feature because they really don't understand what they are missing. They simply assume that what they see on the back of the camera LCD is correct. But, is it really?

A Canon rendering of a file is different from a Nikon rendering and both are different from *Lightroom, Aperture, PhotoMechanic* and any other RAW image processor. Different, yes, but not necessarily any more correct. The color you see on the LCD on the back of the camera is your first impression of your image, so the brain assumes it is accurate. In reality, that LCD rendering is composed of a low-res sRGB display. It's not accurate color of the RAW data captured within the image file.

Another factor to consider is that cameras can vary a lot in color response from camera to camera. Each and every chip is slightly different, so even two cameras of the same make and model may have a slightly different look.

For each *camera RAW* format that is supported, Thomas Knoll created two profiles, which measure the camera sensors under both tungsten and controlled daylight. This is the default for how your camera's files are rendered in *Lightroom*. If Thomas's renderings don't suit your fancy, you can alter them and this is where *Lightroom's* Camera Calibration Panel comes into play.

The Camera Calibration sliders can be used to fine-tune adjustments to the camera's color response. This means two or more cameras can be made to look alike. If your camera is a little magenta or a little green, it can be corrected. Camera Calibration makes it possible to have the look of Kodachrome, Infrared or even the look of Canon DPP, Nikon Capture or even the rendering style of an individual photographer, like a "Jay Maisel look."

The Camera Calibration Panel also has a drop-down menu where you can save specific looks that you create, or that are created by third party products such as the X-Rite ColorChecker Passport.

I PROCESS VERSION

The Process Version specifies which version of *Camera RAW* image processing technology should be used when rendering and editing files. Because the processing engine has been so improved, there is a substantial difference in images processed in *Lightroom 3* and *Lightroom 4*.

A "process version" has been introduced to differentiate between the old process and new processes and to allow you to choose how you want to process. The Process Version allows *Lightroom* to maintain virtually identical representation of images you've edited in the past and will also allow you to take advantage, if you choose, by updating the image to the latest processing version. All images edited prior to *Lightroom 4* are associated with Process Version 2003 or Process Version 2010

Process Versions 1 and 2 have been renamed 2003 and 2010, relating to the year that processing was introduced. Any images with existing settings will be set to the old process version to get an almost identical rendering as in previous versions.

Any new images imported into *Lightroom 4* will be assigned the new Process Version 2012. There's a warning exclamation mark to the lower right of the image if it's set to the old Process Version 2010 and you can click it if you want to update. Process Version is under the Settings menu, in the Calibration panel and the Sync dialog box.

The New Process Version 2012 implements a new tone mapping algorithm, for easy yet powerful contrast management

There is an icon in the lower right-hand corner of the image to let you know that the current image selected in the Develop module is a previous process version (**Figure 8.130**).

By clicking on the process version icon, you have the ability to see a before/after view of the old and new process versions and the ability to update all the selected images or all of the images in the filmstrip at the same time (**Figure 8.131**).

FIG 8.130
Icon in the Develop
module showing it
is a previous

Update Process Version

Lr   New processing technology is available for this image. If you choose to
update, please note that moderate to significant visual changes may occur.
It is recommended that you update only one image at a time until you are
familiar with the new processing technology. You may elect to preserve the
original settings by selecting Cancel.

☐ Review Changes via Before/After

☐ Don't show again

| Update All Filmstrip Photos | | Cancel | Update |

FIG 8.131
Icon options for
updating an image to
Process Version 2010

*CAMERA CALIBRATION WORKFLOW TIP: In the "Camera
Calibration" panel, choose your preferred profile from
the Profile menu. Then hold down the Option/Alt key. The
"Reset" button in the lower right turns into a "Set Default"
button. Click it. Choose Update to Current Settings. Now all
new images for this camera will use your chosen profile.*

FIG 8.132
Camera Calibration setting a new default setting.

I THE PRESETS PANEL

Moving over to the left hand side of the Develop Module, located underneath the Navigator is the Presets Panel. *Lightroom* comes with many Develop Presets. A Preset is a combination of Develop Settings that are already saved that you can apply to one or more images. Scroll over a *Lightroom* Preset and view what the adjustment will look like on the image in the Navigator. If you want to apply that Preset, just click on it. This will synchronize those Preset Develop Settings to your image.

User Presets

Lightroom comes with many Develop Presets, but you can also create your own Custom Presets. These Custom Presets offer a way to save a group of Develop Settings and apply them to other images. Once saved, Presets will appear in the Presets Panel under User Presets. They will also appear in the list of options for Develop Settings when you import images.

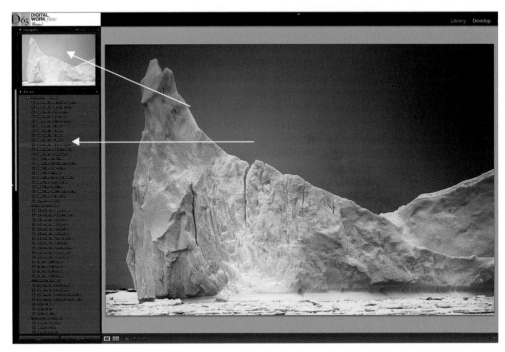

FIG 8.133
Scrolling over a Develop Preset shows the result in the Navigator

Why Save A User Preset?

There are some adjustments that we would like to do to every image we process. These are called "global changes." For example, D-65 shoots with several Canon 1DS Mark III cameras and even though the color temperature may be set identically on the two cameras, the results are slightly different because no two sensors are exactly the same. On one camera, shooting on cloudy produces 6400K and on the other camera, it produces 6350K. To create consistency between the cameras, we create a global setting of 6500K, the traditional industry standard for cloudy and apply that to all files shot on the cloudy setting.

Presets can also be used to create a certain "look". We personally have always liked the saturation from Kodachrome film. Another preset we've created is called Seth Kodachrome which simulates Seth's interpretation of a memorable case of Kodachrome. These presets can be applied in the Develop

Module, and also on files being imported into *Lightroom*. D-65 suggests saving any Develop setting or adjustment that you may want to use again in the future as a User Preset.

Creating a User Preset

We create a Preset that we use over and over again on Import on many of our daylight images.

This Preset does the following:

- Color temperature to 6500K

- Tint to +10

- Contrast to +15

- Clarity to +25

- Vibrance to +15

- Saturation to +12

- **Sharpening:** Amount 40, Radius .8, Detail 50, Masking 20

- **Lens Corrections:** Auto with Remove Chromatic Aberration checked

- Process Version 2012

- Camera Calibration for Canon 5D Mark II (if already created)

1. To create this preset, make the above changes in the Develop Module. For the Camera Calibration you would need to use the X-Rite ColorChecker Passport. If you do not have one, you would leave this step out.

2. Click on the plus (+) sign next to Presets on the left-hand side to open the New Develop Preset dialog box.

3. Check the settings that correspond with the develop settings we are saving.

4. The Preset is given a name of Seth Kodachrome for Process Version 2012

5. After this, we choose Create from the lower right-hand corner of the Presets dialog box (**Figure 8.134**).

New Develop Preset

Preset Name: Seth Kodachrome for Process Version 2012

Folder: User Presets

Auto Settings
☐ Auto Tone

Settings

☑ White Balance

⊟ Basic Tone
  ☐ Exposure
  ☑ Contrast
  ☐ Highlights
  ☐ Shadows
  ☐ White Clipping
  ☐ Black Clipping

☐ Tone Curve

☑ Clarity

☑ Sharpening

☑ Treatment (Color)

⊟ Color
  ☑ Saturation
  ☑ Vibrance
  ☐ Color Adjustments

☐ Split Toning

☐ Graduated Filters

☑ Noise Reduction
  ☑ Luminance
  ☑ Color

☑ Lens Corrections
  ☑ Lens Profile Corrections
  ☑ Transform
  ☑ Lens Vignetting
  ☑ Chromatic Aberration

☐ Effects
  ☐ Post-Crop Vignetting
  ☐ Grain

☑ Process Version

☑ Calibration

[Check All]   [Check None]   [Cancel]   [Create]

FIG 8.134
Creating a
Develop Preset

After naming and saving our Preset, it appears under User Presets, as shown in **Figure 8.135**. This preset can even be applied to images in the future as they are imported.

FIG 8.135
Creating a User Preset

I THE HISTORY PANEL

History saves all Develop adjustments as a state. The History Panel will list any Develop Preset that was applied at import, and also lists all subsequent Develop adjustments as they are applied. These are listed in a chronological order within the History Panel. You can go forwards and backwards in History by rolling over a state and you will see the preview in the Navigator. You can even copy and paste states to other images. As you make these changes, they are recorded in the History panel. Any time you want to compare a previous interpretation, or return to one, just click on that state in the History Panel and you're right there.

FIG 8.136
History Panel

| THE SNAPSHOTS PANEL

The Snapshots Panel is located right above the History Panel. Snapshots are basically saving specific steps of image History to which you might want to revert. When the History List becomes too long, you can create a Snapshot to save a specific state. This allows you to go back to a state in History, once it has been cleared.

Technically, the Snapshot Function is used to perform a sequence of steps in the Develop Module similar to an action in *Photoshop* that can be stored as a single step. Snapshots can be used to store your favorite history states as a saved setting. Rather than use the History panel to wade through a long list of history states, it is often more convenient to use Snapshots. Some folks simply prefer to use Virtual Copies instead of Snapshots but the choice is yours.

To create a Snapshot, click on the History state you want to save for an image. Then click on the plus button next to the Snapshots Panel. Name the Snapshot and click off the field. You can delete Snapshots with the minus button.

FIG 8.137
Snapshots Panel

BEFORE/AFTER WORKFLOW TIP: *When you edit an image in one of the Before/After viewing modes, you can make umpteen adjustments and at any time compare the "After" with the "Before." The problem is that you are always comparing back to the original state. A neat way to compare to the last state is to copy settings from the After image to the Before image. This will update the "Before" with the "After." This is very much like creating a snapshot of the settings, allowing you to make further adjustments and compare these with the latest version. The other method is to take the changes you want to start with and make a Virtual Copy and then make more changes. When you use Before* *and After, the Virtual Copy will show as the Before and your latest changes will show as the After.*

NEW

New In *Lightroom 4* | SOFT PROOFING

Soft Proofing has been one of the most requested features for *Lightroom* and while we were hopeful that it would be included in *Lightroom 3,* it didn't make the final feature list until now. This welcome addition has been a long wait but it is totally worth it. Soft Proofing makes printing out of *Lightroom* a dream. Soft Proofing in *Lightroom* is very different and a big improvement over *Photoshop*.

How to Soft Proof In *Lightroom 4*

Let's go ahead and Soft Proof the image in Figure 8.138.

Once your image is selected, Soft Proofing is enabled by checking the Soft Proofing Checkbox in the Develop Module Toolbar. The checkbox will toggle a Proof Preview on and off. The Keyboard Shortcut for toggling Soft Proofing is "S".

FIG 8.138
Image is selected in the Develop Module and Soft Proofing enabled with a check in the Develop Toolbar

With Soft Proofing enabled, a new panel is opened up above the Basic Panel in the Develop Module where the user can select an installed color profile and rendering intent.

FIG 8.139
Soft Proofing Panel

Using the Profile Dropdown menu, select an installed paper profile. In order select the profile, choose other from the drop down menu and that will open a folder with the installed profiles. We will select a profile for Epson Exhibition Fiber Paper using our Epson 7900 printer (**Figure 8.140**) and the profile and rendering intent are displayed in the panel. **Figure 8.141**

FIG 8.140
Desired paper profile and rendering intent selected from Profile and Intent Menu

FIG 8.141
Desired paper profile and rendering intent displayed

Out-of-gamut pixels are displayed by selecting the clipping indicators in the top right and left of the panel. The indicator on the left will show a blue overlay (**Figure 8.142**) revealing the pixels that are outside of your display's gamut and the indicator on the right shows a red overlay revealing pixels that are outside of the gamut of the selected paper or destination profile.

FIG 8.142
Display of pixels outside of display profile.

With the proof preview enabled, the user can make adjustments to the image to look as good as possible with the selected profile. When Develop adjustments are made to an image with the proof preview on, the user is asked if they want to make a virtual copy to hold the corrections. (FIG 8.143) If yes, a virtual copy is created and selected, the color profile's name is recorded in its "copy name" metadata field, and the adjustment you just made is applied to the copy instead of the original photo.

FIG 8.143
Create virtual copy for soft proofing.

The background color of the proof preview is "Paper White" which simulates the paper white color of the profile. "Paper White" is also displayed when "Lights Out"mode is selected to view proof. When proofing is on, Before/After . (FIG 8.144) shows a comparison of the current proofed copy and the prior version.

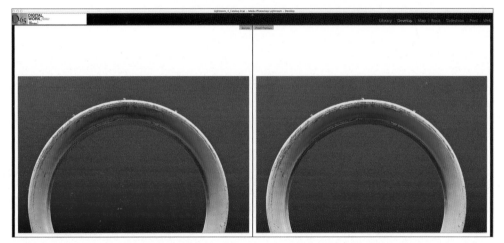

FIG 8.144
Before and After

SOFT PROOFING TIPS:

- *"S" is the shortcut key for Soft Proofing*

- *The histogram is updated as the proofing profile is changed*

- *RGB scale to represent pixel values is the traditional 0 to 255. This is incredibly useful for soft proofing RGB working space profiles.*

| SUMMARY

- The Develop module holds all the controls that you need to adjust images. It is D-65's "Tweaking Command Central."

- The image processing engine used by *Lightroom* is *Adobe Photoshop Camera Raw*, which ensures that digital RAW images processed in *Lightroom* are fully compatible with *Camera Raw* and vice versa.

- Adjustments to images made in *Lightroom's* Develop Module use Parametric Editing and are non-destructive.

- While *Photoshop* has a mix of destructive and non-destructive editing features, all the edits you make in Lightroom are non-destructive.

- A non-destructive edit doesn't alter the original pixels in your image.

- The big advantage of non-destructive editing is that you can undo any edit at any time, and in any order, and you can go back and change the parameters of any edit at any time, keeping the history of a file even after the file is closed. Once you get used to the non-destructive editing system in Lightroom, it will be hard to go back to a destructive system.

- Exposure, Contrast and White Balance will seem very familiar to *Photoshop* users or to earlier *Lightroom* users, plus there is a great deal of added new functionality in *Lightroom 4*.

- The biggest changes that you will find in the Develop Module for *Lightroom 4* are new tone mapping algorithms, for easy yet powerful image adjustment, Process Version 2012 and Soft Proofing.

SYNCHRONIZING DEVELOP SETTINGS

We have seen what all the buttons and controls in the Develop Module can do, and the power of parametric editing. A key to using *Lightroom* effectively is to adjust an image in the Develop Module and apply those changes to other images or groups of images. This is known as synchronizing settings or "Sync." This really makes the work flow quickly within *Lightroom*.

Let's go ahead and adjust an image and then synchronize the settings from one image to a group of others that are similar.

There are two things that are really important to keep in mind as you set out to tweak your images. The first is that *Lightroom* is so good, you may be inclined to start fixing bad images. This is not an efficient workflow. If you waste all your time trying to fix bad images, you will slow down your workflow. If an image is poor to begin with, move on.

Second, try to assess what you want to do to an image before you start working on it. Our friend Jeff Schewe says let the image talk to you. You can always find more areas to adjust, but again, the goal is efficient workflow. If you just keep playing without an end in mind, you will again be wasting time and slowing down your workflow.

I ADJUSTING AN IMAGE IN THE DEVELOP MODULE

We have a group of images that were shot on the Perito Moreno Glacier in Patagonia. We make some basic adjustments to one image including sharpening, lens corrections, tonal corrections and vibrance, and saturation.

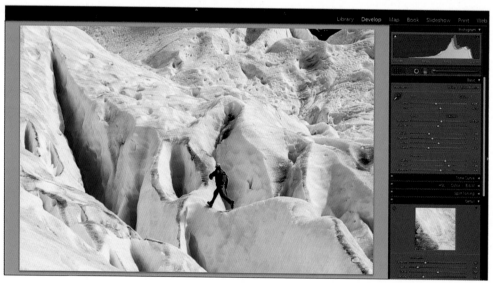

FIG 9.1
We make basic adjustments to one image.

I SYNCHRONIZING DEVELOP SETTINGS
BETWEEN MULTIPLE IMAGES

Now, we want to synchronize these settings to other
similar images.

First, we select the image that we just worked on in the Filmstrip
of the Develop Module.

FIG 9.2

Then, we select the images we want synced with that adjusted
image. **You must** select the adjusted image first, then select the
other images to synchronize to the first image.

FIG 9.3
Then, select the images
we want synced with
that adjusted image.

Then choose the Sync button at the bottom of the
Develop Module.

FIG 9.4
Choose Sync at
the bottom of the
Develop Module.

After we choose Sync, the Synchronize Settings dialog box
appears (**Figure 9.5**). We choose just the settings we want to
sync and click on Synchronize. You can sync all the adjustments,
or any part of the adjustments to the other image(s).

FIG 9.5
Synchronize Settings
Dialog Box

After you Synchronize, a progress bar appears, showing that the settings are being pasted into other images and thus synchronized to the first selected image.

FIG 9.6
Settings are being pasted into other images and thus synchronized.

The Filmstrip will then display the Develop settings being applied to the images.

FIG 9.7
The Filmstrip will display the Develop settings being applied to the images.

I OTHER OPTIONS AVAILABLE WHEN ADJUSTING IMAGES IN THE DEVELOP MODULE

Copy/Paste Buttons

You can adjust one image and choose Copy on the left-hand side of the Toolbar, then select another image(s) and choose Paste (also on the left-hand side of the Toolbar). This will apply the Develop settings from the first image to the newly selected image(s).

Sync Button

You can adjust one image, choose another image(s) and choose Sync, from the right-hand side of the Toolbar. The Synchronize Settings Dialog Box will pop up. You can choose to synchronize all the settings by selecting Synchronize. If you want to synchronize a component or any combination of the settings, for example, a crop, but no color adjustments, then you could uncheck any of the boxes that you didn't want to Synchronize. This is our favorite way of working and the one demonstrated above.

Previous Button

Choosing Shift on the Sync button will change it to the Previous Button. This allows you to sync or copy settings from the last adjusted image to a new image, without having the prior image selected.

Reset Button

The Reset button takes the image back to camera default—the way it was shot without any Develop settings.

Auto Sync

Command-clicking on the Sync button will change it to Auto Sync. Auto Sync bypasses the Synchronize dialog box.

It is critical for you to know what was checked in the Sync dialog box the last time you used it before choosing this option, because all of those settings will be synchronized. Local corrections cannot Auto Sync.

Set Default

Option-clicking on Reset sets a new default. This will allow you to change the basic default Develop settings. For example, you may want black to be 0 instead of 5. *Lightroom* and Camera Raw support the saving of user-defined Develop settings on a camera model, serial number and/or ISO rating basis.

SUMMARY

- *Lightroom* can significantly increase the efficiency and speed of your workflow by decreasing the time needed to tweak your files.

- Don't waste time on bad images, but rather concentrate on improving your good images.

- Analyze your images and decide what it is that you want to accomplish before you start playing in the

- Develop module.

- Look at groups of images that are similar and take advantage of the ability to synchronize the settings from one image to another group of images. You can sync all or just some of the Develop settings.

CHAPTER 10
THE MAP MODULE

New in *Lightroom 4*

There are many ways of organizing and managing your images and *Lightroom 4* introduces a new module to help organize by location. The Map Module is the first of two new modules introduced since version one and it truly gives you the ability to have a visual and permanent representation of where all of your images were taken. The Map Module, geotag images. There will certainly be more work to come on this new module but with Version 4 we have two methods for geotagging.

The Map Module geotags with a basic drag and drop method which will be the preference for the majority of users. The second method which is much more accurate deploys the usage of tracklogs from GPS logging devices like Garmin, Gisteq Phototrackr, Etrex and directly from cameras that support geotagging including Apple's iPhone.

- For traditional DSLR cameras, Nikon leads the pact and has supported geotagging for quite some time with the Nikon GP-1 GPS Unit. Canon supports geotagging with some of their Powershot models like the SX320 but for professional models only the Canon 1Dx supports direct geotagging using the GPS Receiver GP-E1

Images with GPS Coordinates

Visible on Map, Tagged, Untagged, None

Search Map

Map Styles

Map Zoom

Track logs

FIG 10.1
The Map Module Main Window

I MANUAL GEOTAGGING

For many photographers, images will be manually geotagged. This is not an exact science and for this to be close to accurate the photographer needs to have notes or a methodology to remember where a photograph was taken. Once the images are imported into *Lightroom* the user switches to the Map Module and types the location into the search field on the top right corner of the map window (FIG 10.3) . *Lightroom* will search for the location via the internet and generate the corresponding map. In some situations there may be more than one location with the same name, in which case the user must make a choice based on the information provided by Google.

TIPS FOR MANUAL GEOTAGGING:

- *One tip for those who are geotagging manually and have an I-Phone is to photograph each location you are at with the I-Phone which has geotagging and use the I-Phone images as the basis for geotagging your DSLR images.*

- *We at D65 keyword all of our images. If this is done you can select from the Keyword List in the Library Module a group of images based on a location and then search for that location in the Map Module and geotag the corresponding images.*

Steps to Manually Geotag in the Map Module

- Make your selection of images you want to geotag in the Library Module. For this demo we have gone to our Keyword List and selected images keyworded with Paradise Bay, Antarctica. Our images are filtered to this choice and we select all of the images. (**FIG 10.2**)

FIG 10.2
We select 460 images that were keyworded with Paradise Bay in Antarctica from our Keyword List in the Library Module.

- We switch to the Map Module and type in Paradise Bay, Antarctica into the Search Map field.

FIG 10.3
Search Map

- Google Maps returns our search with the pinpointed location of Paradise Bay, Antarctica and reveals the corresponding map.

FIG 10.4
Google Maps shows location from Search Map

- Images are dragged from the filmstrip to the Google marker on the map.

FIG 10.5
Drag and drop images from filmstrip to the marker on Google Maps

- The marker shows how many images are tagged at the location with thumbnails of each image.

FIG 10.6
Geotagged images show on Google Maps.

- After the images are geotagged in the Map Module the metadata will show the GPS coordinates.

FIG 10.7
GPS coordinates shown
in metadata

I GEOTAGGING WITH CAMERAS THAT RECORD GPS

For photographers owning cameras that record GPS coordinates
the process of geotagging is considerably easier than the manual
process. The good news is that from this point forward both
Nikon and Canon should be releasing cameras that record GPS
coordinates which will make this entire process much easier.

Steps to use cameras that record GPS in the Map Module

- Import images into the Library Module. Images that have GPS coordinates will show a GPS badge in the Grid. (**FIG 10.8**)

FIG 10.8
GPS badge in Library Grid

- In the Map Module select your images from the Filmstrip or Collection. The GPS coordinates will show with the corresponding number of images in Google Maps. (**FIG 10.9**)

FIG 10.9
Images with GPS coordinates in Map Module

- Zoom on any Selected Photo or groups of photos for a magnified view in Google Maps and the corresponding thumbnails. (**FIG 10.10**)

331

FIG 10.10
Magnified View in
Google Maps
with thumbnails.

- Zooming to the maximum size on Google Maps provides amazing detail on any Selected Photo. **(FIG 10.11)** is taken skiing some backcountry in Snowbird, Utah and the zoom feature literally reveals trees and rocks.

FIG 10.11
Maximum magnified
view in Google Maps

| GEOTAGGING WITH TRACK LOGS

There are options for Geotagging even for photographers who don't own cameras that record GPS coordinates but desire something more accurate than manually tagging images with approximate coordinates. *Lightroom* can import tracklogs from devices that record GPS as long as the logs are in the GPX format.

Steps to use GPS Track Logs in the Map Module

• Use a GPS recording device like Gisteq Phototrackr, Etrex or Garmin and create a tracklog. The tracklog can be imported into the Map Module as long as it is in the GPX format. The tracklog is loaded by using the tracklog feature to the right of the lock in the Map Module Toolbar.

FIG 10.12
Tracklog loaded into *Lightroom*

FIG 10.13
Recent Tracklogs

• The tracklog is plotted in the Map Module and shows the date and length of time for each tracklog loaded. The tracklog in (**FIG 10.14**) shows an 11 hour journey from Livingston Island to Deception Island in Antarctica on December 3, 2011.

FIG 10.14
GPS tracklog viewed in Map Module

- Choosing Visible on Map yields 108 images from the tracklog at Deception Island in Antarctica.

FIG 10.15
GPS tracklog with thumbnails in Map Module

MAP MODULE WORKFLOW TIPS:

- *The new Map module uses Google maps to allow you to add locations to your photos*

- *Images with pre-existing GPS data will automatically show on the map.*

- *You can add locations by dragging/dropping photos from the Filmstrip directly onto the map.*

- *Lightroom reads GPX format tracklogs.*

- *LR does not read the tracklog off the device. This usually means third party software to ready the log for importing.*

- *You can manually adjust for the camera time not matching the tracklog time just by dragging and dropping photos.*

- *Saved Locations are located on the left hand side of the Map Module and function like a location preset.*

- *You can filter to find photos at that saved location using Metadata filters.*

- *GPS data can be removed on Export by choosing Remove Location info from the Metadata drop down menu in Export.*

- *Markers show where you've taken photos, and when you click on a marker, it shows the photos taken there.*

- *When you click a marker pin, the pin and its photos become selected. Clicking the pin a second time (or double-clicking) will select it and show the pop-up. If a pop-up is already showing, and you click a different pin, its pop-up will show on the first click. If no pop-ups are showing, and you simply hover over a pin, its pop-up will show, and will dismiss when you move off of the pin.*

- *You can advance the thumbnails rapidly with the arrow keys.*

- *You can Search for a particular location using the search bar at the top.*

- *Searching can be accomplished with Search by name, Search by zip code, Search by GPS co-ordinates*

- *Filter using the Location Filter bar at the menu at the top of Map Module using, Visible on Map, Tagged, Untagged or None.*

❘ SUMMARY

- Geotagging images in *Lightroom 4* is a very useful way of adding to the Digital Asset Management Capability of *Lightroom*.

- The Map Module uses Google Maps

- Images with pre-existing GPS data will automatically show on the map

- Drag and drop from filmstrip onto map

- Filtering to find saved locations using Metadata filters.

- GPS can be removed on Export for privacy

- No doubt the future will bring more enhancements to this module.

THE BOOK MODULE

NEW

New in *Lightroom 4*

The Book Module is the second of two new modules introduced since version one and certainly one of the most user requested features. While competing products Aperture and iPhoto have had book modules for a long time, this is still an exciting addition for *Lightroom*. This new module is really very cool and although it isn't as flexible as Indesign it does supports both PDF and direct publishing to Blurb. For those of you who are unfamiliar with Blurb, it is a creative publishing service for self published books and it is the dominant player in the marketplace of self publishing.

Images can be organized in the Library Module using collections or organized directly in the Book Module.

Creating a Book

For this tutorial we are going to examine how to create a book for Blurb. The first step in creating your book is the process of image selection. Select your images for a book in the Library Module and click on the Book Module. The easiest thing to do is to create a collection for the images you want to use for your book. If you have Collections, they will be available directly from within the Book Module on the left side Collections Panel.

BOOK WORKFLOW TIP: *If you want to create a book using images from multiple folders, then create a Collection of those images and select the collection from the Book Module.*

FIG 11.1
The Book Module

We'll go through all the options available in the Book Module in order.

I BOOK SETTINGS

Various presets are available for Book Module creation.

Book

The Book Module can be configured to create using Blurb or PDF.

- **Blurb:** Publishing directly to Blurb.

- **PDF:** Publishing to PDF format

FIG 11.2
Publishing to Blurb or to PDF

Size

Using Blurb you can create your book with several different format options.

- **Small Square:** 7x7 inches

- **Standard Portrait:** 8x10 inches

- **Standard Landscape:** 10x8 inches

- **Large Landscape:** 13x11 inches

- **Large Square:** 12x12 inches

FIG 11.3
Size format options
for Blurb

Cover

You can choose different types of cover layouts and cover stock.

- **Hardcover Image** Wrap features a durable matte finish and library binding.

- **Hardcover Dust Jacket** come with durable library binding and 8pt black linen covers made of a hard-wearing cotton blend which is coated with water-based acrylic for resiliency.

FIG 11.4
Cover choices

Paper Type

You can choose different types of paper for the book project.

- **Premium Lustre** has a bit of gloss and heavier than the standard paper from Blurb.

- **Premium Matte** has a matte finish and is more opaque and heavier than the standard paper from Blurb

- **ProLine Uncoated** manufactured by Mohawk Fine Papers, this premium stock has an eggshell-textured uncoated finish.

- **ProLine Pearl Photo** manufactured by Mohawk Fine Papers, this premium stock is for high-end photo books. It has a lustre finish but is heavier than other papers from Blurb.

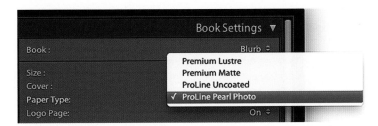

FIG 11.5
Paper options for Blurb

Logo Page

All standard Blurb books are printed with the Blurb logo on the copyright page and final page, but for an additional fee you add your own branding or go "logo free."

FIG 11.6
Option to place Blurb logo or no logo

Estimated Price

An estimated price is calculated on the fly for your Blurb Book.

FIG 11.7
Estimated price
is calculated in
Book Module

Auto Layout

Laying out a book can be done manually or there is a very
convenient Auto Layout feature. Using Auto Layout you can create
and save presets using the Auto Layout Preset Editor (**FIG 11.8**).

- **Presets** can be created, edited, updated and saved in the
  Preset Editor.

- **Auto Layout** generates the layout using the selected images
  (FIG 11.9) be created, edited, updated and saved in the
  Preset Editor.

- **Clear Layout** clears the selected layout and you can start over.

FIG 11.8
Auto Layout
Preset Editor

FIG 10.9
Auto Layout generating layout for book

Page

If you desire more control than what is offered in Auto Layout, there is a manual mode for laying out your book. The Page selection panel has over 180 templates for page types and it also allows you to use layouts you may have created in Adobe Illustrator.

- **Add Page** generates a new page with the specs of the page already used.

- **Add Blank** adds a new blank unformatted page.

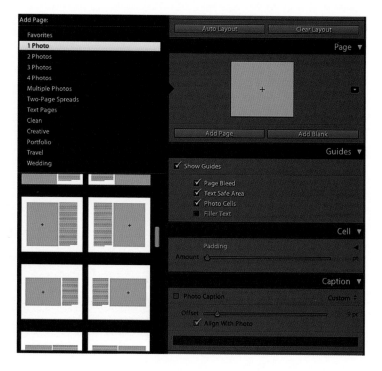

FIG 11.10
Custom layouts or
an assortment of
layouts can be
created with Page.

Guides

The Layout Guides enable you to see various options to help you design your book.

- **Show Guides** All guides can be turned on and off

- **Page Bleed** marked in grey is cut off when it's printed

- **Text Safe Area** is marked with a thin grey line. This line gets cut when trimming after printing is complete, so it is important to keep text within that border.

- **Photo Cells** are shown with a grey fill area which is not included on final export.

- **Filler Text** uses Latin filler text shown where the text cells will go or is says "Photo Title"

FIG 11.11
Guides Panel

Cell

The Cell padding provides flexible photo and text positioning.

FIG 11.12
Cell Panel

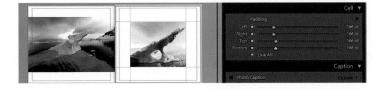

FIG 11.13
Example of Cell Padding

Caption

There are many options for placement of caption information and excerpting metadata. The Caption Panel is flexible and very easy to use.

FIG 11.14
Caption panel

FIG 11.15
Excerpting caption metadata and configuring it in the Book Module is very easy using the Caption Panel.

Type

The type panel is pretty sophisticated and it is possible to configure fonts, text layout, style, character size alignment and opacity.

FIG 11.16
Type Panel

Background

Using the Background Panel you can create individual page color or graphic or apply a graphic or color globally to the entire book.

FIG 11.17
Background Panel

Send Book to Blurb

The finished book is previewed and then sent directly to Blurb.

FIG 11.18
Final book is previewed

FIG 11.19
Sign in and Send
to Blurb

FIG 11.20
Final book produced
and sold through Blurb

BOOK MODULE TIPS:

- *Try Autolayout first as it is the easiest way to layout a book.*

- *Drag and drop behavior for reordering pages or swapping image locations.*

- *Photo captions are based on existing metadata or by manual entry.*

- *Dragging horizontally over a selection adjusts text size.*

- *Dragging vertically over a selection adjusts leading or line height.*

- *Holding down Cmd (Mac) Ctrl (Windows) while dragging horizontally over a selection adjusts tracking.*

- *Holding down Cmd (Mac) Ctrl (Windows) while dragging vertically over a selection adjusts baseline shift.*

- *The document bar at the top of the view area lets you know if the book has been saved. Photos that have been placed in an unsaved book stay there until you choose to celar them using the Clear Layout button .*

• *Saved books can be accessed later from the Collections panel.*

BOOK MODULE SHORTCUTS:

Book Shortcuts

View Shortcuts

Command + Shift + Left Arrow	Go to first page
Command + Left Arrow	Go to previous page
Command + Shift + Right Arrow	Go to last page
Command + Right Arrow	Go to next page
Command + E	Multi-page view
Command + R	Spread view
Command + T	Single page view
Command + U	Zoomed page view

Guides Shortcuts

Command + Shift + G	Show Guides
Command + Shift + H	Show Filler Text
Command + Shift + K	Show Photo Cells
Command + Shift + J	Show Page Bleed
Command + Shift + U	Show Text Safe Area

UI Shortcuts

Tab	Hide side panels
Shift + Tab	Hide all panels
Command + Option + Up Arrow	Go to Previous Module
Command + Option + A	Select all text cells
Command + Option + Shift + A	Select all photo cells

Mode Shortcuts

F	Cycle screen modes
Command + Option + F	Go to normal screen mode
L	Cycle Lights Out modes
Command + Shift + L	Go to Lights Dim mode

FIG 11.21
Book Module Shortcuts

❘ SUMMARY

• Books have been one of the most requested features for *Lightroom*. *Lightroom 4* introduces a brand new Book Module which lets you design books that can be uploaded and printed through Blurb with ease.

• Books can be printed on a local output device as a PDF.

THE SLIDESHOW MODULE

The Slideshow module in *Lightroom* offers an elegant way to assemble your images for a slideshow presentation. Slideshows can be used as a way to deliver images to clients, show your portfolio, or even show your friends and family your favorite images.

The Slideshow, Print and Web Modules all work relatively in the same fashion. The left panels contain a list of templates and collections along with a preview of each template. The center view displays the images. The toolbar contains controls for playing a preview of the slideshow and adding text to the slides. The right panels provide the controls for specifying how the images appear.

Slideshows can be created directly in *Lightroom,* and can include music from your iTunes library and be played from your computer, or the slideshow can be exported as a PDF. If exported as a PDF, one can take advantage of everything that a PDF offers, including password protection for viewing, opening, editing and/ or printing.

Slideshows have an option to Prepare Previews in Advance will ensure that a slideshow is never interrupted waiting for image information to render to the display and slideshows can be exported from *Lightroom* as HD video.

NEW

New in *Lightroom 4* The only change to the Slideshow module is one that also impacts Books, Web and Print. In Lightoom 3, collections stored output module specific settings. A collection could contain for example settings for slideshow, print and web. In *Lightroom 4* you save a specific book, slideshow, print or web gallery. Standard collections no longer store output module settings, and those creations are module-specific, so they can't contain data from other modules. You can however save books, slideshows, prints, web galleries as children of a collection.

This does get a bit confusing but the new Unsaved Slideshow, /print/web/slideshow is basically a temporary play area where you can create things without actually saving them. When you want to keep something, you then save it as a slideshow/book/print/web "creation."

TIP Slideshows, Books, Prints and Web Galleries

When you first enter an output module, you're viewing 'unsaved slideshow,' 'unsaved book,' 'unsaved print,' or 'unsaved web gallery,' depending on the module.

When you want to keep something you've created, you save it as a /slideshow/book/print/web gallery.

Creating a Slideshow

Select your images for a slideshow in the Library Module and click on the Slideshow Module. If you have Collections, they will be available directly from within the Slideshow Module on the left side Collections Panel.

Add and Remove Templates

Options for your slideshow are available from the right side panels.

FIG 12.1
The Slideshow Module

One important notation: The default in the Toolbar is "All Filmstrip Photos," so even if you selected eight or ten images in the Grid, when you switch to Slideshow the Toolbar may still say all Filmstrip Photos.

FIG 12.2
Choose Selected Photos if you are choosing images on an individual basis.

SLIDESHOW WORKFLOW TIP: If you want to create a slideshow using images from multiple folders, then create a Quick Collection of those images and make the slideshow from that collection.

We'll go through all the options available in the Slideshow Module in order.

I TEMPLATE BROWSER

Various presets and custom slideshows can be saved and will be available in the Template Browser. As you roll over the presets, you can get a preview of how the slideshow will look in the Preview Window. User-created custom slideshow presets will appear under the User Templates.

Slideshow Template Presets

The Slideshow Module comes with template presets, or you can create your own custom templates. The included templates are:

- **Caption and Rating:** Centers images on a gray background—the stars and caption metadata are included

- **Crop to Fill:** Displays a full screen image–note that verticals might be cropped to fit the screen aspect ratio

- **Default:** Very similar to Caption and Rating—centers images on a gray background with stars with an identity plate included

- **EXIF Metadata:** Centers images on a black background with stars, EXIF information, and an identity plate

- **Widescreen:** Displays full frame of each image, adding black bars to fill the aspect ratio of the screen

FIG 12.3
Slideshow Template
Browser showing
preview of Exif
Metadata Template

I OPTIONS PANEL

Moving over to the right-hand side of the Slideshow Module you
will find the Options Panel. This is where you begin to control
how the images in the slideshow will appear. Use the Options
Panel to zoom the image to fill the frame, or not, to add a border
with a specific color and size or even to cast a shadow.

FIG 12.4
Options Panel in
Slideshow Module

FIG 12.5
Options Panel in Slideshow Module with Stroke Border set to 4 px black rule, and Cast Shadow set to
Opacity 28%, Offset 58 px, Radius 19 px and Angle -45°

FIG 12.6
Options Panel in Slideshow Module with Stroke Border set to 20 px black rule, and Cast Shadow set to Opacity 66%, Offset 79 px, Radius 53 px and Angle -45°

Stroke Border

Stroke Border provides the ability to add a border around your image in a specific color and pixel size. We have chosen a black border, 4 pixels wide, as shown in **Figure 12.5** and a black border 20 pixels wide as shown in **Figure 12.6**.

FIG 12.7
Setting Stroke Border to 20 Pixels in Options Panel in Slideshow Module

COLOR PICKER WORKFLOW TIP: While the Color Picker is open, drag the cursor (eyedropper) onto the image to sample a color from the image.

FIG 12.8
Sampling color with the Color Picker in Options Panel in Slideshow Module

Cast Shadow

There are four options for working with Cast Shadow:

- **Opacity:** Displays the darkness of the shadow cast

- **Offset:** The distance of the shadow from the image

- **Radius:** The hardness of the edge of the shadow

- **Angle:** The direction of shadow

FIG 12.9
Cast Shadow in
Slideshow Module
Options Panel

I LAYOUT PANEL

The Layout Panel controls the guides and margins for the slideshow. Visual guides can be linked or controlled separately.

FIG 12.10
Layout Panel in
Slideshow Module

FIG 12.11
Layout Panel with show guides using Link All at 200 pixels in Slideshow Module

| OVERLAYS PANEL

If you create an Identity Plate, it will be available in the Overlays
Panel to drop into your slideshow. The Overlays Panel gives
you the ability to control the placement, scale and opacity of
your Identity Plate. You can also create and show text overlays,
watermarking, ratings, and control text drop shadows.

The shadows for the text overlays have the same controls as in Cast Shadows:

- **Opacity:** Adjusts the darkness of the shadow cast

- **Offset:** The distance of the shadow from the image example

- **Radius:** Displays the hardness or softness of the edge of the shadow

- **Angle:** The direction of the shadow

FIG 12.12
Overlay Panel in
Slideshow Module

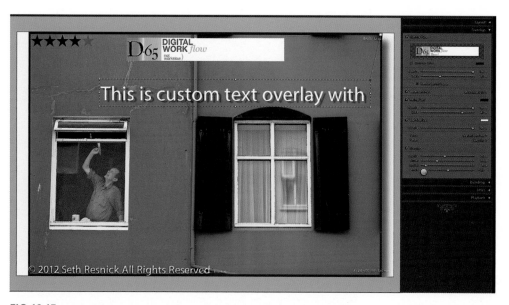

FIG 12.13
Overlay Panel in Slideshow Module with Identity Plate, Watermarking, Rating Stars, Text Overlays and Shadow applied.

I BACKDROP PANEL

The Backdrop Panel allows you to apply a color wash or a gradient shading on the background. You can control the opacity of the wash as well as the angle of the wash.

You can also use an image as a backdrop or set the backdrop color. Color Wash applies a gradient wash on top of the background image.

FIG 12.14
Backdrop Panel in
Slideshow Module

Adding a Background Image to a Slideshow

Drag an image from the Filmstrip into the background of the
slide, as shown in **Figure 12.15**. Use the Opacity slider to adjust
the image's transparency.

FIG 12.15
Drag image from
Filmstrip and adjust
the background
image's transparency

FIG 12.16
Image added as a background image

BACKGROUND IMAGE WORKFLOW TIP: *You can't remove an image from the background, but you can add a new image just by dragging the new image over the old one. You can also set the opacity to 0% or uncheck the background image option to "remove" the image.*

Background Color

The Background Color sets the color of the background.

✔ Background Color

FIG 12.17
The Background Color sets the color of the background.

| TITLE PANEL

The Title Panel allows you to create both opening and closing title slides for your slideshow. The opening and closing slides can be text only, image only, or both.

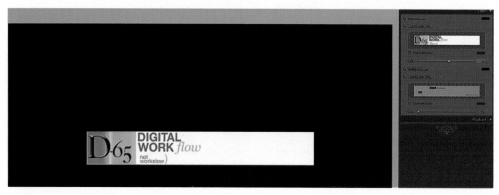

FIG 12.18
The Title Panel in Slideshow Module

| PLAYBACK PANEL

Soundtrack allows you to select music and the soundtrack can be fit to the exact duration of the slide show using Fit to Music.

The Playback Panel settings control the transition and duration of the transition. You can also choose to add music from iTunes or randomize the slides.

The Playback Screen selector comes in very handy with dual monitors. You can choose which screen to play the slideshow on, and blank out the second screen.

Slide Duration controls the amount of time an image is on the screen and the length of time for a fade and includes the addition of color fades.

Random Order will play the slides in a random order.

Repeat will repeat the slideshow from the beginning.

FIG 12.19
The Playback Panel in
Slideshow Module

Prepare Previews in Advance will ensure that a slideshow is never interrupted by waiting for image information to render to the display monitor.

FIG 12.20
Prepare Previews
in Advance

| SLIDESHOW TOOLBAR

Adding Customized Text

The ABC Button located on the Toolbar allows you to add text, including the ability to add metadata and custom metadata from an image. You can scale the text and place it anywhere in the slideshow. The Toolbar also controls going to the next or previous slide, rotation, stopping and playing of the slideshow as well as a text field and a drop-down menu that allows you to choose All Filmstrip Photos, Selected Photos or Flagged Photos.

FIG 12.21
Slideshow
Module Toolbar

| EXPORTING AND PLAYING

The Export PDF button allows you to export the slideshow as a PDF file. Holding down the Option/Alt key while clicking on the Export PDF button toggles the button to Export JPEG and allows you to make slideshows to your own specifications using any third party slideshow product. Preview provides a preview of the show and Play will play the full slideshow. Export Video allows export as HD Video.

FIG 12.22
Slideshow Module
Export as PDF,
Export JPEG, Export
as HD Video

FIG 12.23
Slideshow Module
Preview and Play

Quality: Sets the quality using JPEG options: the lower the number, the lower the quality. The photos are automatically embedded with sRGB.

Width and Height: Pixel dimensions for the slideshow. The pixel dimensions of your screen are the default size.

D-65 exports the slideshow to a job folder, using a file naming convention that corresponds to the job name, such as 20120201_clientx_slideshow.pdf. We then send that slideshow to a client for viewing.

EXPORTING AS A PDF WORKFLOW TIP: With the full version of Adobe Acrobat, the user can apply security settings to the PDF saved from within Lightroom. This means you have control over an end user opening the document, printing or editing it. So for a client who may have presented payment problems in the past, you could save the document with a password required to open the document. The document can be delivered but not opened. When payment is received, the password can then be relayed and the document opened.

SUMMARY

- The Slideshow module in *Lightroom* offers an elegant way to assemble your images for creation of a slideshow presentation.

- The left panels contain a list of templates and a preview of each.

- The center displays the photos.

- The toolbar contains controls for playing a preview of the slideshow and adding text to the slides.

- The right panels provide the controls for specifying how the photos appear.

Lightroom really makes printing a breeze with many features for all your printing needs. You can place multiple size images on a single page and have multiple pages of multiple picture layouts. You can even use draft mode printing which renders from the Previews. This is even more amazing because you can select a group of images, print them as a PDF and accomplish the task in seconds.

Another plus is the ability to print straight to JPEG and to attach a profile. That means that you can produce print packages for a client and allow the client to print their own photos at their local lab. You can print more than one image at a time. In fact, you can actually send your entire catalog to the printer, or just one image at a time. There are pre-configured presets which provide all kinds of options including contact sheets. You can also create your own custom presets and save them for future use. The coolest feature of all is the ability to render an image automatically at the native resolution using Dimensions.

NEW

New in *Lightroom 4*

- **Although it is located in the Develop Module, Soft Proofing is a most welcome addition has been a long wait but it is totally worth it. Soft Proofing makes printing out of *Lightroom* a dream.**

- **Print Adjustment (Brightness/Contrast)**

- **There are 2 new quick & dirty sliders, to compensate for printers that are always a bit dark/light/lacking contrast. This was a much debated feature because the real answer is proper color management and profiling with a device like X-Rite i1 Display. So while It's not intended to be a replacement for proper color management, it can help those who still have problems with slight mismatches. It is important to note that *Lightroom* isn't usually the cause, but it's the easiest place to fix it. The setting is sticky and should not need to be adjusted per image but rather specific for a printer/paper/ink combination**

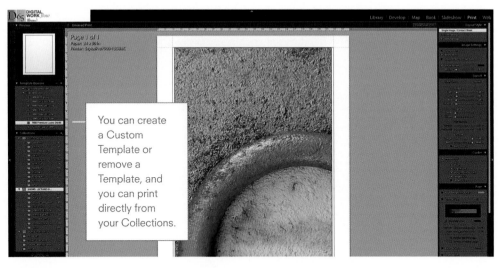

You can create a Custom Template or remove a Template, and you can print directly from your Collections.

FIG 13.1
The Print Module

| THE TEMPLATE BROWSER PANEL

The Template Browser holds many preconfigured layouts for printing, or you can completely create your own custom layouts and add them to the Template Browser. You add and delete templates from this panel by clicking on the + and - signs. In *Lightoom 3*, collections stored output module specific settings. A collection could contain for example settings for print, slideshow and web. In *Lightroom 4* you save a specific print, slideshow, book or web gallery. Standard collections no longer store output module settings, and those creations are module-specific, so they can't contain data from other modules. You can however save books, slideshows, prints, web galleries as children of a collection.

FIG 13.2
The Template Browser
in the Print Module

Creating a Custom Print Template

To create a new template, you can modify existing templates or start from scratch. The easiest method is:

1.   Select a template from the Template Browser.

2. Use the settings in the right panels to setup the layout you want.

3. Save it as a custom template by clicking on the + button on the right of the Template Browser.

4. Give the template a name and choose Create.

5. The template will be saved in the User Templates folder of *Lightroom*.

| THE COLLECTIONS PANEL

You can make selections for the Print Module from the Library Module or directly from your Collections, which appear in the Print Module. You can also make print-specific collections. Either choose the images you want to print from the Library Grid, or choose a Collection from the Collections Panel in the Print Module.

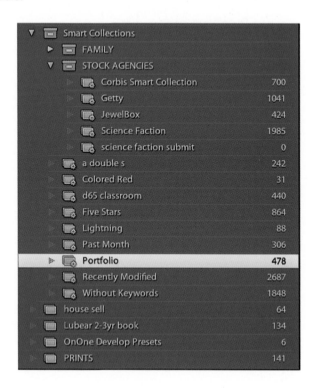

FIG 13.3
The Collections
Panel in the *Lightroom*
Print Module

| PAGE SETUP AND PRINT SETTINGS BUTTONS

On the lower left-hand corner of the Print Module is Page Setup and Print Settings. Here is where you select your paper size, orientation, color management and printer.

FIG 13.4
Page Setup and Print Settings in the *Lightroom* Print Module

FIG 13.5
Page Setup Dialog with Epson 7900 and 24 x 30 inch paper selected.

Print

Printer:	StylusPro7900–15DB8C ‡
Presets:	Default Settings ‡
Copies:	1
Pages:	⦿ All
	◯ From: 1 to: 1

Printer Settings ‡

Basic | Advanced Color Settings

Page Setup:	Roll Paper
Media Type:	Exhibition Fiber Paper ‡
Ink:	Photo Black ‡
Print Mode:	AccuPhoto HDR ‡ ☑ 16 Bit Output
Color Mode:	Off (No Color Management) ‡
Output Resolution:	SuperPhoto – 1440 dpi ‡
	☑ Super MicroWeave
	☐ High Speed
	☐ Flip Horizontal
	☐ Finest Detail

(?) | PDF ▾ | Hide Details | Cancel | Save

FIG 13.6
Print Settings Dialog
Box with our choices
for Epson Exhibition
Fiber Paper

I THE LAYOUT STYLE ENGINE PANEL

On the right side of the Print Module is the Layout Style Panel.
The Layout Style Panel contains the Single Image / Contact
Sheet, Picture Package and Custom Package options. Single
Image / Contact Sheet is what you use to print contact sheets or
single images of your selected images.

Layout Style ▼

Single Image / Contact Sheet

Picture Package

Custom Package

FIG 13.7
The Layout Style Panel

FIG 13.8
Single Image/
Contact Sheet

Picture Package creates multi-page layouts for an individual image in several different sizes. Picture Package allows you to create wallet size, 5x7 and 8x10 outputs all at the same time. What is really neat is that *Lightroom* sizes the images to the page. If they won't fit on one page, *Lightroom* creates a new page. You can even create custom image sizes by simply grabbing a border with the mouse and extending it. Shift-click and drag to keep the aspect ratio.

FIG 13.9
Picture Package

Custom Package which truly lets you customize any layout.

FIG 13.10
Creating a Custom Print
Template by dragging
and dropping and sizing
on the fly.

When Custom Package or Picture Package are selected from the
Layout Style menu, the Cell Panel is activated.

FIG 13.11
The Cell Panel is activated when Picture Package or Custom Package are selected.

I THE IMAGE SETTINGS PANEL

Image settings are used to rotate, crop and fit images in a layout. The menu choice will change depending on whether you have Single Image / Contact Sheet selected or whether you have Picture Package or Custom Package selected.

FIG 13.12
The Image Settings Panel when Single Image / Contact Sheet is selected. Rotate to Fit and Stroke Border selected.

- **Zoom To Fill Frames:** Fills the frame, cropping the edges as necessary

- **Rotate To Fit:** Rotates images to produce the largest image for the layout

- **Repeat One Photo per Page:** This option allows you to repeat a photo multiple times on a page

- **Stroke Border:** You can add a color border to your image to be printed by clicking on the color picker, choosing the appropriate color and adjusting the width of the border with the slider.

I THE LAYOUT PANEL

The Layout Panel is available for the Single Image / Contact Sheet Layout Style. The Cell Panel (**Figure 13.11**) is available for Picture Package and Custom Package. The Layout Panel controls margins, page grid, cell spacing and cell sizes.

FIG 13.13
The Layout Panel

- **Ruler Units:** Sets the ruler to either inches, centimeters, millimeters, points or picas

- **Margins:** Sets the page margins. Changing the margin will move the image in the layout in real time

- **Page Grid:** Provides control over the number of cell rows and columns

- **Cell Spacing:** Controls the space between cells for rows and columns

- **Cell Size:** Controls the size of the image cells

| THE GUIDES PANEL

The Guides Panel shows or hides rulers, page bleed, margins and gutters, and image cells. The guides can be turned on and off for Page Bleed and layout purposes.

The coolest feature of all in Guides is Dimensions, which really belongs under Print Job. By checking Dimensions and unchecking Print Resolution in the Print Job Dialog box, the file will be ripped at the native resolution with no upsizing or downsizing. This in itself makes *Lightroom* worth every dime.

PRINTING WORKFLOW TIP: Uncheck Print Resolution in the Print Job Dialog box and check Dimensions and the file will be printed at the native resolution, yielding the best possible print.

FIG 13.14
The Guides Panel

FIG 13.15
With Dimensions checked and Resolution in the Print Job box unchecked, the print will be made at the optimum native resolution which in this case would be 343 PPI.

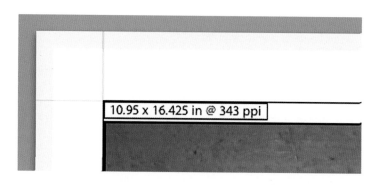

10.95 x 16.425 in @ 343 ppi

| THE PAGE PANEL

Lightroom provides the ability to print various metadata as an overlay from the Photo Info dialog box, along with your Identity Plate and/or watermark. Many photographers like to put their copyright or logo on proof images and this is the place to create those overlays.

FIG 13.16
Page Panel

Identity Plate

If you have created an Identity Plate, you can choose to include it in your printing by checking this option. You can rotate the Identity Plate with the degree option on the right by clicking on it and selecting No Rotation, Rotate on screen 90°, 180° or -90°. To move the Identity Plate, simply drag it to the desired location. The Identity Plate can be moved with precision by selecting it and using the arrow keys.

- **Opacity:** Controls the opacity of the Identity Plate

- **Scale:** Controls the size of the Identity Plate

- **Render behind every image:** The Identity Plate will appear behind the photo

- **Render on every image:** The Identity Plate will appear centered on every photo in a multi-photo layout. It can be further scaled using the controls in the Overlays panel

Watermarking

If you have created a Watermark, you can choose to include it in your printing by checking this option.

Page Options

- **Page Numbers:** The page numbers will be printed on the bottom right of each page

- **Page Info:** The sharpening setting, profile setting and printer name will be printed on the bottom of each page

- **Crop Marks:** Crop marks can be printed around the image for use as a cutting guide

Photo Info

You can include the filename, title, keywords and caption excerpted from the metadata printed below each image. Select Photo Info and click the drop down menu to the right.

- **Date:** Prints the creation date of the photo

- **Equipment:** Prints the camera and lens information

- **Exposure:** Prints the shutter speed and f/stop

- **Filename:** Prints the name of the image

- **Sequence:** Prints sequential numbers based on how many images are printed as in 1/4, 2/4, 3/4, 4/4 for a sequence of 4 images.

- **Custom Text:** Prints any custom text entered

- **Edit:** For editing in the Text Template Editor

Font Size

You can set the size of the font chosen in point size.

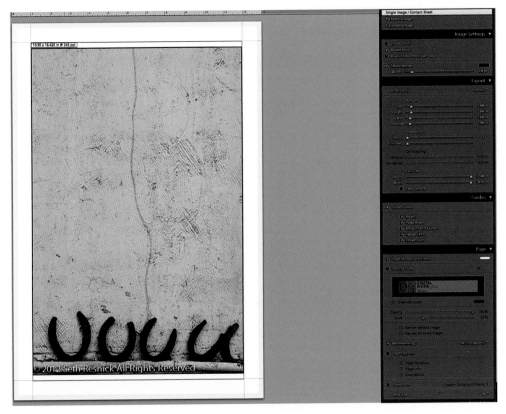

FIG 13.17
Page Panel showing an image with watermarking and other metadata options

I THE PRINT JOB PANEL

This is really the "Control Central" for the Print Module. Color management, print resolution, rendering intents and sharpening are controlled in this panel. You decide whether to print to a printer or to output straight to JPEG and to attach a profile. That means that you can produce print packages for a client and allow the client to print their own photos at their local lab. You can decide to allow the printer to control color management (not recommended by D-65) or choose a corresponding paper profile and allow *Lightroom* to control your color.

On a Mac running OS X 10.5 or greater, you can even output in 16-bit mode (not available on the PC). D-65 suggests that you let *Lightroom* handle color management. If, however, you choose Draft Mode, the printer automatically handles color.

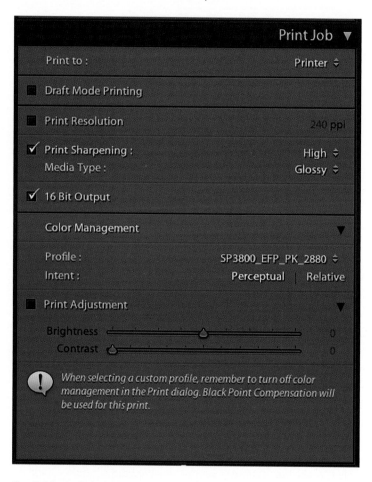

FIG 13.18
Print Job Panel

Draft Mode Printing

Draft Mode Printing is good for printing contact sheets and quick prints. It is also very cool to print to PDF. You can select some or all the images in your library and print them fairly quickly to a PDF contact sheet based on the preview resolution chosen in the Catalog Preferences. In Draft Mode, the cached preview is used for the print.

If you choose an image without a fully cached preview, the thumbnail data is used and the prints may suffer from "jaggies" and artifacting. Sharpening and color management controls aren't available when using Draft Mode Printing.

You can also deploy PDF security if you have the full version of *Adobe Acrobat* which allows the ability to lock out printing and/or copying.

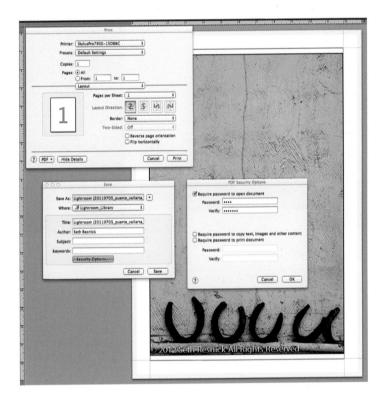

FIG 13.19
Choosing Draft Mode Printing and Printing to a PDF with PDF Security.

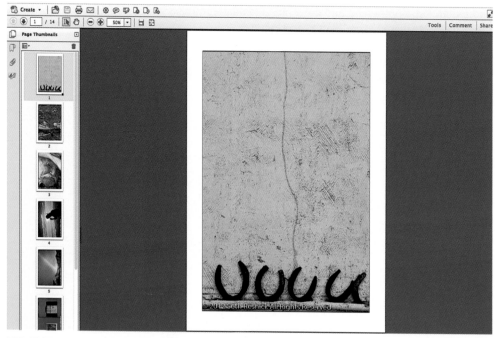

FIG 13.20
PDF output with PDF Security using Draft Mode Printing.

Print Resolution

The print resolution defines pixels per inch (ppi)—for the printer. The default value is 240 ppi. As a side note, the Epson print engine can handle any resolution between 180 and 720 ppi.

Maximum print resolution is 720 ppi. The ideal resolution for an image is the one which has the least change from the native resolution of the file.

TIP: The native resolution is best achieved by unchecking Resolution in the Print Job Panel and checking Dimensions in the Guides Panel. This will output the file at its native resolution.

Print Sharpening

Lightroom includes output print sharpening based on Pixel Genius PhotoKit Sharpener algorithms. Output sharpening accounts for pixels being converted to dots on paper. You can choose the type of paper you are printing to, and the degree of sharpening. When Draft Mode Printing is enabled, Print Sharpening is disabled.

16-Bit Output

Lightroom includes the ability to output as 16-bit printing for Mac OS X 10.5 or above.

Color Management

Profile: Other

If you have loaded paper profiles into your computer, they will be available in Color Management under Profile>Other. If you choose a custom printer profile, make sure that all color management is turned off in the printer driver software. This is controlled in the Print Settings Button under Color Management.

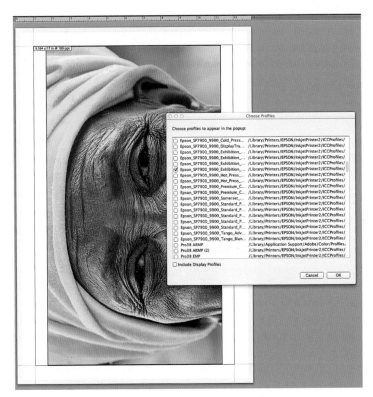

FIG 13.21
Selecting custom profile for printing

Managed by Printer

If no profiles are installed in your computer, color will automatically be managed by the Printer. If you do use Manage by Printer, make sure to select ColorSync in the Color Management settings (Mac OS) or enable ICM Method for Image Color Management on the PC.

Depending on the print driver software, you can usually find the color management settings below the Presets menu after the Print dialog box opens on a Mac and after the Print Document dialog box opens at Setup>Properties>Advanced on a PC.

Rendering Intents

The printer's color space is likely smaller then the color space of the image to be printed. The rendering intent you choose will compensate for these out-of-gamut colors. Rendering intents options are Perceptual, Relative Colormetric and Relative.

Perceptual is for strong vibrant colors. Perceptual preserves the visual relationship between colors. Colors that are in-gamut may change as out-of-gamut colors are shifted to reproducible colors.

Relative Colormetric is for muted colors. Relative Colormetric rendering preserves all in gamut colors and shifts out-of-gamut colors to the closest reproducible color.

The Relative option preserves more of the original color and is a good choice when you have few out-of-gamut colors.

| THE PRINT BUTTON

After you have used all of the tools in the Panels to configure your print settings, press the Print button and you will wind up with a gorgeous print!

| DEMONSTRATION: MAKING A PRINT

Printing seems to confuse a lot of folks, so we are going to do a quick step-by-step tutorial, reviewing the areas that seem to cause confusion. We are going to print a 13x19 A3 print with the Epson 3800 using Epson Exhibition Fiber Paper.

Every printer manufacturer will yield a different response to color and changing inks. Paper will also affect how the print will look. *Lightroom's* working color space, ProPhoto RGB, is an extremely wide and accommodating color space. The range of colors that are available from printers today may exceed the Adobe 98 color space. Epson K3 inks and papers like Epson Premium Glossy or Epson Premium Luster are capable of a gamut well beyond Adobe 98.

To achieve the best results and the widest gamut, it is critical to have your monitor profiled. You can rely on the colors that you see displayed as being the actual colors that you are trying to print.

We are going to make a print and take you through the basic steps.

1. Select an image from the Library, or if the image is part of a collection, select the image from the Collections Panel directly in the Print Module. Soft Proof in the Develop Module and make appropriate changes.

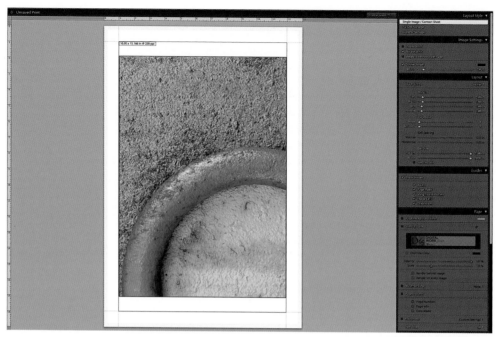

FIG 13.22
Select the image

2. Choose Page Setup from the bottom left of the Print Module to configure your paper size and choose your printer. We select our Epson Stylus Pro 3800. Choose your orientation and Scale to 100%. It is a good idea not to scale images in the Page Setup Dialog.

FIG 13.23
Page Setup

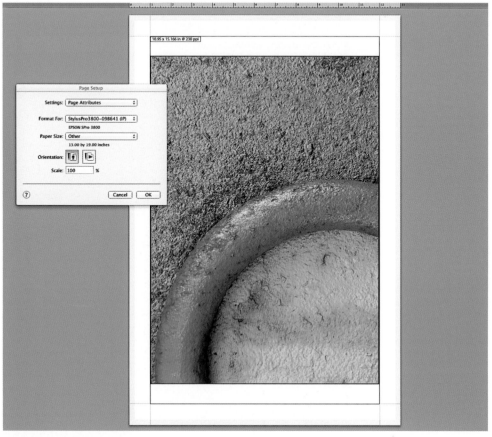

FIG 13.24
Choosing Printer and Paper Size from Page Setup Menu.

3. We use Image Settings and Layout to create a 2-point black border and 1 inch margins all around the image.

Single Image / Contact Sheet
Picture Package
Custom Package

Image Settings ▼

☐ Zoom to Fill
☑ Rotate to Fit
☐ Repeat One Photo per Page

☑ Stroke Border
    Width ———▲———————————— 2.0 pt

Layout ▼

Ruler Units :   Inches ⬍

Margins
    Left ——▲———————————— 1.00 in
    Right ——▲———————————— 1.00 in
    Top ——▲———————————— 1.00 in
    Bottom ——▲———————————— 1.00 in

Page Grid
    Rows ▲———————————————— 1
    Columns ▲———————————————— 1

Cell Spacing
    Vertical ═══════════════════ 0.00 in
    Horizontal ═══════════════════ 0.00 in

Cell Size
    Height ════════════════▲═ 17.00 in
    Width ═════════════════▲ 10.95 in
    ☐ Keep Square

FIG 13.25
We set Stroke Border to
2 and margins to 1 in.

4. In order to determine the ideal resolution for printing on
Exhibition Fiber paper to the Epson printer, we want to
output at the native resolution. By checking Dimensions in
the Guides Panel and unchecking Print Resolution in the Print
Job Panel, we see that the output will be 230 ppi.

FIG 13.26
Resolution is unchecked and Dimension is checked and we can see that the native resolution will be 230ppi.

5. Now comes the confusing part for many photographers, how to handle color management and how to handle the Print Job Panel?

There are two choices when it comes to Color Management. You can use a custom printer profile and have *Lightroom* manage the color, or turn over the color management to your printer. D-65 chooses Application Color Management, which means that *Lightroom* manages the color, doing the conversions and handling the information off to the print driver.

First, you must turn off color management in the print driver. **Set Color Settings to Off (No Color Adjustment).** This option is the single most important one and also the one that causes the most confusion.

To utilize Application Color Management, you need an ICC profile associated with a particular paper/ink combination. You can download excellent profiles from many printer and paper companies. Epson has excellent free profiles on their website.

Color Mode
Off. No Color
Adjustment

FIG 13.27
Color Mode Off No
Color Management

6. In In the Printer Settings Dialog Box (**Figure 13.27**), first choose the Media Type that matches your paper. We choose Exhibition Fiber Paper.

7. **Print Quality:** We choose 1440 in part because it saves a substantial amount of ink. 2880 versus 1440 is debatable, as it is impossible to see the difference at a normal viewing distance. For the best quality print, it's usually better to leave High Speed off while choosing Finest Detail if it is available.

Adding Custom Printer Profiles

To add custom printer profiles, place the profile in your computer's Colorsync (Mac) or Color (PC) folder. On the Mac, place the ICC profile in the Colorsync folder in the main Library folder. In Windows, navigate to the Color folder in C:\Windows\

System32\Spool\Drivers" and drop the ICC profile into the "Color" folder. After placing the new profile in the folder, restart *Lightroom* and under Color Management/Profile toggle to Other. Your profile list will appear.

Printer Manages Color

We don't recommend it, but if you don't have profiles, you have no choice except to select Printer Manages Color. The print driver runs the show, and there can be many OS issues associated when printing this way, as drivers are not always up to date with the OS. The critical thing here is to select Colorsync (Mac) or ICM Color Management (PC) as a Color Correction option. Even with these options, you may still have difficulty getting a print to look exactly the way you expect.

8. To choose the paper profile, click on Other next to Color Management and select the paper profile for the 3800 using Epson Exhibition Fiber. We already had it loaded, but if it wasn't preloaded, you would simply select the appropriate profile from Other.

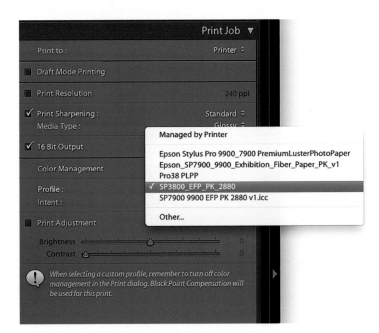

FIG 13.28
We have selected standard sharpening and glossy for the Media Type and we have selected our profile SP3800_EFP_PK_2880

9. The Media Type is Glossy and we are going to output in 16-bit mode which is possible with Mac OS X 10.7. The rendering intent for this image is set to Perceptual as we have strong saturated color.

10. The last series of steps are the most confusing of all. You can choose either Print Settings or Print.

Print Settings will allow you to save the settings while Print offers the same settings but does not allow you to save.

D-65 suggests choosing Print Settings so that you can save these final steps to use over again.

FIG 13.29
We have selected Print Settings to save the settings

11. Click the Save button when all the options are set correctly. This will ensure that the settings are stored and ready for creating a Print Template.

12. We are almost home free. Select Print One or Print from the lower right-hand panel of the Print Module. We choose to select Print One as long as we are only printing one print. If you select Print, you first get the print dialog box and will have to choose Print on the lower right of the module.

FIG 13.30
Print One

13. Go check the printer and see the results. In **Figure 13.31** we have a print in front of the screen after following the steps above, and it is pretty darn good. If for some reason your print is dark you can use the Print Adjustment sliders for Brightness and Contrast to fine tune the print. With proper color management this step should not be needed.

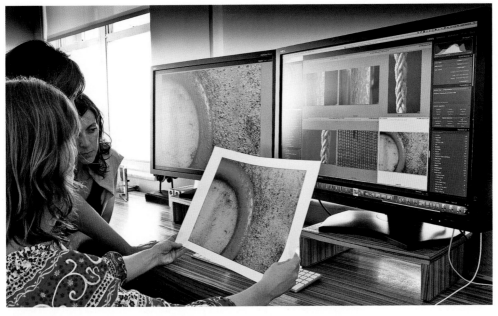

FIG 13.31
The Print is almost identical to the image on screen

14. We We will probably use these exact settings again in the future, so let's create a custom template.

    Choose the + sign next to the Template Browser on the left-hand side of the Print Module. Name the New Template and choose Create.

    Now the next time we want to print with Exhibition Fiber at 13x19 on the Epson 3800 all we need to do is select the image and the saved template and hit Print.

    This just rocks!

SUMMARY

Lightroom really makes printing a breeze with all the features in the Print Module. *Lightroom* can place multiple size images on a single page and have multiple pages of multiple picture layouts.

Draft mode printing renders from the Previews, enabling speedy prints. Another plus is the ability to print straight to JPEG and to attach a profile.

You can produce print packages for a client and allow the client to print their own photos at their local lab. You can also print more than one image at a time. In fact, you can actually send your entire catalog to the printer, or print just one image at a time.

There are pre-configured presets that provide many options including contact sheets. You can also create your own custom presets and save them for future use.

Best of all is the ability to render the file at the native resolution. Just as in the Slideshow, Book and Web Modules, the left panel contains templates of page layouts and collections and the right panel contains all the options and controls for each layout.

THE WEB MODULE

Lightroom's Web Module allows you to create web galleries directly from RAW images with very little effort and no knowledge of programming. The galleries can be previewed in *Lightroom*, exported to a folder or uploaded to a website. There are a wide variety of templates to choose from or you can create your own using Flash or HTML. There is also an array of third party templates available on the web.

The Web Module is designed to be very similar to the Book, Print and Slideshow Modules, with templates and collections on the left-hand panels, and features on the right-hand panels. Web Galleries are an excellent way for clients to view your images and you can use your tweaked RAW files to create a gallery for a fast streamlined workflow.

Web Module Features

You can add an Identity Plate with a web link and an e-mail address. You can also choose from a wide array of metadata to display or even create custom tokens of almost any metadata available in *Lightroom*. You can even apply output sharpening to keep the images crisp even when they are small in size on the web. There is also a very cool built in FTP function, allowing you to upload your web gallery directly to your web site.

NEW New in *Lightroom 4* **The default flash gallery has been rewritten to use color management in supported browsers.**

FIG 14.1
The Web Module Features.

Creating a Web Gallery

A web photo gallery can be created by selecting images in the Library Grid Model or from a Collection that is available inside the Web Module. Let's build a Web Gallery and discuss the available features along the way.

1. Choose your selection of images that you want to use to create your web gallery from the Library Module or the Collections Panel in the Web Module. You can choose which images to use: all, selected or flagged. This is the same procedure used for the Slideshow, Book and Print Modules. For this demonstration, we have selected 40 images from a Collection called Antarctica 2011.

FIG 14.2
We have chosen to use all 40 photos from the filmstrip from a collection called Antarctica 2011.

Template Browser and Preview Panels

On the top left-hand side of the Web Module is a Template Browser and a Preview Panel to see what the templates look like. The Template Browser provides two distinct methods of Web Gallery displays. You can choose a traditional HTML style with thumbnails on a main page and enlarged images on individual pages or a Flash Gallery with features like Autoplay.

HTML Galleries use static XHTML, CSS and Javascript. A user can customize these galleries as they contain standard HTML components. The Flash templates are totally cool and offer some of the unique technology of flash directly to the user inside of *Lightroom*.

We have chosen the default HTML gallery for this demonstration.

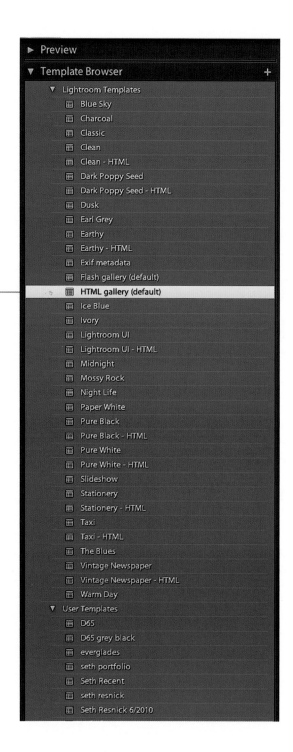

Rollover style preset and custom previews

FIG 14.3
Template Browser.
We select the
Default HTML gallery
to start customizing.

Layout Style

Layout Style is on the top right-hand side of the Web Gallery Module. The Layout Style provides *Lightroom* users with some very interesting third party template and custom options. Although we are going to build our gallery with HTML, we want to show you a few other options available in the Engine.

FIG 14.4
Web Gallery
Layout Style

Figures 14.5 through **14.7** show some of the possibilities from third party vendors for producing web templates.

FIG 14.5

FIG 14.6

FIG 14.7

Site Info Panel

The Site Info Panel offers controls for:

- **Site Title:** Your Name

- **Collection Title:** Your Job Name

- **Collection Description:** What you shot. For example, "Images shot in Antarctica for Client XYZ"

- **Contact Info:** Your E-mail Address

- **Web or Mail Link:** http://www.yourwebsite.com

- **Identity Plate:** You can add your identity Plate or Logo with a link to your website. Click on the drop-down menu next to identity plate to create a new one, or use what you have already setup in *Lightroom*. Under Web or Mail Link, put in your website. This creates a link on the logo or identity plate.

2. The next step in producing our web gallery is to fill out the Site Info Panel located on the top right-hand side of the Web Module.

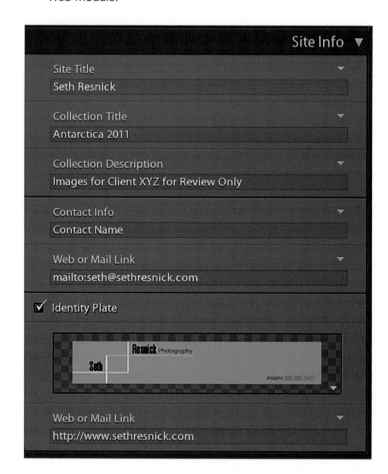

FIG 14.8
The Site Info Panel in the Web Module

Color Palette Panel

The next Panel is the Color Palette. You can choose colors for a variety of options. Choose colors that are different for Text and Detail Text. Detail Matte is the area around the image when it is enlarged, so you might like to create a frame around the image with a different color. Rollover is when you scroll over the images on the index page. The Grid Lines and Colors are also for the index page.

3. We chose black for our Background, dark gray for our Rollovers. We chose gray from our logo for Cells and an off white for our Text.

FIG 14.9
Color Palette Panel in the Web Module

FIG 14.10
Sampling color for Cells from Logo

Appearance Panel

The Appearance Panel is where you choose how many rows, and columns you want, the size of the images on the page, and whether you want a border around the images. You can also choose to display a cell number for each image and section borders too (the dotted lines above and below the cells) and whether there is a drop shadow on the background from the image.

4. We choose no drop shadow, a light border defining each section of the gallery, an 8 column wide gallery, a border around each image of 70 pixels and an image size of 800 pixels.

FIG 14.11
Appearance Panel in
Web Module

Image Info Panel

Image Info allows you to decide what metadata you want to display with the images. The Title and Caption can be applied by simply checking the box next to each option. Additional metadata can be displayed by clicking on the drop-down menus.

5. We have chosen to use Title and Caption and to apply customized metadata for Filename. For this to work, the images need to contain title and caption metadata. This is the same for the Print and Slideshow Modules as well. Customized information can be edited and saved in the drop down menu.

FIG 14.12
Image Info Panel in
Web Module

FIG 14.13
Creating Custom
Metadata for the
Image Info Panel

Output Settings Panel

The next choice to make is for Output Settings. You can select the Quality for the JPG output and the degree of Output Sharpening needed for the web gallery. The sharpening algorithms are based upon Pixel Genius PhotoKit Sharpener and make a major difference in how the images will look on the web. Lastly, you can choose to show a copyright watermark as well as other metadata.

6. We have chosen to render our images at a JPG quality of 70, show all metadata, apply a copyright watermark and apply standard sharpening for web output. The copyright info is being extracted from the IPTC metadata and will add your copyright to the image as an overlay. We always choose to check this box.

FIG 14.14
Output Settings Panel
In Web Module

Upload Settings

You can configure your Upload Settings so that you can accomplish an FTP transfer directly from *Lightroom* to your website.

FIG 14.15
Upload Settings Panel
in Web Module

There is a drop-down menu on the right of the panel so that you can put in your username and password for the FTP transfer and save the settings as a preset.

FIG 14.16
Custom settings for FTP
Transfer can be saved
as a preset

We filled out all of our FTP information and saved it as a New Preset.

Export / Upload

On the bottom right of the Web Module there is a choice to Export or Upload. Upload initiates the FTP transfer settings set up in Upload Settings. Export will export the web gallery files to a folder and location of your choice for offline viewing, or upload the gallery at a later time using FTP software such as Transmit or Fetch. One word of caution: for FTP, the gallery is always INDEX.HTML, so unless you have a subfolder selected, it might overwrite an existing INDEX.HTML. The subfolder gets created automatically if it isn't there or you can just be careful about to which directory you upload.

FIG 14.17
Export and
Upload button

Preview

Before Exporting or Uploading, you can preview your web gallery in the default browser.

7. Choose Preview in Browser on the lower left-hand corner of the Web Module to view your web gallery.

FIG 14.18
Preview in Browser

So let's take a look at what our gallery looks like in our default browser, which in our case is Safari. **Figure 14.19** shows the index page and **Figure 14.20** shows an image page. If we wanted to keep this as a template to use in the future, we could save it by clicking on + sign to the right of the Template Browser or we could save the web gallery with the images by choosing Create Saved Web Gallery **Figure 14.21**.

FIG 14.19
Index Page for our web gallery

FIG 14.20
Preview in Browser with an image page

In *Lightroom 4,* collections no longer store output module settings. For this demo, when we first entered the Web Module we were viewing "Unsaved Web Gallery". Now that we are finished with our gallery if we want to save it we select Create Saved Web Gallery.

FIG 14.21
Create Saved
Web Gallery

You can also create your own customized Layout Style and save it in *Lightroom* to give your web galleries a complete customized look and feel.

FIG 14.22
Customized Layout
Style web gallery

SUMMARY

Lightroom's Web Module allows you to create web galleries directly from RAW images with very little effort and no knowledge of programming. The galleries can be previewed in *Lightroom* or exported to a folder.

There are a wide variety of templates to choose from or you can create your own using Flash or HTML. There is also an array of third party templates available on the web.

Lightroom adds many features and controls along with a very cool built in FTP function, allowing you to upload your web gallery directly to your web site.

Web Galleries are an excellent way for clients to view your images and you can use your tweaked RAW files to create a gallery for a fast streamlined workflow.

CHAPTER 15
D-65'S *LIGHTROOM* WORKFLOW

Now that we have reviewed all of *Lightroom's* Modules and concepts, it's time to put *Lightroom* into action and tie it all together to achieve efficient digital workflow. This chapter covers the D-65 *Lightroom* Workflow. This is where all of your organization and digital asset management system begins.

With D-65's workflow, all of your files are imported, renamed, keyworded, captioned, ranked, processed, and exported in a systematic, standardized methodology adaptable to any photographer's needs. With this system, you will manage your workflow efficiently, effectively and effortlessly, allowing you more time behind the camera and less time behind the computer.

Before we begin with our workflow and importing our files, it is important how we are going to name files and folders so they can be found in a hierarchical, industry-standard fashion.

File Naming Standards

Digital photography has increased the importance of naming conventions because the digital camera creates the initial name assigned to a file. That's convenient, but these file names, such as "UY74O822," are cryptic and random.

The solution to this problem is for every photographer to develop a naming convention, based on standards, and use it consistently to name your files. This will give you a standardized nomenclature that will help you categorize, organize, and later locate your images. A good file naming system will not only ensure consistency, but will also form the backbone of the file retrieval process.

To create a file-naming system, you need to essentially generate your own secret code. Now, this code does not have to be worthy of an über-geek award. In fact, it doesn't have to involve anything more complicated than giving each image a sequential number or a descriptive name. It may even include IPTC (descriptive information about the image) or EXIF (technical data taken from the camera) data as well as other information of your choosing.

Adhering To Standards

There are some basic rules to follow when it comes to naming files. First, all file names should be limited to a total character length of 31, including the file type extension. Second, all file names must include the correct three-letter file type extension. Examples of file type extensions are JPG, TIF, DNG, PSD and PDF.

To address cross-platform usability, file names should not contain special characters or symbols other than underscore "_" or hyphen "-". In fact, it is best to avoid punctuation characters in file names altogether because some characters are reserved for use only by the operating system. It is wise to use only lower-case characters because some operating systems, such as UNIX, are case-sensitive.

Once you have a system in place, it should meet these technical guidelines and still provide enough information about the image so you do not have to open the file to identify the image. The file name should give you everything you need to know. Searching on a file name should yield results.

Finding a Simple Solution

Yes, naming a file is important, but doing so correctly is also crucial—and is all too often overlooked by many photographers. Some use relatively generic names, such as "cat1.JPG," but these make it difficult to locate files later. Others simply ignore naming conventions, increasing the risk that the files will not be readable on other computers.

Again, the file-naming convention you come up with needs to address two separate issues: one, a naming system that works for you, and that you can use on the fly—ideally, file naming should be done at the time of capture, not later on; and, two, adherence to certain known standards that will ensure the file names remain intact across a variety of platforms and systems.

The Right Name

Files should be named using a convention that provides accurate information about each file and why it was created. A naming system based on the date you capture the image and a series of letters defining the file is a great place to start. With such a system, you can address criteria such as high-resolution files, layered files, or when they were published.

We will be using images in this tutorial shot in Dallas on January 26, 2012. In this case, the file name would be:

20120126_dallas_0001.cr2

- "20120126" defines the date, as in January 26, 2012—because computers arrange files in a hierarchical fashion, this system ensures that every file will be organized chronologically

- "dallas" defines the actual subject in our naming convention

- "0001" defines the sequential image number

- ".cr2" defines the type of file, in this case, Canon's RAW file format

Your exported images will have the same filename, with a different extension. Using this basic formula, you can add in other components to your file name, which can further help you describe the image files and job. Some additional examples follow:

- 20120126_dallas_0001.tif: This is the exported file as a TIFF.

- 20120126_dallas_bw_0001.cr2: This is a variation of the file in black and white.

Organization in the Library Module Folders Panel

To start, D-65 organizes the Lightroom_Library hard drive with folders of images with the same file naming convention; by the year, month, day and subject name, such as 20120126_dallas. Because we shoot so many "jobs" or subjects each year, the scrolling list in the folders panel would become unruly. For that reason, we create Parent Year folders to nest all of our jobs for that year (see Figure 15.1). We also name our images with the same file naming convention as described above.

The steps for creating parent folders in the Folder Panel follow.

1. Go to the Folders Panel in the Library Module.

FIG 15.1

2. Click on the + sign. Choose Add folder. Make sure Folder Name Only is also selected

FIG 15.2

3. Navigate to the Lightroom_Library Hard drive.

4. Select New Folder from bottom left.

FIG 15.3

5. Name the Folder (in the above example we called it 2012, because we already have a 2011 folder).

6. Click on Create.

7. Click on Choose on the lower right.

8. You should now have a new folder called 2011 in your Folders Panel.

D-65 suggests creating parent folder for all the years of images that you will be importing into *Lightroom*. It totally aids in organization.

D-65's Workflow

For this tutorial, we are going to start with a flash memory card with images from a shoot. D-65 always advocates shooting in the RAW format, but this workflow works with JPEGs, too. These RAW files will be:

1. Downloaded from the memory card and imported in *Lightroom*

2. Edited and ranked

3. Metadata and Keywords applied

4. Renamed

5. Color corrected and "tweaked"

6. Shown to client via Web Gallery, PDF Contact Sheet or Slideshow

7. Exported (if necessary) into the type of files we need for our job

8. Organized into a job folder for archiving

As we go through this tutorial, each major step of the workflow is colored **RED**.

First, make sure that *Lightroom's* preferences are set up correctly and that you have created a Lightroom_Catalog, and a Lightroom_Library to store images in your desired location (refer to Chapters 5 and 6).

| STEP 1: IMPORTING IMAGES INTO *LIGHTROOM*

There are several ways to import images into *Lightroom*. Images can be imported in the following ways:

• New images directly from a memory card

• Existing images on your computer

- Existing images on external media such as a hard drive, CD or DVD

- Tethered from a camera

While all methods work well with *Lightroom*, each requires different import setup. The D-65 Workflow outlined below is specifically for shooting RAW files and importing from a flash memory card into *Lightroom*.

When you insert a memory card into a card reader, an icon of the card will appear on your desktop and *Lightroom* will automatically open the Import dialog box (below). (*Lightroom* may not automatically launch an import dialog when a memory card is attached to a Windows Vista computer. Please select the Import button in the Library and select the attached card reader to begin the import.)

1. Open *Lightroom*. Load your memory card into your card reader and wait for Import to pop up.

Icon of the card on your desktop

EOS_DIGITAL

FIG 15.4
Memory card
on desktop.

Figure 15.5 displays the Import Dialog in expanded view.

FIG 15.5
Import Dialog in Expanded View

FIG 15.6 displays the Dialog in Compact View. To change between Expanded and Compact View, click on the arrow on the bottom left-hand corner of Import. When the arrow points up, you are in Expanded View. When the arrow points down, you are in Compact View. D-65 prefers using the Expanded View in our workflow.

FIG 15.6
Import Dialog in Compact View

I SOURCE PANEL

Let's go through the Import window in Expanded View. The Source Panel allows you to browse your hard drives and devices that are available on your computer or network.

The top left corner, above the Source Panel displays your primary source, from which you have chosen to import. When you load a card into a card reader, *Lightroom* will automatically load that card as your source. (As long as the preference has been setup—refer to Chapter 5).

D-65 checks "Eject after import" in the Source panel, so that our card is automatically ejected from the desktop after the images have been imported.

FIG 15.7

D-65'S LIGHTROOM WORKFLOW

2. In most cases, your source (card) will be selected automatically. If not, choose your source from the Source Panel.

Now, we will move across the top of Import. Once you have chosen what you'd like to import, you have four choices how to handle your files:

- **Copy as DNG:** Convert to DNG in a new location and add to catalog

- **Copy:** Copy photos to a new location and add to catalog

- **Move:** Move photos to a new location and add to catalog

- **Add:** Add photos to catalog without moving them

D-65 firmly believes that DNG will prevail and become the adopted universal RAW format, but it is not yet universal with all software manufacturers. For this reason, D-65 still believes in keeping the original proprietary RAW file from the camera manufacturer along with a DNG copy after the tweaks have been applied to the RAW files. We want our DNG to have the same information as our proprietary RAW files, which is why we create them after we are done working on them in *Lightroom*.

To accomplish this, D-65 chooses Copy, and this will copy our photos from the card to a new location, our Lightroom_Library hard drive, and add them to the catalog. Further down the line in our workflow we will make DNGs and save them in our archive.

3. Choose an option of how you would like to handle your import.

All Photos | New Photos | Destination Folders

FIG 15.8

I DESTINATION PANEL

Now, from the Destination Panel in Import, we have to choose the destination, our 2010 folder within our Lightroom_Library hard drive.

4. Choose Choose the location you are copying TO.

5. Go to the Destination Panel.

6. Check "Into Subfolder" and name your subfolder with your subject or job name, such as 20120126_dallas. It is important to hit return or enter after you create the name.

TIP:
You can see the year, month and day that the images were shot by hovering over the image with your mouse (Figure 15.9).

FIG 15.9
Hover the mouse over an image to see the year, month and day it was shot.

_MG_6303.CR2 | _MG_6304.CR2 | _MG_6305.CR2 | _MG_6306.CR2

_MG_6304.CR2
1/26/12 5:54:46 PM
22 MB

7. Organize: Choose "Into one folder."

8. Highlight or select your Lightroom_Library hard drive from the list of devices located in the Destination Panel.

9. Then select the 2012 folder, or whatever parent folder you wish to import into. If you do not use parent folders, then select the Lightroom_Library drive.

FIG 15.10

I FILE HANDLING PANEL

10. Open the File Handling Panel (**Figure 13.11**).

FIG 15.11

11. Render Previews: Choose 1:1 from the drop-down menu (refer to Chapter 5 – Catalog Settings for more information on Preview size).

12. Check "Don't Import Suspected Duplicates."

13. Check "Make a Second Copy To."

D-65 always recommends backing up to a secondary location. We suggest an external hard drive or a second internal drive (if you have one) for your backup. If you do have an external drive to dedicate for this import backup, choose it now.

D-65 has a dedicated drive that we call Import_Backup (**Figure 15.11**). This backup is a "Murphy's Law" backup. It is a copy of what is on the card and it won't have everything that you have chosen on import. It is purely a second copy of the structure of the card only to be used in the event of an emergency. After a shot is complete and archived D-65 reformats the Import_Backup drive in order to get it ready for the next shoot.

Import_Backup

FIG 15.12

| FILE RENAMING PANEL

D-65 renames our images on import with the same file naming convention that we use for the folders holding the images. *Lightroom* comes with a number of presets for renaming your images. To make the workflow really flow, we are going to create our own custom File Naming Preset. This preset will name our files with a naming convention consisting of yyyymmdd_subject_sequence#(0001).cr2 (the 3 letter file type extension). This will allow you to batch-rename your files, giving them a meaningful name for easy retrieval from an archive. Our demonstration images are from a shoot in Dallas that took place on January 26, 2012. Hence we are renaming the proprietary RAW files in the following way:

2000126_dallas_0001.cr2

Creating a File Naming Preset

To create our File Naming preset, follow the steps listed below.

1. From the File Renaming panel, go to the drop- down menu next to Template and choose Edit

FIG 15.13

2. The Filename Template Editor window will pop up. The default in the example window is Filename.

3. Delete the token Filename in the example window by clicking on it, and hitting the Delete key. Now you are starting with a clean template. (A token is the term for the field you are inserting or deleting in this window)

4. Go to the fourth window down, Additional, and choose YYYYMMDD from the drop-down menu and click on Insert. Your first token will contain the year, month and day the image was shot. *Lightroom* extracts this information from the metadata coming from the camera, so make sure your date/time is correct in the camera.

5. Your cursor should now be in the Example window after the newly inserted date token. Manually type in an underscore after the first token. This will separate the tokens we will be stringing together.

6. Go down to Custom, and click on Insert to the right of Custom Text. This will insert Custom Text as your next token.

7. Again, manually type in an underscore next to Custom Text to separate the tokens in the example window.

8. Go down to Numbering and from the third drop-down menu, Sequence, choose: Sequence #(0001) and click on Insert. This is your final token to insert, but do not click on Done yet.

Filename Template Editor

Preset: [Custom ▾]

Example: 20120205_untitled_0001.cr2

[(Date (YYYYMMDD) ▾) _ (Custom Text) _ (Sequence # (0001) ▾)]

Image Name

[Filename ▾] [Insert]

Numbering

[Import # (1) ▾] [Insert]

[Image # (1) ▾] [Insert]

[Sequence # (0001) ▾] [Insert]

Additional

[Date (YYYYMMDD) ▾] [Insert]

[Dimensions ▾] [Insert]

Custom

Shoot Name [Insert]

Custom Text [Insert]

[Cancel] [Done]

FIG 15.14

9. Now we will save this as a Preset, so we can use it over and over again. To save the preset, go to the drop-down menu at the top of the window, under Preset, and choose Save Current Settings as New Preset.

Filename Template Editor

Prese ✓ Custom

Exampl

Date
Sequ

bookimport
Custom Name (x of y)
Custom Name – Original File Number
Custom Name – Sequence
Custom Name
Date – Filename
Filename – Sequence
Filename
Preserve Filename
Session Name – Sequence
Shoot Name – Original File Number
Shoot Name – Sequence

Image N:

Numberi

Save Current Settings as New Preset...
Restore Default Presets

Additional

| Date (YYYYMMDD) | ⬍ | Insert |
| Dimensions | ⬍ | Insert |

Custom

| Shoot Name | Insert |
| Custom Text | Insert |

Cancel   Done

FIG 15.15

10. Name the preset yymmdd_subject_0001.ext (This describes how exactly your file will be named) and choose Create.

FIG 15.16

11. Now choose Done in the Filename Template Editor window.

12. You will automatically be back in Import in the File Renaming Panel. You can apply this File Naming Preset to your images from the Template drop-down menu by choosing yyyymmdd_subject_0001.ext. Next to Custom Text, type in your subject or job name. In our example below, we typed in dallas.

13. Our Start Number is 1, since this is the first image of our shoot.

FIG 15.17

The cool part of saving a File Naming Preset is that it can be used over and over again every time you shoot. The only thing that will ever need to be edited is the actual subject name under Custom Text and possibly the Start Number.

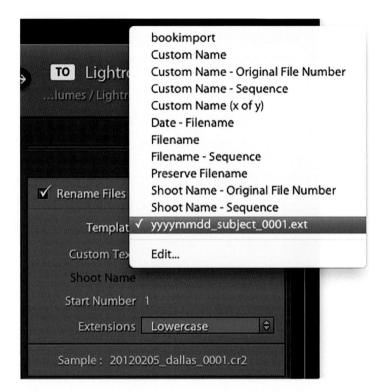

FIG 15.18
File naming template
saved for use each time
there is an import.

I APPLY DURING IMPORT PANEL

Develop Settings

You can further increase your workflow efficiency by applying
Develop Presets to images on import. *Lightroom* comes with
many Develop Presets and you can also create your own. D-65
has created a Develop Preset that we like to apply to all images
on import. The setting adjusts vibrance, saturation, clarity,
sharpening and a camera calibration to simulate the look of
Kodachrome film. We created this Custom Preset in the Develop
Module (see Chapter 8). Depending upon your needs as a
photographer, you may or may not apply a Develop Setting on
import from the drop down menu.

14. Choose to apply a Develop Setting or not at this time.

FIG 15.19
Applying a Develop
Preset on import.

Metadata

D-65 creates a basic Metadata Preset with our copyright and
contact information. We apply this preset on import to all of our
images (see Chapter 7 for steps on creating a Metadata Preset).
We add further metadata using the Metadata Panel in the Library
module to add specific information on each job.

What is Metadata?

Metadata is a set of standardized information about a photo,
such as the author's name, resolution, color space, copyright,
and keywords applied to it. For example, most digital cameras
attach some basic information about a file, such as height, width,
file format, and the time the image was taken.

Lightroom supports the information standard developed by the
International Press Telecommunications Council (IPTC) to identify
transmitted text and images. This standard includes entries for
descriptions, keywords, categories, credits, and origins, gps and
more. You can use metadata to streamline your workflow and
organize your files.

File information is stored using the Extensible Metadata Platform
(XMP) standard. XMP is built on XML. In the case of *camera RAW*
files that have a proprietary file format, XMP isn't written into the
original files. To avoid file corruption, XMP metadata is stored
in a separate file called a sidecar file. For all other file formats
supported by *Lightroom* (JPEG, TIFF, PSD, and DNG), XMP
metadata is written into the files in the location specified for that
data. XMP facilitates the exchange of metadata between Adobe
applications and across publishing workflows. For example, you

can save metadata from one file as a template, and then import the metadata into other files.

Metadata that is stored in other formats, such as EXIF, IPTC (IIM), and TIFF is synchronized and described with XMP so that it can be more easily viewed and managed.

Applying Metadata Preset

In our workflow, we create a basic copyright preset that we apply to all our imported images. (refer to Chapter 7 for the steps on creating this Metadata Preset). If you already have a metadata preset created, you can choose to apply it at this time from the drop-down menu, or choose New from the drop-down menu to create a new preset.

15. If you do create a new preset at this time, after you save it, you will automatically be placed back in Import in the Apply During Import Panel, and you can apply this new Metadata Preset to your images. From the Metadata drop-down menu, choose 2012_copyright.

FIG 15.20
Applying a Metadata
Preset on import.

Keywords

Lightroom gives you the ability to apply a set of keywords to your images upon import. Depending on the circumstances of your shoot, you may want to do this for all images, do it selectively at a later date, or both. We find it easier to use the Keyword Panel in the Library Module and add keywords after the images are imported. If you are going to add keywords, add only global keywords at this point. Keywording can be reviewed in Chapter 7.

16. Add keywords if you would like at this point.

FIG 15.21
Applying global keywords on import.

Import Bottom Toolbar

On the bottom of Import, all the way to the left is the compact/expanded view arrow. The text to the right of the arrow illustrates the number of images you are importing and the size of the import.

There is also a button for Grid Mode or Loupe Mode, and a checkmark to check all images for import or uncheck all images for import. You can sort with different options in the drop-down menu, as well as set the size of the thumbnails with the Thumbnail Slider.

In the center of the screen at the bottom is an Import Preset tab where you can create or select import presets that you have setup.

D-65 always imports our images to a new folder specific for that subject/job, so we do not use Import Presets. On the bottom right are the Import and Cancel buttons.

17. Click Import to import your images or cancel if you don't want to go through with the Import.

FIG 15.22
Import or Cancel
buttons are at the
bottom right of the
Import Module.

Import

After completing all of the above steps, you are now ready to import your files into *Lightroom*.

1. Click on import on the lower right of the Import Photos Dialog Box. The files will be imported into *Lightroom* and start to render one by one. We choose 1:1 previews as discussed in Chapter Five. You can monitor the import progress via the activity viewer in the top left-hand corner of the Library Module.

FIG 15.23
Images importing into
the Library Module.

FIG 15.24
After Import Previews
are rendered

2. Now that you are in the Library Module, notice that your Previous Import is selected under the Catalog Panel (top left-hand side). Navigate to the Folders Panel. Make sure you select (highlight) the folder of images you are importing. This assures that you are working on the correct folder.

FIG 15.25
Images in designated folder in Library Module.

I STEP 2: EDITING

The next step in our workflow is to edit. Editing and ranking works in much the same way that a film-based photographer works on a light table.

Checking Focus

First, we go to the Secondary Window button and take advantage of using multiple monitors. Then we click on an image and go to full screen. We then use the Tab key and Shift-Tab key combination to expand our view and collapse the panels. Using the arrow keys, we start moving through the images. We use the Navigator Tool with an appropriate zoom level to move through each image and check focus.

Rating Images

After checking focus, a photographer typically threw rejects in the trash, used a star or dot to mark a select, two stars to mark second tier selects and three stars to mark and cull "keepers." We can do exactly this within *Lightroom*.

We can add and remove stars from an image using the number keys 1 thru 5. We can also add color labels by using the numbers 6 through 9. We can rate and color label by using the Photo Menu and then choosing Set Rating, Set Color Label or Set Flag. Additionally, we can select an image in *Lightroom* and manually add or subtract stars by clicking on the dots immediately below the thumbnail. In essence, there are a number ways to rate and color label your images. These rankings and color labels will stay with the image, in its metadata, even after you process the files.

FIG 15.26
Using dual monitors and rating images.

Rating Shortcuts

- You can use the] key to increase the rating and the [key to lower the rating; Command Z will undo a rating

- Having CAPS LOCK on while you are rating images automatically moves to the next image after you rate the first image

- You can also Set a Flag as a Pick, instead of rating and color labeling: for our workflow, we stick with ratings and color labels

Deleting Images

You can delete images in *Lightroom* in two ways:

- Hitting the delete key when an image is selected in the Grid View to delete images one by one

- Using the X key on an image to Flag as Rejected: after you are done editing the entire shoot and hitting the X key on all images you want to delete, go to the Photo Menu and choose Delete Rejected Photos

FIG 15.27
Delete Rejected Photos Option.

FIG 15.28
After you choose to Delete Rejected Photos, the images marked as rejected will be filtered automatically, so you can see what you are deleting before you do it.

D-65 suggests choosing "Delete from Disk," not "Remove from *Lightroom*." We have no use for outtakes in our Lightroom_Library hard drive. They just take up room, and can't be seen in *Lightroom* once they are deleted from the catalog.

1. Rank and edit your images.

2. Rotate images if needed.

3. Delete your outtakes.

I STEP 3: ADD KEYWORDS AND ADDITIONAL METADATA

After we edit, we add keywords and additional metadata to all of our images. We start by adding global keywords and metadata if we didn't apply any on import, and then local keywords and metadata on smaller groups and individual images (see Chapter 7).

TIP: D-65 has created a keyword list of over 6000 keywords in a hierarchical order to allow you to easily keyword your images in Lightroom. To purchase the keyword list, go to http://www.D65.com.

FIG 15.29
Use the Keywording, Keyword List and Metadata Panels to add information to your images.

I STEP 4: RENAME YOUR IMAGES

Before we move into the Develop Module, we will rename our images since we have deleted some in our editing process. While this is not critical, you may like your images numbered sequentially. Images also may have been shot over multiple days, so you may want to begin each day with 000. If you want to rename , you can rename (renumber) your images now.

1.   Select all images or images by date

2.   Go to the Library Menu and choose Rename Photo in the drop-down (F2).

FIG 15.30
D-65 suggests renaming your images after editing so that they are in sequential order with gaps.

3. The Rename Photos Dialog Box pops up. Choose the template we just created (yyyymmdd_subject_0001.ext), put in your subject or job name next to Custom Text and make sure the Start Number is 1. Choose OK.

Rename 33 Photos

File Naming: yyyymmdd_subject_0001.ext

Custom Text: dallas   Start Number: 1

Example: 20120128_dallas_0001.cr2   Cancel   OK

FIG 15.31
The Rename Photos window

| STEP 5: APPLY GPS, IF NOT DONE IN CAMERA
(OPTIONAL STEP)

Before we move into the Develop Module, we may want to apply GPS coordinates if not done automatically in camera. Please refer to Chapter Ten. In our demo we will apply a GPS Tracklog recorded with PhotoTrackr and MyTracks.

1. Click on the Map Module.

2. Import GPS Tracklog and apply GPS Coordinates to images.

FIG 15.32
GPS Tracklog applied to images.

| STEP 6: COLOR CORRECTING, "TWEAKING" YOUR
FILES AND SYNCHRONIZING SETTINGS IN
THE DEVELOP MODULE

1. Click on the Develop Module.

2. Move through all of your files in the Develop Module, tweaking and synching.

3. Any additional work that you need to do on a file in *Photoshop* would be done at this time by using Edit in *Photoshop*, and then saving the edited file back into *Lightroom*.

FIG 15.33
Work on your images in the Develop Module, either individually or by synching similar images.

| STEP 7: SAVING THE METADATA TO THE FILES

As mentioned in Chapter 5, there is no Save feature in *Lightroom*. Everything is always saved automatically to the catalog. However, if the catalog were to crash and you didn't have a backup, your data would be at risk. For this reason, just like an insurance plan, D-65 also takes the extra precaution to Save the Metadata to the files. This writes out a sidecar .XMP file for every proprietary RAW file and writes the date directly to the file for JPGS, PSD, TIFFS and DNGS.

1. Go back to the Library Module.

2. Select all your images.

3. Go to the Metadata Menu and choose "Save Metadata to Files."

FIG 15.34
Save the metadata to your files.

| STEP 8: CREATE A WEB GALLERY, BOOK, SLIDESHOW OR PRINTS FOR YOUR FRIENDS, FAMILY OR CLIENT

D-65 would typically prepare a web gallery for the client to see the images and make their selects. D-65 does not send an entire shoot to a client. We prepare the client's selected files for their specific specifications depending upon usage and media. For personal work, we create web galleries to show our friends and family. Now, we also can upload directly to Facebook.

FIG 15.35
Create Web Gallery for Client.

I STEP 9: EXPORTING YOUR FILES AND CREATING A JOB FOLDER

At this point, depending upon what type of photographer you are, and the workflow that you need, you may be done working in *Lightroom*. For example, if you're making exhibition prints using your own printer, then you're all done. Or if you are shooting for yourself, and don't need to deliver files to anyone, you are done too. Everything you need is already saved in *Lightroom,* and you can move onto the next shoot. If you need to deliver files to a client, D-65 continues the workflow described below.

Lightroom is capable of exporting TIFF, PSD, JPEG, and DNG files. This is how *Lightroom* processes files. Whether you need any or all of these files will depend on your specific workflow and your needs as a photographer.

For D-65's workflow, we always create two types of files from our tweaked RAW files:

- DNG (Digital Negative format) for archiving

- JPG in sRGB color space at 72 ppi, and 600 pixels wide for copyright registration and submission to stock agents

   Then, after our client reviews our images from our web gallery, we export the finals that they have selected. The third type of file that we export is:

- Any type of file our client requests on a per job basis. D-65 usually delivers client finals as TIFFs.

Creating a Job Folder

We export from the Library Module. On export, we will create a new job folder on our desktop, or on our hard drive(s) dedicated for our job folders. We use the job folder to organize files for archiving. This folder will be archived on multiple external hard drives, both on-site and off-site. The files are tweaked in *Lightroom*, then exported (processed) into the file type(s) you need for the job. All of these processed files go into a job folder for that specific job. This is all for organization and archiving. Let's explain this concept a bit more:

In the film world, when you returned to the lab to pick up your film, it was given to you in a nicely organized manner. The E-6 slides were in a box, the C-41 negatives were in sleeves and the prints were in glassine envelopes. You then took those chromes or negatives back to the office and filed them away.

We are going to simulate that same concept by creating a job folder for each and every job. The job folder will contain subfolders for all of the different file types and information required for that job; such as DNG, JPG, TIFF, PSD, Invoice, Model Releases, Layouts, etc. The job folder and subfolders will use a naming convention similar to what you used for your image names. For example, for our job in Dallas, we would create a job folder called 20120126_dallas_job. The subfolders we create on Export within this job folder will be:

- 20120126_dallas_dng

- 20120126_dallas_jpg

We always use the year, month and first day of the job with an underscore and then job name for our file naming convention.

We choose to leave the proprietary RAW files from the camera on our hard drive named Lightroom_Library, not in our job folder. Any database will slow down as it accumulates information. *Lightroom* will currently slow down with more than 200,000 files. For this reason, we choose to only keep our RAW files in *Lightroom* and our processed files on external hard drives dedicated to holding just our job folders, outside of the Lightroom_Library hard drive.

Should we need to browse through these job folder hard drives, we would do so using *Lightroom* or *Bridge*.

Let's export some files from our Dallas shoot job into a job folder. For our workflow in this job, we are going to create a set of DNGs, a set of small JPGs for the copyright office, and four full size TIFFs of our client's selects chosen from the web gallery that we had already posted for their review.

| STEPS FOR EXPORT

1. Select all your images in the Library Grid Mode (you don't have to select them all unless you wanted to process them all—this all depends on your workflow).

2. Click on the Export Button (left of the Toolbar).

3. The Export dialog window will open.

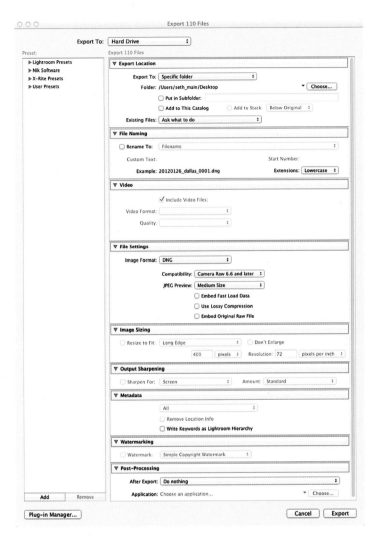

FIG 15.36
Export Dialog before
D-65 setup.

4. **Export Location:** We are choosing to Export To: Specific Folder. Choose your hard drive where your job folders are located (we have a hard drive called 20120101_current_job_folders already dedicated to holding all of our job folders for this year).

FIG 15.37
D-65 exports to a specific job folder.

5. Create a new job folder on that drive by clicking on New Folder.

FIG 15.38
Creating the job folder.

6. Name the folder with the file naming convention for the job. Our job folder name is 20120126_dallas_job.

7. After you name the folder, choose Create.

8. Then click Choose back in the directory window. You will be brought back to the Export Dialog Box.

9. Check Put in Subfolder: give the subfolder the file naming convention for your job and file type you are creating. We will create DNGs for our first type of file for this job. Our subfolder is 20120126_dallas_dng. For our workflow, we do not choose "Add to This Catalog" or "Stack with Original."

FIG 15.39
Export Location setup
to D-65's workflow

10. **Existing Files:** Chose "Ask what to do."

11. **File Naming:** If you wanted to rename your files to a different naming convention for your client's needs, this is where you could do it. D-65 does not check "Rename To:" because we have already renamed our files during our workflow in the Library Module.

FIG 13.40
Lightroom has the ability to Rename your files on Export.

12. **File Settings:** This is where you choose what type of file you will be exporting. After choose the format, you will get different options for each type of Format. Under Format choose "DNG."

New in *Lightroom 4*

DNG Format Enhancements

For those who convert to DNG on import, users can specify a preference to use a new lossy compression (only enabled for ACR 6.6 and later) to generate the DNG from proprietary raw files.

The imported DNG will always keep the same pixel size as the original. This compression can also be applied during the Update DNG Preview and Metadata command.

The new Lossy DNG is an extension of the linear DNG – it's demosaiced and JPEG compression is applied – so it's not the traditional DNG raw DNG that we've all been used to.

NEW

The full resolution lossy DNG files are considerably smaller than their lossless counterpart – a 24mb lossless becomes a 6mb lossy, with minimal loss (but loss nonetheless) of quality and the full flexibility of raw.

This is Adobe's answer to sRAW used by some camera companies. You can also reduce the resolution resulting in an even smaller DNG file. KEEP IN MIND HOWEVER, THAT IT IS LOSSY COMPRESSION so we do not suggest doing this to all your originals. Lossy DNG's are also NOT backwards compatible. *Lightroom 3.6* and ACR 6.6 understand them but most other programs don't yet.

Here is the thought process of why you might want to consider this for your workflow.

You might consider keeping full resolution lossless DNG files on your main computer but working with smaller versions on your laptop when you are on the road. The format has been designed to make their settings interchangeable, so you can make Develop adjustments to a small lossy DNG copy and then apply those same settings to the full resolution originals when returning to the office.

If you usually convert to JPEGs, you could now consider using lossy raw, retaining their editable state. The file sizes are comparable.

Lightroom 4 also includes an option to embed "Fast Load Data. This preference allows compatible programs such as *Lightroom 4* to show you a preview much more quickly than a proprietary raw file or a DNG file without Fast Load data. It's fully backwards compatible, so it won't break other programs.

To update existing DNG files, change it in Preferences and then select all in Grid view and go to Metadata menu > Update DNG Previews & Metadata.

Since we prefer to work on proprietary raw files and archive a DNG we are not going to alter our DNG methodology and watch how all this progresses in the future.

The DNG options that we choose are:

Compatibility: *Camera Raw 6.6* and later (this depends on version of *Photoshop* you have and what version of *Camera Raw* you have installed)

JPEG Preview: Medium Size

▼ File Settings	
Image Format:	DNG ⬍
Compatibility:	Camera Raw 6.6 and later ⬍
JPEG Preview:	Medium Size ⬍
	☐ Embed Fast Load Data
	☐ Use Lossy Compression
	☐ Embed Original Raw File

FIG 15.41

13. **Image Sizing:** This is where you can up-res/down-res and resize your files if needed. Since DNG files are RAW, we cannot check any of these options. We would choose our parameters in this section for any JPGS, PSDS or TIFFS.

14. **Output Sharpening:** *Lightroom* allows output sharpening for Screen or Print, using algorithms based on Pixel Genius's Photokit Sharpener. Since we are creating DNGs, there is no output sharpening, but we would use this feature for other processed files.

15. **Metadata:** There are two choices under Metadata. You can minimize the embedded Metadata (which only includes the copyright and which D-65 does not recommend), or you can choose "Write Keywords as *Lightroom* Hierarchy." D-65 does not choose either of these options. If you have private metadata, it will be revealed in the *Lightroom* hierarchy.

16. **Watermarking:** We do not choose "Add Copyright Watermarks" on our files, but it is a great idea for proofs for wedding photographers, and works great in *Lightroom*.

17. **Post Processing:** We might or might not do any post processing from export depending upon the job. Refer to Chapter 16 for more information on Post Processing on Export.

18. Click on Export. Your RAW files will be converted to DNG and wind up in a DNG subfolder of the job folder in your job folder hard drive.

FIG 15.42

We will repeat this same Export step for JPGs (or whatever type of file you may need for the job). *Lightroom* can export more than one file type at the same time. You do not have to wait until one group is done to export another group; the export is being done in the background. If you wanted to cancel the Export, just click on the X key.

I EXPORTING JPEGs:

The following steps are for exporting JPEGs for the copyright office. We send small JPGs and not high-res files because since it is a public place, there have been cases of theft at the copyright office.

1. Select the images in the Library Grid Mode.

2. Choose Export. The Export dialog box will pop up.

3. Change the subfolder name to 20120126_dallas_jpg.

4   Do not check "Rename To:" under File Naming.

5. Under File Settings: Format will be JPG, Quality is 80 and Color Space is sRGB.

6. Under Image Sizing: Check "Resize to Fit" and under Long Edge, set the long edge to 400, and Resolution to 72 pixels per inch.

File Settings

Image Format: JPEG ⬍   Quality: ————————○—— 80

Color Space: sRGB ⬍   ☐ Limit File Size To: 100 K

Image Sizing

☑ Resize to Fit: Long Edge ⬍   ☐ Don't Enlarge

400 | pixels ⬍   Resolution: 72 | pixels per inch ⬍

FIG 15.43
Export as JPEG.

UP-RESING ON EXPORT

Lightroom does an excellent job with up-resing as well. The up-res is done with a proprietary algorithm similar to the Bicubic Smoother in . Above, we demonstrated going down in size to make smaller JPGs for the copyright office, but you can also create larger files very easily. Follow the same steps as above, and then under Image Sizing, put in the width and height either in inches, pixels or centimeters for your needs. If you wanted to make a 13-x19 print, put in those numbers. It's that easy!

7. **Output Sharpening:** Check "Sharpen For Screen, Amount Standard." Sharpening is not critical for the copyright office, but if we are going to this extent, we might as well sharpen them for screen use at the same time.

8. **Metadata:** Do not check either option.

9. **Post Processing:** Choose "After Export, Do Nothing."

10. **Click on Export.** Your RAW files will be converted to JPGs and wind up in a JPG subfolder of the job folder in your job folder hard drive.

EXPORTING TIFFs FOR THE CLIENT

We are delivering these TIFFs in ColorMatch RGB. Ideally, we would deliver in CMYK for print use, but we only deliver in CMYK if we get complete cooperation from the client. When we deliver in RGB, we like to deliver in ColorMatch RGB because it is very close to CMYK. Delivering in Adobe 98 is sort of like saying "See all of this color? Well, you can't have it." When delivering in ColorMatch, the client can see and have all of the color they see.

1. Select the images the client chose in the Library Grid Mode.

2. Click on Export.

3. The Export dialog box will pop up. Change the subfolder name to 20120126_miami_tif.

4. Do not check "Rename To:" under File Naming.

5. Under File Settings, select:

   Format: TIFF
   Compression: None
   Color Space: Choose Other

6. The Choose Profiles dialog box will appear. Check "Include Display Profiles" at the bottom left. Then check "ColorMatch RGB." Choose OK. Now you will have ColorMatch RGB as a choice in your Color Space drop-down menu.

FIG 15.44

7. **Under Image Sizing:** Do not check "Resize to Fit." We are sending full size files to the client. Resolution is 266 pixels per inch, which is two times the line screen of 133 for the press the client is using.

8. **Output Sharpening:** *Lightroom's* Output Sharpening is for screen and InkJet Printing. For web press printing, we

would opt for the third party plug in Pixel Genius Photokit Sharpener, or leave output sharpening up to the client.

9. **Metadata:** Do not check either option

10. **Post Processing:** Choose "After Export, Do Nothing."

11. **Click on Export.** Our RAW files that the client selected will be converted to TIFFs and wind up in a TIFF subfolder of the job folder in your job folder hard drive.

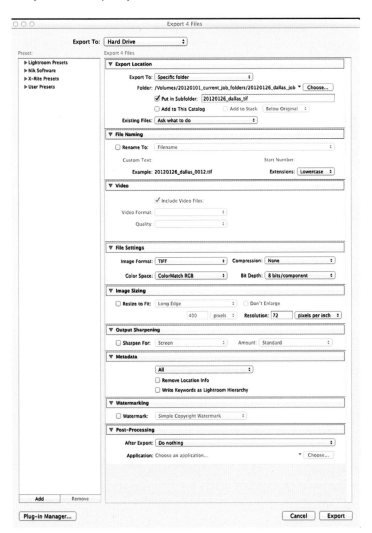

FIG 15.45
Export options for
ColorMatch Tiff's.

12. Go to your job folder hard drive and you will see the job folder, with three subfolders of the images you just created.

20120101_current_job _folders

FIG 15.46
Hard Drive dedicated to holding your job folders

FIG 15.46
Hard Drive dedicated to holding your job folders

FIG 15.47
Dallas Job Folder with three subfolders of different types of files within them

SUMMARY

- D-65's workflow can be adapted to any type of photographer.

- Our digital asset management system will lead you thought the maze of technical problems and challenges that stand between you and a seamless digital workflow with *Lightroom* at the core.

CHAPTER 16
INTEGRATING *PHOTOSHOP* AND *LIGHTROOM*

What is advanced to some, is basic to others, but we are pretty sure that most of you will find that this chapter definitely takes it up a notch. Integrating *Photoshop* and *Lightroom* can even further enhance the power of *Lightroom,* and speed up your workflow. We are going to explore a few features such as Edit in *Photoshop* and Post Processing on Export.

I EDIT IN *PHOTOSHOP*

The first feature to examine is Edit in *Photoshop,* or keyboard shortcut Command-E. *Lightroom* provides the ability to go directly from a file in *Lightroom* into *Photoshop,* work on the file in *Photoshop,* and then to save the file with those changes back into *Lightroom.*

In **Figure 16.1**, we took a RAW file from *Lightroom* with *Lightroom* adjustments, 20100509_bimini_0101.cr2, and hit Command-E. This opens the file in *Photoshop* in a non-destructive fashion, recognizing all of the *Lightroom* adjustments.

We then applied some *Photoshop* adjustments, specifically, Content Aware Fill to remove the toy. The file is saved and closed and automatically saves an edited version of the file, as a TIF, next to the original RAW file in *Lightroom's* Library. The new file from *Photoshop* has the name, 20100509_bimini_0101.cr2-Edit.tif. If the file is not saved next to the original, check the sort criteria. If you choose sort by Capture Time, the files will be next to each other.

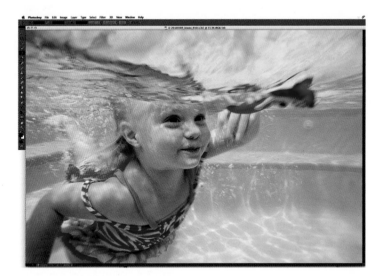

FIG 16.1
Original RAW file with *Lightroom* adjustments.

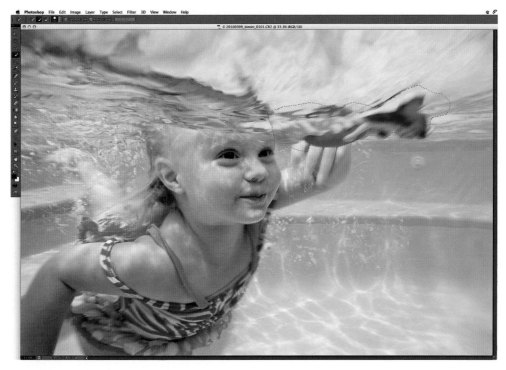

FIG 16.2
Command-E opens the file in Photoshop and we make a selection around the toy.

Fill

Contents

Use: Content–Aware

Custom Pattern:

OK

Cancel

Blending

Mode: Normal

Opacity: 100 %

☐ Preserve Transparency

FIG 16.3
Using Content Aware
Fill to remove the toy in
Photoshop CS6

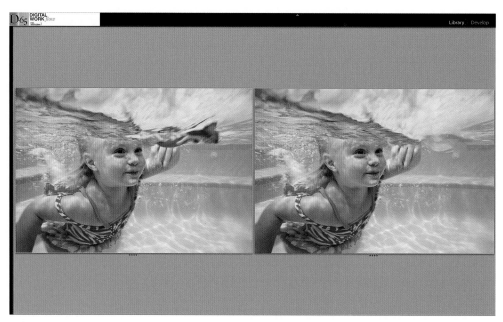

FIG 16.4
File saved next to the original back in *Lightroom*.

I EDIT IN *PHOTOSHOP:* MERGE TO PANORAMA

You can select multiple images in *Lightroom* and take advantage of *Photoshop*'s Merge to Panorama, or Merge to HDR. For this demonstration, we are going to create a panorama of Miami Beach with images shot Jan 4, 2012.

1. We select five RAW files in the Library Module Grid Mode.

FIG 16.5
Five RAW files are selected in *Lightroom*.

2. From the Library Module Photo menu, we select "Edit In" and drop down to "Merge to Panorama in *Photoshop*."

FIG 16.6
Edit In>Merge to Panorama in *Photoshop*

3. The Photomerge dialog box opens and we select Auto for the layout, Blend Images Together, Vignette Removal and Geometric Distortion Correction.

FIG 16.7
Photomerge Dialog box in CS6

4. The files are opened and the layers are blended together.

FIG 16.8
Align Selected Layers
Based On Content.

Progress

Aligning Layer 20120108_miami_beach_0032.cr2

[Cancel]

FIG 16.9
Blend Selected Layers
Based On Content

Progress

Blend Selected Layers Based On Content

[Cancel]

5. When the process is complete, we have a 200-plus degree panorama of Miami Beach. We choose Save and the composited panorama is saved back in *Lightroom* next to the five original files with the name 20120108_miami_beach_0032_Edit.tif

FIG 16.10
Composited file saved
back into *Lightroom*.

FIG 16.11
New file is renamed in *Lightroom* 20120108_miami_beach_0032_Edit.tif

6. The file is rendered as an 384 MB TIF file. If we check the dimensions in *Photoshop*, we can see we now have a panorama which is over 77 inches wide. How cool is that?

FIG 16.12
New file is
384 MB. Wow!

7. But wait—there's more! We could make non-destructive edits to this file in *Lightroom* and then if we choose Command-E or Open in *Photoshop* we could take advantage of those non-destructive edits and again open the file in *Photoshop*. If we choose Command-E we would get the following dialog.

FIG 16.13
The file could now
be edited back
in *Photoshop*.

Edit A Copy With *Lightroom* Adjustments: Edits a copy of the original file with *Lightroom* adjustments visible.

Edit A Copy: Edits a copy of the original file without *Lightroom* adjustments. This is not for RAW files. It is for JPG, TIF and PSD only.

Edit Original: Edits the original file without *Lightroom* adjustments. This is not for RAW files. It is for JPG, TIF and PSD only.

It is you choice how far you want to go with this file, but it is important to understand the dialog box options nonetheless.

I POST PROCESSING ON EXPORT WITH ACTIONS FOR POWER PROCESSING

There are a number of options available under Post Processing in the Export Dialog Box. To really bump the workflow up a notch, we customize this feature for our workflow. We write *Photoshop* actions and have them execute on our images as we export them from *Lightroom* as Droplets. This truly integrates *Lightroom* and *Photoshop*, and speeds up workflow.

As a photographer, how often do you find yourself working in *Photoshop* performing repetitive tasks over and over again? If you are like most folks, the simple answer to this question is way too often.

Well, if you enjoy all that wasted time in *Photoshop* you have no problems, but if you want to reduce your time in *Photoshop* and get back to shooting, there is a solution. Actions automate repetitive tasks and are key to taming workflow. An action allows you to automate your workflow and batch process your files. An action is a recording of the steps needed to process one image, which can be played back and applied to a group of images. Learning how to write actions can help you get your life back or at least some of the precious time.

Consider this scenario, which was in fact a very real set of tasks we needed to accomplish. We had 400 RAW files that we worked on in *Lightroom* and wanted to prepare them for a multimedia presentation. The requirements for the multimedia presentation were to have the images with a ¼ inch white frame and to have the images in sRGB at a resolution of 144. The verticals needed to be 768 tall and the horizontals needed to be 1024 wide.

If we were doing this one file at a time, we would likely still be working in *Photoshop* two days later. Instead, we were able to hit a keyboard shortcut, go to Starbucks and all the files were processed when we returned home, thanks to Post Processing on Export with Actions.

I ARE ACTIONS PART OF *PHOTOSHOP?*

Some actions come with *Photoshop* and those are known as the default actions. You can also write your own actions or gather them from other sources. Actions are located in *Photoshop's* main menu under Window>Actions.

Actions in the Actions palette are arranged in sets, each of which can contain one or more actions. To open an action set, click the right-pointing arrow to the left of the action set name. Now you'll see the list of actions in the set. This panel and Actions in general are not the most intuitive things in *Photoshop*. For example, after creating an action, you will find that you can't save an individual action. You can only save a set of actions. Sets are sort of like holding pens that hold individual actions. For example you might have a retouching set and a processing set and a sharpening set. In each of these sets you might have many actions to accomplish different tasks.

The actions included in *Photoshop* are only a small example of what can be done with actions. You can write your own actions and can record commands like open, close and save as part of the action. In fact just about everything you can do in *Photoshop* is actionable.

Before creating an action to perform a complex task (particularly if you're unsure exactly how to begin), search the web to see whether an action already exists to do the job. A good place to start looking is the Adobe Studio Exchange, which is a shared resource for many *Photoshop* tools. If you find an action you like, you can load an action by opening the Actions palette menu, choosing Load Actions, navigate to where you saved the action and select the ATN file, and click Load to load it. You can then play the action by opening the actions set, selecting the action to play, and clicking the Play Selection button. **Big note: you have to have an image open to play the action on.**

I CREATING YOUR OWN ACTION

Once you're comfortable with finding the actions and using them, you can try creating your own custom actions.

We like to have our destinations designated by the action so we suggest that you create a folder on your desktop that is permanent destination for all your actions. We call ours "D-65 Lab." By having this permanent "lab" on the desktop, all of the actions run to the same destination eliminating any problems with folders no longer in existence or disappearing files.

One further problem is that *Lightroom* doesn't really play actions. The good news is that you can turn an action into a Droplet and have the Droplet executed by *Lightroom*. Following is a demonstration on Post Processing in *Lightroom* for our presentation scenario described earlier.

I BEFORE YOU BEGIN WRITING THE FOLLOWING ACTION:

1. Edit and rank the images in the *Lightroom* (delete all outtakes).

2. Verify that the images have been properly named, keywords added and that metadata has been applied.

3. Make sure that all developing is finished and the images are pretty much the way you want them.

4. Make sure that you have a destination folder for your actions. Ideally, set up the folder with sub folders for all the processing you are going to do. For the action below I have a D-65 Lab folder and one sub folders inside, called Multimedia.

We will write a simple action that will access your processed full-size JPGs located in your job folder (these jpegs would have processed during export from *Lightroom*) and will size them to a resolution of 144 with a .25 inch white border and deposit the processed files into a folder called Multimedia. The horizontals will be 1024 wide and the verticals will be 768 tall. All the metadata applied from *Lightroom* will be embedded in this new set of JPEGs. Even your rankings will be there, too!

I LET'S WRITE THE ACTION

1. Make new folder on desktop called D-65 Lab or "white border for client x," or whatever you want to call it. We already have a folder called D-65 Lab and inside that folder we have various folders for many different actions. For this exercise create a folder inside the D-65 Lab called multimedia.

d65_lab

6 items

FIG 16.14
Folder called D65_lab on Desktop.

FAVORITES		
All My Files	d65_class_files	CMYK
Desktop	d65_lab	holga_infrared
Applications	DealMaker...reakers.rtf	holga_resize
Music	Dear Unit Owners.docx	Iphone
	dpdheader2.jpg	multimedia
	FIG 16.12.tif	whiteborder

FIG 16.15
D65_lab has folder inside called Multimedia Images

2. Process one RAW file in *Lightroom* into a JPG using the specifications below:

• Color Space is sRGB

• Resolution at 144

• Check Resize to Fit Dimensions at 987x732

Because we are making a ¼ inch white border around the image, the image size is 987x732. When we add the border the final size will be 1024 x 768.

FIG 16.16
Export Dialog Box

3. Open the one JPG you just created in *Photoshop*.

4. Go to the Actions Palette in *Photoshop*, located under Window>Actions

FIG 16.17
Actions Palette in CS6

5. Using the flyout arrow, create new set called *Lightroom* Actions. You will put any action your write for *Lightroom* into this set.

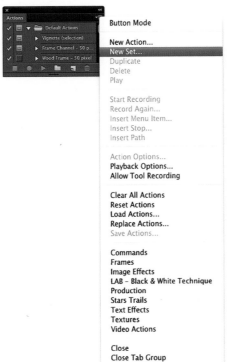

FIG 16.18
New Set Is created in CS6.

FIG 16.19
Set is named in CS6.

FIG 16.20
New Action created in
Set in CS6.

6. Name the action "xxx action (i.e., whatever action you are writing)"

FIG 16.21
New named Action
in CS6.

7. Click Record.

8. Go to image that is already open and from the Image Menu, choose Canvas Size.

9. Type in .25 x .25 under width and height. Make sure Relative is checked, and that the Canvas Extension Color is white.

10. Choose OK.

Canvas Size

Current Size: 1.86M
Width: 6.854 Inches
Height: 4.569 Inches

OK
Cancel

New Size: 2.03M
Width: .25 | Inches ‡
Height: .25 | Inches ‡
☑ Relative
Anchor:

Canvas extension color: White ‡ ☐

FIG 16.22
Canvas Size in CS6.

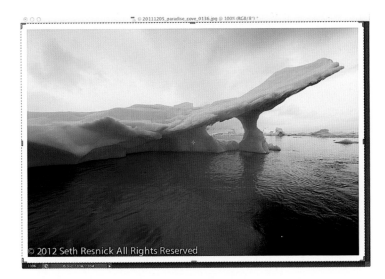

FIG 16.23
Image with ¼
white canvas.

11. Go to the File Menu and choose Save As.

12. Save as a JPG to the new "multimedia" folder that you
    created in the D-65 Lab on your desktop.

FIG 16.24
Image saved to
multimedia folder
in D65_lab

FIG 16.25
Image saved as JPG.

13. Close the image that is open in *Photoshop*.

14. Stop the Action from the Actions Palette (button to the left of the Red button at bottom).

Stop playing/recording

FIG 16.26
The action is stopped.

15. Now you need to convert the Action into a droplet: select Action Called ¼ Inch White Border from the Actions Palette.

16. Go to File Menu>Automate>Create Droplet.

FIG 16.27
Create Droplet

17. Save the droplet in User>Library>Application
    Support>Adobe>Lightroom>Export Actions.

    For a PC, the location is Documents and Settings>UserNam
    e>ApplicationData>Adobe>Lightroom>Export Actions.

18. Check "Suppress File Open Options Dialogs" and
    "Suppress Color Profile Warnings" And select
    Destination NONE.

19. Save Droplet and give it a name that makes sense, like
    quarterinchwhiteborder.

FIG 16.28
The droplet is created
and save

To Run the Action/Droplet in *Lightroom*

1. Open *Lightroom*.

2. Select the images that you want to export and process with
   this new droplet in the Library Module.

3. Choose Export.

4. Go through the Export Dialog box choosing the
   correct parameters.

5. Under Post Processing—After Export, choose the droplet
   from the drop-down menu.

FIG 16.29
Post-Processing
drop down menu—
choose droplet

6. Click on Export

7. Your selected images will export to the correct specs and the droplet will run on them.

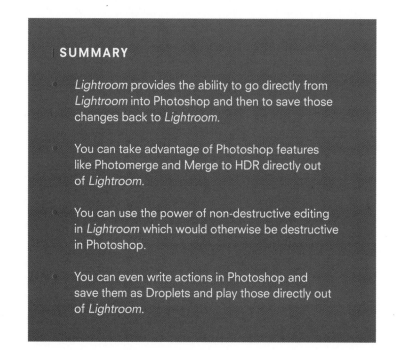

SUMMARY

Lightroom provides the ability to go directly from *Lightroom* into Photoshop and then to save those changes back to *Lightroom*.

You can take advantage of Photoshop features like Photomerge and Merge to HDR directly out of *Lightroom*.

You can use the power of non-destructive editing in *Lightroom* which would otherwise be destructive in Photoshop.

You can even write actions in Photoshop and save them as Droplets and play those directly out of *Lightroom*.

The dilemma is:

"I use a Laptop in the field when shooting, and a desktop at the studio/home for processing and management in *Lightroom*. If the "main" Library and Catalog live on my "main" computer's secondary internal drive, or external drive in the studio/home, how do I sync the Catalog on my laptop or other computers with the "main" Library and Catalog?"

There are several ways to do this and we will review them here. Most folks make this very confusing but D-65 has found work-around solutions that run effortlessly and flawlessly. Your methodology for accomplishing this needed task will be dependent upon what you need to do to your files in the field. We will go through each scenario starting at the most basic and build to more complicated scenarios in this tutorial.

I D-65 CONCEPTS FOR SYNCING

Concept One:

You maintain your archive on your studio or home desktop computer. You have a shoot on location, so you will be bringing a laptop with you. You may do some work on the files you capture in the field, and you are going to want to sync the laptop back to the desktop when you return home.

Solution for Concept One:

1. The easiest and most reliable way to accomplish this is use a large capacity portable drive at home with your catalog and images, and simply take this hard drive on the road with your laptop when you travel. This drive will be shared between the laptop and the desktop. There are several companies that make one terabyte 7200 speed drives which will hold your catalog and the images. We usually take Western Digital My Passport Studio or Lacie Little Big Disk 1 terabyte drives but any decent fast large portable drive will do. For absolute protection, we like to bring two or three external drives on location, duplicating the contents.

2. This sounds simple and it is! You share one external drive between both computers.

Lightroom_Library

FIG 17.1
Drive named Lightroom_
Library contains Catalog
and images and is
shared between laptop
and desktop computer.

3. There is only one issue to worry about. Make sure that the portable drive is mounted on your desktop BEFORE you start *Lightroom*. If you start *Lightroom* and the drive is not connected or mounted you will get a dreaded message that *Lightroom* can't find your catalog and will create a new default catalog in your User>Library>Pictures>*Lightroom* Folder.

FIG 17.2
Lightroom application
started without
Lightroom_Library
drive connected.

4. Oy Vay! Where the #@$*are my pictures? What do I do if I get the dreaded message? Quit *Lightroom* and connect your hard drive with the correct catalog. Make sure it is mounted. In our case, it is the drive named Lightroom_Library and the catalog named Lightroom_4_Catalog. When *Lightroom* starts again it is still going to go to the wrong catalog (the default catalog in your Pictures Folder). You will need to point it to the correct catalog and relaunch *Lightroom* with the correct

catalog. Go to the File Menu and choose Open Catalog. Then navigate to where your correct catalog is located on your external drive. Don't Freak Out!!!!

FIG 17.3
Once *Lightroom* is started without the Lightroom_Library drive connected, even when the correct drive is connected again, *Lightroom* is going to open up the default Catalog and you will need to point *Lightroom* to the correct catalog by choosing File> Open Catalog.

FIG 17.4
Navigate to the correct catalog and relaunch *Lightroom*.

5.   There is one more step when the wrong catalog opens by accident. The default catalog in *Lightroom's* General Preferences needs to be reset. Go to *Lightroom's* Preferences > General > Default Catalog>When starting up use this catalog. Navigate to your correct catalog located on your external drive, in our case the Lightroom_4_Catalog on the drive named Lightroom_Library

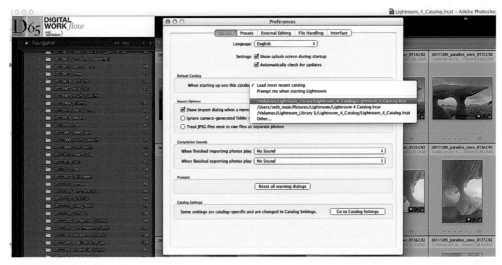

FIG 17.5
Set *Lightroom's* preferences to open the correct catalog which defaults to most recent every time the wrong catalog is opened.

6. OK, you are golden! This method is really foolproof and very simple and allows you to go between a laptop and desktop with minimal problems.

Concept Two:

You maintain your archive on your studio or home desktop computer. You have a shoot on location, so you will be bringing a laptop and external hard drive on location with you. You may do some work on the files you capture in the field, but your main goal is simply to take the images you captured in the field and bring them back to the studio, placing the images from the field onto the studio/home machine. In this scenario, you don't need to bring your entire archive of images with you on your shoot.

Solution for Concept Two:

1. The easiest and most reliable way to accomplish this is to bring a laptop and a hard drive on location. For absolute protection, we like to bring two or three external drives on location, duplicating the contents to all three drives just to protect against drive failure or theft or any other unforeseen

circumstance. The system below is what we use for 99% of our location shooting. Following the steps for Concept Two will transfer all metadata and images from your laptop to your desktop successfully and easily.

The only items that won't transfer are Collections, Smart Collections and Virtual Copies. We always suggest that you wait until you get home to make Smart Collections, Collections or Virtual Copies, unless you are sharing the one drive between both computers, as in Concept One.

2. Ideally, reformat the hard drive before the trip. We usually take Western Digital My Passport Studio's or Lacie's Little Big Disk, 1 terabyte drives, but any decent fast large portable drive will do. The drive is named Lightroom_Library. This is the exact same name as our main *Lightroom* drive at home. We keep the same name because *Lightroom* is path specific. As long as the path is the same for both the home and laptop there will be no problems finding the catalog. We do use different icons for each drive to visually distinguish the drives, but this in not a necessity, only a convenience.

FIG 17.6
Internal or External *Lightroom* drive at home called Lightroom_Library with a shareware drive icon.

Lightroom_Library

FIG 17.7
Portable drive for road formatted and named Lightroom_Library.

Lightroom_Library

3. Before we leave home, we create a new *Lightroom* Catalog on the freshly reformatted drive for the portable computer. We

name the catalog yyyymmdd_Lightroom_4_Catalog. If you have questions on how to create a catalog, refer to Chapter 6.

FIG 17.8
Lightroom Catalog named 20120126_ Lightroom_4_Catalog created on the Lightroom_Library portable drive.

4. We go on location with the laptop computer and shoot the job(s) on location. We import from the card to the portable drive into a folder named yyyymmdd_jobname and back up to another drive called Import_Backup just for safety.

FIG 17.9
Import from card to the portable drive into a parent folder named YEAR and a child folder named yyyymmdd_ jobname and back up to another drive called Import_Backup just for safety.

5. Our portable external drive (Lightroom_Library) will have a *Lightroom* Catalog (20120126_Lightroom_4_Catalog) and a folder of images from that job.

6. We tweak our files in the field and apply metadata and keywords, edit out ones we don't want, rank, and essentially accomplish as much as we can. We try and avoid Collections, Smart Collections and Virtual Copies on the road because that information is contained only in the catalog and not in the .xmp metadata.

7. After we are done tweaking all our files, we select them all in the Library Module Grid Mode and choose Save Metadata to File (Command-S) or if you prefer, you could also have Automatically Write Changes into XMP selected in Catalog Preferences (although it does tax the system to automatically write XMP).

FIG 17.10
XMP has been saved
to the RAW file
using Command-S

FIG 17.11
Back home, external
drive named
Lightroom_Library is
plugged into the main
computer. Note that if
you are on 10.7 (Lion)
you can have two drives
with the same name but
if you are on a previous
operating system
change the name of
the portable drive.
We suggest adding
an (x) in front of
Lightroom_Library
(portable drive) as in
xLightroom_Libarary.

Lightroom_Library

8. When we return from location, we plug the external drive
    Lightroom_Library into our main computer at the studio or
    at home. Note, if you are on OSX 10.7 you can have two
    drives with the same name. If you are on a prior operating
    system you can't have two drives with the same name so add
    an (x) or other character in front of Lightroom_Library like
    xLighroom_Library.

Lightroom_Library   Lightroom_Library

9. We start *Lightroom* on the main computer and choose Import from the lower-left hand corner of the Library Module. We select the folder to import as in 20120126_dallas

10. **The Import Photos Dialog Box will pop up:**

   - Choose "Copy photos to a new location and add to catalog."

   - **File Handling:** Choose 1:1 Initial Previews because we always want 1:1 previews

   - Don't re-import suspected duplicates

   - **File Naming:** Uncheck Rename Files—because we named the files in the field

   - **Apply During Import:** None, because we have applied Develop Settings, Metadata and Keywords in the field

   - **Destination:** Organize: by original folders

   - To the location that all of our image files reside, our Lightroom_Library hard drive on our main computer. In our case it would be /volumes/Lightroom_Library/2012

11. The files are imported and all material is now on our main drive. The portable drive can be reformatted and readied for the next location shoot.

Concept Three:

You maintain your archive on your studio or home desktop. You are leaving for a location shoot and you want to bring your entire catalog and some images from studio/home with you. You plan on working on old images from the existing catalog but you also want to be adding new material. You have a shoot on location so you will be bringing a laptop and external hard drive on location with you. When you return to the studio / home, you want to update the catalog on your main computer with the material you captured in the field, and with the material changed in the field. Now we must sync the field catalog and the studio/home catalog.

Solution for Concept Three:

1. The easiest and most reliable way to accomplish this scenario is to bring a laptop and an external hard large enough to hold the entire *Lightroom* Catalog and image files you want to bring. For absolute protection we like to bring two or three drives on location duplicating the contents to all three drives just to protect against drive failure, theft or any other unforeseen circumstance.

2. Before we leave for our trip, we copy our Lightroom_Catalog and folders of images from our main Lightroom_Library to the external drive that we are taking on location.

3. We start *Lightroom* on the Laptop and all of the files that we took with us will be available. We will still be able to see full size previews of the files we did not take. Their respective folders will be grayed out and have a question mark. The question mark is present because we did not take all of the files.

FIG 17.12
External drive named Lightroom_Library is plugged into the laptop on the road. We have taken our Lightroom_Catalog and some folders of images. The images we have are available and the images we did not take are grayed out but because we built 1:1 previews, we can still see those on the laptop. **(FIG 17.13)**

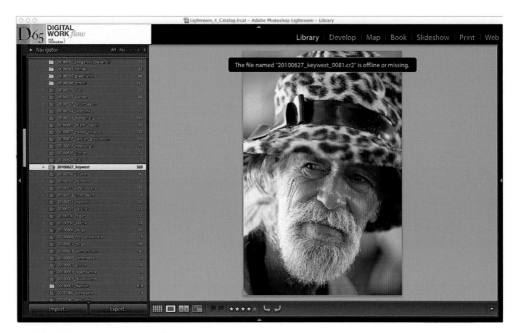

FIG 17.13
External drive named Lightroom_Library showing an image that is offline. Folders of images that were taken on location are fully usable in *Lightroom*. Folders that were not present on the laptop drive are visible because we have taken the entire Lightroom_4_Catalog and have generated 1:1 Previews. These offline files are visible in *Lightroom* but they can't be developed because they are not physically present.

4. We shoot on the road and import the files. We then tweak our files in the field and apply metadata and keywords, edit out ones we don't want, rank, and essentially accomplish as much as we can. We avoid making collections and avoid making virtual copies.

5. As in Concept Two, after you are done tweaking all your files select them all in the Library Module Grid Mode and choose Save Metadata to File (Command-S) or if you prefer, you could also have Automatically Write Changes into XMP selected in Catalog Preferences although it does tax the system to automatically write XMP.

6. The new job will be imported when you get home exactly the way we described in Concept Two. The new twist is that on the road you have decided to work on another folder of

images. We always advise that you write down on a piece of paper what folder or folders you are going to do work on.

7. As in Concept Two, after you are done tweaking all your files, from an existing folder, select them in the Library Module Grid Mode and choose Save Metadata to File (Command-S).

8. We return back home and check to make sure that all the files we worked on with the laptop are the way we want them and that the metadata has been saved. We open up *Lightroom* on our main computer and we navigate to the folder or folders that we worked on while on the road with the laptop. We select all the images on the desktop computer and we choose Delete From Disk. After deleting the images we Control Click on the folder with no images and delete the folder as well. There is now no trace of the images or folders that we worked on while on the road, on the desktop computer.

9. Once the folder is deleted from the computer at home, we choose import from the lower left-hand corner of the Library module and we will now import the new folder created on the road as well as the folder or folders that we worked on while on the road. The steps are the exact same steps as outlined in Concept Two.

Concept Four:

You maintain your archive on your studio or home desktop computer. You have a shoot on location, so you will be bringing a laptop and external hard drive on location with you. You will do some work on the files you capture in the field and you are going to work on files that you bought from home. You haven't kept track of the files you bought from home so you are now forced to completely sync both catalogs.

Solution for Concept Four:

1. The easiest and most reliable way to accomplish this scenario is to bring a laptop and an external hard large enough to hold the entire *Lightroom* Catalog and image files you want to bring. For absolute protection we like to bring

two or three drives on location duplicating the contents to all three drives just to protect against drive failure, theft or any other unforeseen circumstance.

2. Before we leave for our trip, we copy our Lightroom_Catalog and folders of images from our main Lightroom_Library to the external drive that we are taking on location.

3. We start *Lightroom* on the Laptop and all of the files that we took with us will be available. We will still be able to see full size previews of the files we did not take. Their respective folders will be grayed out and have a question mark. The question mark is present because we did not take all of the files.

4. We shoot on the road and import the files. We then tweak our files in the field and apply metadata and keywords, edit out ones we don't want, rank, and essentially accomplish as much as we can. We may even make collections and smart collections and virtual copies. We also work on several other folders of images, so now we must sync the Laptop *Lightroom* Catalog to the desktop.

5. We truly try to avoid this method because it is complicated and it will take a long time and use a lot of space. For most of our work we use Concept Two, but this is yet another way.

6. Select all the photographs or folders of photographs or even the entire catalog in the catalog that you want to export from.

7. Choose Export as Catalog from *Lightroom's* Library File Menu.

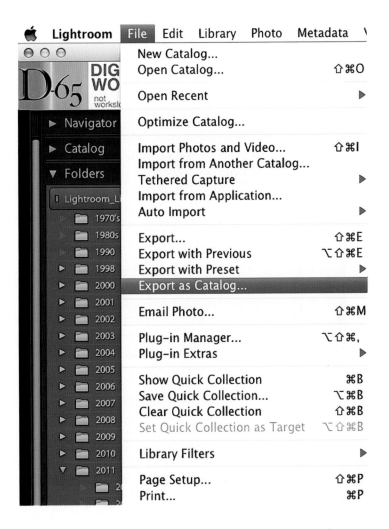

FIG 17.14
Export as Catalog.

8. We chose Save As, name the file for_Export and save it to an external drive or any place that is large enough to hold all the information.

Export as Catalog

Save As: Laptop_Catalog

Where: Desktop

Exporting a catalog with one photo.

☑ **Export selected photos only**
☑ **Export negative files**
☑ **Include available previews**

Cancel   **Export Catalog**

FIG 17.15
Catalog is exported.

9. Now the exported catalog is imported into the office or desktop Computer. To do this, we choose Import from Catalog from *Lightroom* File Menu. The information from the exported catalog is merged into the master catalog on the desktop computer. While this method works and will preserve virtual copies, collections and smart collections, it can be a very tedious and time consuming process.

Concept Five: Only for Advanced or Power Users

We contemplated not putting this part in the book, but here goes. This concept can be used for several advanced scenarios. We are going to present a very advanced concept and if you understand this, you can extrapolate quite a few possibilities. *Lightroom* is not a network application yet, but you can force it to be a networked application with a little help.

1. All of the images above are placed on a drive or on a server.

2. Each person in the office has a copy of *Lightroom* and builds their own *Lightroom* Catalog on their respective computers. One person is deemed to be the Master and no one touches that catalog except the Master. He or she imports all the images from the server, either by copying to a new location or by adding the images from the existing location.

3. Each person in the office does exactly the same thing. They each have a catalog with images.

4. Person A is going to be working on Captions and Person B is going to be working on Keywording and Person C is going to be working in the Develop Module. The key is that each person has a specific task that they work on.

5. At the end of the day, after the Master has made sure that each person (or slave if you will) has correctly done their task, the catalogs are exported but without negatives and without previews. This is totally cool. This will take only minutes or less but it would take days to do this and include the previews and the negatives.

6. Each person selects All Photographs from the Catalog.

7. Each person chooses Export as Catalog.

8. Uncheck "Export negative files" and uncheck "Include available previews." In essence, you are exporting metadata only to import this metadata into the Master catalog.

9. The catalog is exported from each "slave" computer.

10. The catalog contains only a catalog file and the export is very fast. This is imported into the Master Computer and effectively the Master computer is updated with all the changes from the slave computers. This process effectively turns *Lightroom* into a feasible network application.

SUMMARY

You use *Lightroom* on a main computer and you take a laptop on location. How you go about synching the work done on your laptop on location to your main computer is a critical part of workflow.

There are several methods that will accomplish this task in *Lightroom*. The choice you make will be dependent on whether or not you are simply acquiring new information on location that you want to bring back to the main computer, or whether you are taking information from the main computer and working on that in the field and then syncing that information back to the main computer.

At a very advanced level, *Lightroom* can even be forced to become a network application synching multiple catalogs on different computers.

ARCHIVING YOUR IMAGES AND CATALOG

Back-up is important, but back-up is not preservation. The goal of D-65 is to have an EXACT DUPLICATE of our catalog and of all of our image files on multiple media in multiple locations.

An archive should be made regularly because computers are not 100% reliable. Hard disks malfunction, viruses and worms corrupt data, and people can make simple mistakes like inadvertently deleting files. Having an archive means you can recover from such faults, with little, if any, lost data.

In the Summer of 2011 I was up on our roof watching a storm develop on Miami Beach. The massive thunderstorm started to rotate creating a sudden but intense Supercell less than a ¼ of mile away. The television was flashing tornado warning and it looked like the end of the world. Miraculously this storm just moved out to sea and we had little more than heavy rain and wind. A few years back we were not as lucky. As Hurricane Wilma passed over Miami Beach, we watched and took photographs from our 17th floor apartment, which faces the Atlantic Ocean on the front side and the Intercoastal Waterway on the backside. We live on a very narrow section of Miami Beach, which is roughly one foot above sea level. Our building flooded, our docks were destroyed, and as the storm intensified, we watched the roof come off of the building next door. As we looked out at the raging storm, we realized that our building was actually swaying a few degrees in this Class 3 Hurricane.

Hurricanes, typhoons, tornados, fires, volcanoes, blizzards and even tsunamis are a fact of life and they wreck lives and destroy property. After each of these events, you can usually always find a news clip where a reporter asks someone if they were able to save or salvage any of their belongings. You know the scenario because you have seen it hundreds of times. There is man or woman crying at the seen of what was once their house, devastated because they lost everything. When they can salvage items they typically grab the memories like wedding pictures, baby pictures or family pictures. While having little financial value, these items contain tremendous personal value and are irreplaceable. Did you ever stop to think what would happen to your image collection even if it were on multiple media but all stored in only one location?

If you are a digital photographer, your data is the heart of your business. Not having an archive strategy in place means that a single malfunction can leave your business without any data, thus placing the future of the business in jeopardy.

D-65 suggests having a place that is a safe place for the computer in the event that one has to evacuate. We wrap all of the hard drives and computers in garbage bags and put them in the bathtub at the approach of a hurricane. The bathtub will hopefully drain if there is water and most bathrooms have doors to offer extra protection. Ideally a bathroom on an upper floor would be a wiser choice than one in the basement.

| DUPLICATE BACKUPS IN MULTIPLE PLACES

While basic computer backups are a good start, a backup is not necessarily an archive and does little good if your home or offices are destroyed. Not only do you need backups, but it is critical to have multiple backups, both off-site and on-site in the case of an emergency. Redundancy, redundancy, redundancy: you simply can't have too much.

An archive should be made to separate media that you can pick up and take with you. This way, copies of your data can be kept off-site, such as in another building. This helps protect against disasters, which may obliterate the building where your computer is held.

| BACKUPS

Ideally, the copies made onto backup media should be performed with a system that verifies the data. This is fundamental difference between a backup and an archive. Most folks simply perform a Finder Copy better known as drag and drop. These are very unreliable and permissions, preferences and other needed files may or may not copy this way. We personally like to use SuperDuper from Shirt Pocket and Retrospect from Dantz but there are other products as well. These products perform a bit-for-bit duplication and then verify that the data has been duplicated correctly.

The frequency of your "backups" should be dictated by how much data you would like to lose if there is a problem on your machine. For example, if you enter a significant amount of data every day, you should be backing up every day. If you rarely enter new data, then backups once per week might be okay.

"Backups" should be tested. Make sure that you can read the backup you just wrote. Nothing is worse than having a disaster and discovering that your backups are unreadable for some reason or another. If you are burning CDs or DVDs, it is usually sufficient to have the burner program "verify" the disk after it is written.

Of course, if you don't have a computer or power, you won't be able to access the data, but just knowing your personal and business documents are safe is reassuring. A good battery backup system is always a wise idea, but if power is out for an extended period of time even this will fail.

| EMERGENCY POWER

In case of an emergency, you may or may not have access to power, phone service, or the Internet, and the need for power is the foundation of maintaining communication. Power alternatives include extra batteries, conversion battery kits, power cords that hook up to a car cigarette lighter, solar packs, and manual power generators.

Preparation is the best defense against nature and other unforeseen disasters. While a personal bomb shelter might help you rest easily at night, there are more practical ways to protect your personal treasures. In the event of a catastrophe, take care of your family, friends, property, and community. Knowing that you're prepared will let you do just that. Personal safety is always first, of course. But after that, it's the insurance companies and state and federal agencies that bear the burden of helping families rebuild and replace material possessions.

| ARCHIVING *LIGHTROOM*

Archiving is different than backing up during processing or in the field. An archive is duplicated bit-for-bit, verified for integrity, duplicated for both on- and off-site storage.

| IMPORT BACKUP

There are several backups available within *Lightroom* but it is important to understand exactly what they do, and more importantly, what they don't do. When we first import files into *Lightroom*, the import dialog box offers a backup. This is a copy of what is on the card and not your Develop Presets or other metadata that might be applied. It is certainly useful but it is more of a temporary backup, rather than a permanent archive.

| THE CATALOG BACKUP

The Catalog Backup in *Lightroom's* Catalog Preferences is a backup of the Catalog only. While the preferences clearly state "Catalog Backup," most photographers fail to recognize exactly what this means.

It means exactly what it says. It is a backup of the Catalog. **It is not backing up any of the images associated with the catalog.** So if you have your catalog and your images on Drive A and you have chosen to backup to Drive B, the only backup occurring is a backup of the catalog, not the images. If Drive A fails, and this is the only place where you had your images, you would have just lost all your images.

In the Catalog Settings Preference we choose "Never" because we like to back up our catalog and our images twice a day.

| THE D-65 ARCHIVE

We want to duplicate and back up our images and our *Lightroom* Catalog. As we said earlier, the *Lightroom* Library and Catalog are held on an internal drive with nothing else on it. We duplicate the *Lightroom* Library and Catalog on a second internal drive as well as on two external drives, one of which goes off-site.

| MEDIA CHOICE FOR ARCHIVE

D-65 chooses hard drives as our main means of archiving for many reasons. Do you remember SyQuest drives? Eventually, they became obsolete. The same happened with the ZIP format, optical drives, and on and on. The only standard that has been around to stand the test of time is the hard drive. The only problem with hard drives is that they will all die. It is not a matter of if only a matter of when. Therefore, multiple redundant drives with even offsite storage is simply mandatory. The key word here is REDUNDANY!

When a newer and faster drive comes out, it is easy to simply duplicate an entire drive. Recently we just upgraded our internal drives to 7200 speed 4 TB drives. Many people make their main archive on CD, but there are many problems with CDs. The average CD may only last for 3-10 years and that is a potential disaster for archiving. Further, if one has 20 GB of data per photo shoot, there could easily be 50 CDs or more per shoot.

| D-65 DRIVE STRUCTURE

As discussed in Chapter 4, D-65 chooses to have a large internal drive holding our images (*Lightroom* Library) and our Catalog. The structure of that drive looks like **Figure 18.1**.

Internal 4 Terabyte hard drive holds the images and the *Lightroom* Catalog. The drive is named Lightroom_Library

Folders of images and .XMP files are organized by yyyymmdd_jobname in each calendar year.

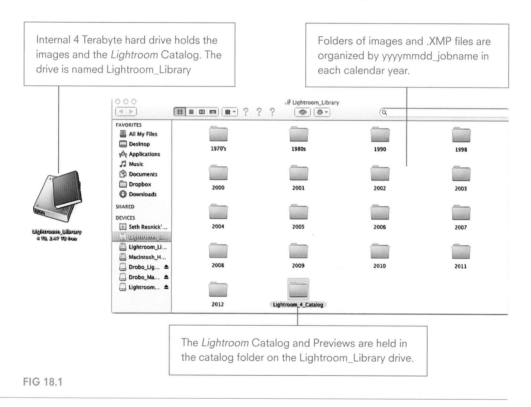

The *Lightroom* Catalog and Previews are held in the catalog folder on the Lightroom_Library drive.

FIG 18.1

In each year folder are folders for each job named yyyymmdd_
jobname and in each job folder are the RAW files and
corresponding .XMP files as in **Figure 18.2** below.

The folders are
organized by
yyyymmdd_
jobname. These
folders contain the
RAW files and the
.XMP sidecar files

FIG 18.2
Folders with RAW files
and XMP files

The Lightroom_4_ Catalog folder contains two files, and the
Lightroom_4_Catalog.lrcat and the Lightroom_4_Catalog
Previews.lrdata

FIG 18.3
The Lightroom_4_
Catalog showing the
Lightroom_4_Catalog.
lrcat files which holds
the catalog information
and the Lightroom_4_
Catalog Previews.lrdata
whch holds the
preview information.

I MAKING THE BACKUPS

The Lightroom_Library gets duplicated to a second internal
drive called Lightroom_Library_bk and that drive gets duplicated
to one Drobo which then gets duplicated to a second Drobo.
Even the Drobo gets duplicated to a third Drobo that gets
stored off-site. For detailed information on Drobo, see:
http://www.datarobotic.com.

We do not use the drag and drop of Finder copies as they are not very accurate. Instead, we use software specifically designed for archiving. We currently use SuperDuper. SuperDuper runs on a schedule in the background and does a complete backup of all the drives multiple times a day. For a PC we suggest Retrospect.

FIG 18.4
SuperDuper can schedule a backup to work behind the scenes several times or more a day.

SUMMARY

- Backup is important, but backup is not preservation. The goal of D-65 is to have an EXACT DUPLICATE of our catalog and of all of our image files on multiple media in multiple locations.

- Archives should be made regularly because computers are not 100% reliable. Hard disks malfunction, viruses and worms corrupt data, and people can make simple mistakes like deleting files inadvertently. Having an archive means you can recover from such faults, with little, if any, lost data.

- If you are a digital photographer, your data is the heart of your business. Not having an archive strategy in place means that a single malfunction can leave your business without any data, thus placing the future of the business in jeopardy.